Some Day
THE SUN WILL SHINE

AND HAVE NOT WILL BE NO MORE

"If we are to achieve results never before accomplished, we must employ methods never before attempted."
—Sir Francis Bacon (1561–1626)

Some Day
THE SUN WILL SHINE

AND HAVE NOT WILL BE NO MORE

BRIAN PECKFORD

FLANKER PRESS LIMITED
ST. JOHN'S

Library and Archives Canada Cataloguing in Publication

Peckford, A. Brian
    Some day the sun will shine and have not will be no more / Brian
Peckford.

Includes bibliographical references and index.
Issued also in electronic format.
ISBN 978-1-77117-024-6

    1. Peckford, A. Brian. 2. Premiers (Canada)--Newfoundland and
Labrador--Biography. 3. Newfoundland and Labrador--Politics and
government--1972-1989. 4. Newfoundland and Labrador--History--
1949-. 5. Federal-provincial relations--Canada. 6. Canada--History--
20th century. I. Title.

FC2176.1.P43A3 2012   971.8'04092   C2012-905009-1

PRINTED IN CANADA

MIX
Paper from
responsible sources
FSC® C016245

This paper has been certified to meet the environmental and social standards of the Forest Stewardship
Council® (FSC®) and comes from responsibly managed forests, and verified recycled sources.

Cover Design: Adam Freake   Edited by Erika Steeves

FLANKER PRESS LTD.   PO BOX 2522, STATION C   ST. JOHN'S, NL CANADA
TELEPHONE: (709) 739-4477   FAX: (709) 739-4420   TOLL-FREE: 1-866-739-4420
WWW.FLANKERPRESS.COM

16 15 14 13 12   1 2 3 4 5 6 7 8 9

 Canada   Canada Council
for the Arts   Conseil des Arts
du Canada   Newfoundland
Labrador

We acknowledge the financial support of the Government of Canada through the Book Publishing Industry Development
Program (BPIDP) for our publishing activities; the Canada Council for the Arts which last year invested $24.3 million in writ-
ing and publishing throughout Canada; the Government of Newfoundland and Labrador, Department of Tourism, Culture and
Recreation.

CONTENTS

I dedicate this book to all those Newfoundlanders and Labradorians who remained steadfast against difficult odds so that we were able to achieve our goal.

AUTHOR'S NOTE

The title is taken from a line in a speech I gave, which of course is quoted in the book. The actual wording was, "One day the sun will shine and have not will be no more." Although this book is based on my life, a fifty-year-old memory, while good, may tend to spice a little for effect.

PREFACE

FOR MANY YEARS NOW I have been planning to write this book. The stories, events, and people have been rolling over in my mind on almost a daily basis.

When I began writing about my experiences as a social worker in rural parts of the province, I discovered the most unusual thing. It happened one afternoon when I had begun the exercise. I was writing away in what I thought was a third-person account of these experiences. I stopped for a moment, and when I looked at what I had written, I was shocked. I had been writing in the first-person, complete with dialogue, without my knowing it. And there were pages and pages of it. I could not believe that I had just written that material!

I am sure there are those who would say that these short stories are fodder for another book. For me, they must be in this book since it is only through such stories that I think one has the opportunity to realize why I was so passionate about our place. I was lucky to experience both the older way of the early fifties as a boy and then to see it repeated later in northern Newfoundland and southern Labrador as a university student before the roads, electricity, and jukeboxes came to be, and then to experience the transition as it began, and simultaneously to have been a part of the "new" in Lewisporte and St. John's.

These experiences as a student have had a profound effect upon me. I remember my first political adventure, not counting high school and university. I decided to run for the presidency of the Green Bay Liberal Association at the last minute, and against the person who was being supported by Premier Smallwood, who was also in attendance at the meeting. In this, my first political speech (discounting the school and university politics), I remember using the experiences of my student days to describe my understanding of the province and hence why I was qualified to run for the office. Of course, it also signalled that from the start I was anything but an insider. And during my political career I always seemed most at home when I was in rural parts: yes, asking for a vote, but being impacted by what I saw and heard, especially the resilience and tolerance of the people. These experiences seem photographed in my mind and are an integral part of my sensibility.

It is really not the story of one person, but through one person the lives of many who thought like me and fervently desired to see a more prosperous place and our history respected.

The process by which we were able to help to effect this change was anything but smooth. Of course, there were moments of joy, but most were a struggle and often it looked impossible.

I am sure there are those who would argue that I overemphasize Newfoundland's struggles. Well, my life seems to replicate that view, both my own early experiences and those in public life. I make no apologies.

Better times have arrived, and let us hope that we have learned from distant and recent history. I still hold out the hope that, now, through these better times, we can address our fishery, achieve more influence, and see a revitalized rural Newfoundland.

CHAPTER 1: BEGINNINGS

"Being grown up is not half as much fun as growing up."
—Anonymous

BESSIE R LEFT BAY Bulls with a cargo of salt for Port aux Basques and intended to load a cargo of fish at the latter port. It arrived in Fermeuse on the Southern Shore on Sunday, February 17, 1918, and its master, Sandy Thistle, fully expected to harbour at Trepassey that night. However, once out and en route, the fickle forces of nature took command.

Thistle had an experienced crew; most like himself belonged to Hickman's Harbour on Random Island: Mate Joseph T. Blundon (or Blundel) and Levi Benson. Cook John Anderson lived in British Harbour, but he later moved to Britannia on Random Island. W.J. Peddle hailed from Little Heart's Ease and Lewis Rice from Bay Bulls. Joseph Peckford, a well-known citizen of St. John's, was supercargo on the schooner. As supercargo he would have managed the business transactions of the *Bessie R*, whose main work seems to have been trading fish and supplies along the coast.

The skills of Thistle's crew were soon to be tried, for the schooner ran headlong into a snowstorm with southeast winds. Within hours this swung around to a gale from the northwest—the worst winds for sail-driven vessels off southeastern Newfoundland. For twenty-four hours *Bessie R* was pushed to sea, and during the gale the jumbo boom broke off. The log—towed on its line behind the ship, which would give some indication of speed and distance—broke and Captain Thistle had no idea how far his schooner had drifted off.

1

Slowly he and his crew worked the vessel back to within sight of land, perhaps somewhere on the east side of St. Mary's Bay. Thistle figured this was the general area, but *Bessie R* was near a rock called by local folks The Bull. Thistle didn't recognize it at the time, but he realized he needed to keep his schooner out to sea. Despite the best intentions of his crew, contrary winds pushed *Bessie R* near Holyrood Arm and there was no way to swing the schooner around to get out. The vessel made its last-ditch standoff the town of Point LaHayse, or as it is known today, Point La Haye.

Meanwhile, the residents of Point La Haye had gathered on a headland and were watching the valiant efforts of the six seamen. When *Bessie R* sailed in, they ran to the beach to help if they could. At first it seemed as if it would ground and break up offshore. There seemed to be no recourse but disaster and death. One account of the wreck says, "The people on the shore never thought that any of the crew would reach the shore alive, and they gathered on the beach praying for their safety."

But Captain Thistle drove *Bessie R* right up on the beach and the crew were able to jump off from the bowsprit to the shore, much to the amazement of Point La Haye residents. Joseph Peckford sustained the only injury. During the two or three days of fighting the storm, Peckford had taken his turn at the wheel and bent over to examine the compass. The main boom swung, hitting him in the middle of the back, and his chest struck the wheel with considerable force. One of the wheel spokes injured his chest.

Despite their close call and two or three days of exciting and anxious hardships, the crew, all but businessman Peckford, went about their life work on the sea. They found employment at Harbour Grace and went there to join the schooner *Henry L. Montague* for another stint on the ocean.

This was not the last word on the wreck of *Bessie R*. Apparently one man was so impressed with the self-rescue of the hardy seamen, he wrote an unsigned letter to the St. John's newspaper *Evening Advocate* dated March 11, 1918. The heading says, "Nothing Can Daunt Our Brave Seamen."

Dear Sir:

Please allow me space to say a few words about the loss of *Bessie R* at Point La Haye, St. Mary's Bay, in one of the heaviest seas of thirty years and in the height of a winter storm. She ran ashore and everything was handled so well that every man was landed in twenty-five minutes in a way that no one but Newfoundland fishermen could do.

My pen cannot tell you what a hero Mr. Joseph Peckford is. He nobly stayed to the wheel until the vessel grounded on the beach and the first place he was up to was the middle of the storm trysail which was set. If there are any medals to be given, those men deserve them. There are brave men in all ranks, but I think seamen beat them all.

Another matter I would like to mention is that I think outport men might have a little more rum than men in the city. When you drag a man out of the surf the bottle seems mighty small nowadays. I hope we will be able to get some more.

Yours very truly,
"A Good Hand to Throw a Line"

Point La Haye, St. Mary's

In the June 22 edition of the *Trade Review*, as quoted by Patrick O'Flaherty in his book *The Lost Country: The Rise and Fall of Newfoundland*, the following article appeared:

One other development in the 1907 fishery should be noted. In June a fishing craft of "ordinary open boat style" about twenty feet keel "propelled by a 4 1/2 horse power one cylinder gas engine was in use in St. John's. The owner of this "motor boat" was the fisherman, Joseph Peckford. The engine for those who could afford one—Peckford's cost $350—was a major development.

In volume four of *The Book of Newfoundland*, one finds the following concerning Joseph Peckford:

> Peckford fished from the Battery and Bay Bulls for most of his life and spent 49 years spring sealing. He was a survivor of the Greenland disaster and was once master watch of the sealing steamer *Florizel*. He is said to have been the first Newfoundlander to use a gas-powered engine in the shore fishery. The Knox engine had originally been used in oil exploration at Parson's Pond and was purchased by Peckford in 1905. Crowds of people gathered around the St. John's waterfront to watch the motorboat on its trial run. (p. 244)

This was my grandfather Peckford, who came to St. John's from Fogo Island after jumping a sealing ship in St. John's in the 1890s. In St. John's he met Clara Brett, also from Fogo Island, and married. Joe fished out of St. John's harbour for fifty years and reportedly went to the seal fishery for forty-nine years, and my grandmother kept a small store. The Peckford home that Joe built still stands; some of his wharf and rooms were at the bottom of Temperance Street, now all filled in as part of harbour enlargement and on which the Terry Fox Memorial now stands.

In 2009 I visited Fogo Island to further investigate the birthplaces of these two grandparents: Locke's Cove and Lion's Den. Walking a wonderful new walking trail on a glorious August day, I visited Lion's Den and Locke's Cove. It was only then that I realized that Joe and Clara had likely known one another before their St. John's days, as the distance between both places was not great. Who knows? They might have been earlier lovers and Joe's jumping ship was to find his lost love. Curiously, no headstone remains of the Peckfords on Fogo Island. After some crawling around in one of three cemeteries, I found a fallen headstone of my great-grandfather Jonathan Brett, Clara's father, who it is reported was a shipbuilder.

My maternal grandparents were Hiram Young and Queen Victoria Ross. Great-grandfather Young moved from Greenspond, his birthplace, when my grandfather was a young boy. Queen Victoria was born on the Ross farm, now Pleasantville. The Rosses were originally from Margaree Valley, Cape Breton Island. My grandmother, who kept a diary, recorded the following:

> I was born on March 23, 1885, in St. John's, Newfoundland. As far as I know I was born in an old farm house called Grove Farm, Quidi Vidi Road, North Side. At that time I had seven sisters, six of whom were born in Margaree, Cape Breton Island, Nova Scotia. The Ross name is a well-known name in the Margaree area seeing five different families of Rosses immigrating there from Scotland in the 1700s, each claiming they were unrelated to the other.

Great-grandfather Ross owned 100 acres of what is now Pleasantville, formerly Fort Pepperell, and farmed there, supplying St. John's with vegetables, milk, and cream, including the General Hospital and the Governor's House. He operated a store on Water Street at one time, imported cattle from the Maritimes, and raised thoroughbred horses. Grandmother Ross actually taught weavery at Mount Cashel orphanage at one time. An enterprising lot!

Of course this enterprise came naturally, if one studies this Ross family. My great-great-great-grandfather David Ross was brother to James Ross, the first of his clan to settle in Margaree and third husband to Henriette LaJeune. She fought with the French (coming from France herself) at Louisbourg when it fell to the English. She had a medical background and became famous in Cape Breton for nursing, administering the smallpox vaccine that she had brought from France. She became affectionately known to all as Granny Ross and lived to the age of 117. At St. Patrick's Church in northeast Margaree, there is a cedar sign which reads:

> Welcome to St. Patrick's Church
> Built in 1871 on land granted
> To James Ross, English Pioneer
> For fighting at Louisbourgh in 1758.
> Buried in this graveyard is his wife
> 'The Little Woman'
> Who fought for the French.

A memorial (although there is now some dispute over the veracity of her age) on the south side of the church reads:

> In Memory of
> The Little Woman
> Henriette LeJeune
> Wife of
> James L. Ross, pioneer
> The first white woman to settle
> In North East Margaree
> Born in France 1743
> Died in Margaree in 1860
>
> Fought with the French in the
> Second Siege of Louisbourgh 1758
> Administered smallpox vaccine
> Brought with her from France
> To the settlers of this valley
> Benefactress of both white
> And Indian.
>
> Erected by her Great Grandson
> Thomas E. Ross

I WAS BORN IN Whitbourne, a small railway town just sixty miles from St. John's, one of a handful of communities in Newfoundland that was not next to the ocean. Although both my parents were St. John's people, my father's position with the Newfoundland Ranger Force necessitated that he be stationed at the force's training facility in Whitbourne. I remember the train passing through the town and how we kids would play close to the moving train, almost daring it to touch us. I remember taking it to St. John's with my mother, and riding the streetcar in bustling St. John's. Years later as a university student I would take the train home for Christmas to Lewisporte, and even later I was to take the train in an unsuccessful attempt to save it.

My first three years of school were in Whitbourne, the Anglican School; the Catholic one was just across the road, just close enough so that we could throw snowballs at one another in winter. You did not have to attend church to know that there were major separations in the community. You knew through school. And it was weird since it was the same God, same Jesus, and same book. But little was said other than you were United, Salvation Army, or Anglican, or that real strange one, Catholic. And that is the way it was. But fate was soon to bring me closer to that strange denomination, only we called them religions then.

In December, 1951, when I was the age of nine, the family moved to Marystown, my father having changed from being a law enforcement officer and small business owner to a social worker. After his social worker training he was posted to Marystown, a small, undeveloped community over 200 miles from St. John's on the Burin Peninsula. It was more isolated than Whitbourne and without electricity; farther along the peninsula were the more developed towns of Burin, Grand Bank, and Fortune, all economically active with fish plants serviced by offshore trawlers.

It's a bit of family lore as to how the family arrived in Marystown. Father had gone to Marystown a few weeks earlier in December to finalize arrangements for a house and to meet with the outgoing social worker and other such matters. Mother and her brood of five were to follow later. There was a ninety-nine-mile drive from the Goobies railway station to Marystown, and we were to travel there by train from St. John's, a further 100 miles. Father would pick us up there in a rented vehicle and drive all the family to our new community, to our new home. Ah! The best-laid plans . . .

To Goobies we arrived—in a snowstorm—and Father was somewhere on the ninety-nine-mile gravel highway, stuck in snow. So here we were—no doubt a forlorn-looking group. Someone at the railway station who knew of a boarding house nearby took pity on us and we were brought there to reside overnight. The next day we learned that it would be impossible for Father to meet us—the road was blocked. In those days, without the mechanical machinery of today, it would be blocked for quite some time. Father would go back to Marystown. A new plan had to be devised. Back to St. John's we were to go, and to take a train as soon as we could (a half-day journey) to the port of Argentia, where we could catch a coastal passenger freight boat, which plied Placentia Bay communities including Marystown.

By the time this was arranged and executed, Christmas was upon us—well, just about—and we took the coastal boat, *Bar Haven*, at Argentia in a hell of a snowstorm on Christmas Eve morning and, like everyone else on board, the whole family was sick as dogs. I almost get sick today thinking of that experience, more than fifty years later. I don't know if we thought we would ever make it or not. We did not know enough to be afraid—that was left to Mother as she tried to care for five vomiting youngsters in a cramped cabin in the bowels of a rolling ship. It was six or seven o'clock in the evening when we were told that the rolling would subside a bit since we were coming into Marystown Harbour. Once the *Bar Haven* tied to the wharf, this distraught family clambered to the deck, and with snow and wind still bellowing all around, we stumbled off the gangplank, seeing through the blur, at long last, our Father! We were to walk with him up over a hill and pasture in two or three feet of snow to our new house. We were all carrying something and struggling as we trekked, making a path as we went. Finally, we arrived and burst into the house. What a treat! It was all ablaze with a Christmas tree and decorations that Father had prepared!

We were one of the few Protestant families in Marystown and the only non-Catholic children attending the convent school operated by the Sisters of Mercy. I remember one incident at lunchtime when I was engaged in a snowball fight with one of my classmates. After a bull's-eye throw by me I heard the recipient cry out, "You black Protestant!" One of the kids told the Sisters and there was heavy punishment dispensed to the foul-mouthed student. In five years this was the only incident of this kind that I remember.

There were many prayers and such at school and our parents said that we should just participate—the Sisters had made arrangements for us to leave the classroom during such religious events. However, obeying our parents, we stayed and it wasn't long before we had memorized all the prayers and did the "Stations of the Cross" at the church nearby. We enjoyed it all, and hence what potentially could have been difficult years for my brothers, sister, and I turned out to be a very positive experience. And I attribute a lot of my personal good habits to the Sisters of Mercy, who were relentless but fair in dispensing "education" to us all. It was not all book work: the music and concerts displayed the Sisters' love of culture and brought to these activities a discipline and joy that has never left me. There were no school buses or central heating or cafeterias—each student took turns bringing "splits" to start the fire in the pot-bellied stove—yet there was something special; everyone had to help out to make it all work. This produced a unity and spirit that was as "hard as a rock." These were formative years, and I learned a lot about punctuality, discipline, and getting by with whatever one had at the time. There was no whining or excuses, at home or in school.

Many years later, one of my ministers would have occasion during an election to solicit support from a convent in St. John's that hitherto was somewhat unfriendly to the Conservatives. He was to discover that there were a number of Sisters who had been part of the Marystown convent during our family's years in Marystown, and who were eager to lend their support. I remember a final rally in St. John's, during my first election as premier in 1979, and in referencing the Sisters' role in my education I was quickly informed that there were some in the audience.

My father's work took him to visit many communities in Placentia Bay, many of them islands. I was interested in going with my father on these jaunts, and I well remember a particular trip by a small boat owned by a gentleman in Baine Harbour.

Leaving Baine Harbour one morning, we were quickly surrounded by fog, and with only a compass to go by, it was for me a harrowing experience, and judging by the expressions on the faces of my father and our operator, it was not fun for them either. But our skipper knew the bay well. Our destination was Oderin Island. So the skipper simply said, "Okay, we have to steam so many minutes in a certain direction using the compass, then so many minutes in a slightly different direction using the compass." And so this was done. After some anxious moments—presto, we see through the dispersing fog land on both sides of us—we were smack dab in the centre of Oderin Island harbour! There are some on the water who say they can smell the land in the fog. I was to remember this incident many years later when I travelled Green Bay, White Bay, and the Labrador Coast in small boat. Anyway, here we were in Oderin harbour.

Father had to visit some clients—widows and disabled people who qualified for government assistance. After a quick lunch that day, Father had to travel to the other side of the island, walking along a small pathway. Noticing my boredom, he invited me along. Along the way, Father informed me that there were but a few families on the other side and that he had only one visit to make. However, in mentioning this, he went on to describe to me a mysterious tale that was told on the island. He said that we would soon arrive at a small gully or pond near the beach on the back side of the island, not far from the ocean. It was said that the famous pirate Peter Easton had frequented these parts, and being chased by his enemies he had actually buried a treasure at the bottom of the pond. The tale relates that the pirate drained the pond, being of higher elevation than the beach, placed the treasure in the bottom of the waterless pit, cut a number of trees, and after removing branches placed the "longers" across the bottom of the pond, and then the natural spring of the pond filled it up. A real place of safekeeping!

Father said that we should check this tale out by taking off our boots and socks and walking out in the water of the pond to see if we could feel something like a floor. This we did. It was eerie—we could feel that there was something like a floor! A mystery to this day!

Socks and boots back on, we proceeded to a large two-storey house on the far side of the beach to Father's lone client here. On approaching the house, I noticed that a curtain in an upstairs window parted slightly. Upon entering, we were warmly greeted by a middle-aged woman, and Father proceeded to complete some necessary forms. In the course of the conversation the woman mentioned that her young daughter had become frightened, since visitors were few, and we being total strangers, she ran to an upstairs room to hide.

In the 1980s I was relating my early experiences on a local CBC radio show, and one of the stories I described was this one about Oderin Island, the treasure, the walk in the pond, and the visit to the house of the lady and her daughter. In just minutes, a lady called the radio station to inform us that she was that little girl who had run upstairs and nervously parted the curtain to glimpse the approaching strangers.

So my time in Marystown from age nine to age fourteen was a pleasant one, filled with childhood memories: of homework by Aladdin lamp, snow sledding in the winter, bike riding, and swimming in local ponds in the summer, and our share of beachcombing, digging for "cocks and hens," and smoking cigarettes made from stolen tea, and cigarette papers purchased from older friends. A few crabapple trees were also the victims of wayward childhood ways and saw on one occasion some serious reprimand by my parents.

I think I travelled to St. John's once during that time. I was told that I had large tonsils and that they were to be removed. Really, it was a sinus problem, I was to discover years later. But the medical fad then was that if a child suffered from a cold and cough, it had to be those darn tonsils and adenoids. So at a convenient time when a friend of the family was travelling by car to St. John's, I travelled with my mother to the big city. Well that was some ride. I never thought that we would get there. What I remember most about that visit is not the city, large and different as it was, or the time at the hospital, frightening and unusual as it was, but rather seeing TV for the first time. I think I was twelve. I sat in my grandmother's room too dumbfounded to speak—there was a game show and then some ads about buying some type of food. I would not see TV again for another two years.

It was in Marystown where I gained an appreciation for baseball. Yes, baseball. There was no baseball in Marystown, of course, but across Placentia Bay from Marystown was the American Naval Base at Argentia. It was easy to pick up the Armed Forces radio on our battery-operated radio (a much-used instrument in our family), and in the evenings of spring, summer, and fall there were many baseball games broadcast. It was from the radio I learned the names and the rules of baseball, and my favourite player was Willie Mays. A young boy's imagination fuelled by the noise of the game and the descriptive play-by play-of the announcers brought me into the wonderful world of baseball.

In 1954 my father had to take a trip to visit his counterpart in Grand Bank, and of course I tagged along for the ride. After entering the house I was immediately struck by the sight of a small magazine on baseball (it was *The Baseball Digest*, still publishing today) lying on a chair in the kitchen. My focus was so fixed on this magazine that my father's friend took notice and suggested that I pick it up and read it while my father and he conducted their business in an adjoining room. Excited beyond words, I was eager to see the two adults depart to the other room so that I could hold this magazine. On the cover was my baseball hero, Willie Mays. I had never seen his picture before, and now here he was featured on the front page of this important magazine. I devoured the article and was still busily engrossed when the adults returned. Feeling a little embarrassed, I put the magazine down and got up to leave. And then my father's friend uttered the words, "You really seem to like that magazine. You can have it!" Months after, I was still rereading the articles and studying the statistics. And now the radio broadcasts were even better.

There was one really magical part of our family lives. Each birthday we would receive a card and money from our Aunt Bessie in faraway Boston. There was a time before Confederation in 1949 when

Newfoundlanders gravitated to the "Boston States" for employment. My aunt was one of them. She travelled to Boston in her early twenties, enrolled in nursing courses, and graduated with an RN from Leonard Morse Hospital Training School for Nurses in 1926. She never forgot anyone in the family. She was affectionately known as Auntie Bett to all the people connected to my father's side of the family. And at Christmas you could be as sure that snow would fall that a large parcel would arrive before Christmas (never late) from this great lady. And what a parcel it would be—from clothes for all of us, to books and other practical and needed things; we were, each season, aghast at the quantity and quality of what she would send. My brothers and I would have modern clothes to wear to school each new year right from America's fashion houses. So we grew up with our own fairy godmother. In Whitbourne, on my seventh birthday, this shiny blue Buick pulled up to our door that afternoon, and on top of the car was an unusual thing. Once the car stopped, out stepped Auntie Bett; she fiddled with the thing on top with my father's help, removed it from the car, and placed it on the ground: a birthday present—my first bike! Our house was full of magazines, compliments of you-know-who.

As I grew up I became fascinated with Auntie Bett: her stories of nursing terminally ill wealthy people in the Boston area, receiving postcards from her from other continents as she travelled with her employers around the world, to coming home each year to see her mother, this lady led an interesting and productive life. Her generosity was exceptional, and her commitment to family unlimited. When she was much younger, she had told her mother that if the day ever came when she, her mother, could not look after herself, she would come home and care for her. And she did. The last two years of my grandmother's life saw Auntie Bett leaving Boston to care for her mother in St. John's until her passing.

My aunt was always interested in seeing her nephews and nieces succeed. And if they showed they were willing to work and commit, she was always there to help. On entering university I was to receive from Auntie Bett annual complimentary tickets to all the happenings at the local Arts and Culture Centre. When I travelled to remote rural parts in the summertime as a temporary social worker, I was sure to receive a parcel of recent magazines and newspapers from Boston or St. John's.

No one knew her politics. But one evening, after inviting me to her favourite St. John's Chinese restaurant, she did confide to me that she was a financial contributor to the Republican Party and was therefore invited to many of their political dinners and events. I got up enough courage to ask her why she was a Republican.

Her answer was simple: "I believe in hard work," she said. "Everyone must earn their keep, if they are able."

My aunt was eighty-five when she died in St. John's; and in death as in life, she ensured that all the immediate family received a generous part of her estate.

My father was transferred to Lewisporte in 1956, a far more "advanced" town in northeast Newfoundland. It was quite a change. Here were hotels and the shunting of trains and a bustle and activity not present in the more isolated Marystown. And now, instead of being in a largely Catholic town, we were in a predominantly Protestant town, with a large United Church of Canada congregation as well as a viable Salvation Army church, a small Anglican church, and a quickly growing Pentecostal group. There were shops and restaurants, more than one doctor (which had been the case in Marystown), and even a dentist. Lewisporte owed some of this activity to the fact that it was the terminus for a number of CN coastal boats. It was strategically located to serve the transportation and passenger needs of northeastern and northern Newfoundland and Labrador. A railway spur line of nine miles joined the town to the railway's main line at Notre Dame Junction. So there was a large workforce at the dock, loading and unloading freight from railcars, and the processing of passengers. The people of the town were entrepreneurial and independent. I completed my high school education there. This was a much larger school, and it did not have the rigour and discipline that we experienced in Marystown. This was a shock at first. Of course, like most kids of my age, it did not take long to get used to it.

There was one shining exception to this, and that was our main grade eleven teacher. I say main in the sense of a homeroom teacher who also taught us a number of subjects. His name was Mr. Paddock (Brose); he later moved on to teach at Memorial University and become Dean of the Faculty of Education. We were a lucky forty-two students to have him as our teacher. For the first time (outside of Father's admonitions) I was encouraged to think about things, not to accept things at face value, that reason was a very valuable commodity, and that dogma and entrenched positions often retarded advancement. This was all new to me but very exciting. I had been so involved in sports and friends and all the normal adolescent things that this was the first time I had been forced to stop and consider the larger world.

The culmination of this new thinking occurred one day when Mr. Paddock asked me to stay for a few minutes after school. After school! This was unusual, and I didn't know what to expect. Sitting in the back of the room, I had become a bit of a distraction for the teacher, and while I was doing well in most of my subjects, I think Mr. Paddock felt I was unfocused and just a little too carefree as a high school senior. He approached my desk and abruptly asked, "Brian, what do you intend to do with your life?"

I stuttered something stupid in reply. And then it was over. Mr. Paddock turned and left the room. I struggled to my feet and left the room and school, pondering that simple but provocative question. I knew this was an attempt to shock me to my senses, and it worked. I had given little thought to my future, and it was time. Within several months, high school would be over, and what then?

I enjoyed my Lewisporte years and became heavily involved in sports, especially baseball and hockey. Now, we had few facilities at the school or in the town generally. Across from the school was an outdoor rink, and just "up the road" from the school was a level ground that was supposed to be the sports field. We made the best of it, and in my last year we had organized games on that rink and actually played hockey with other teams in nearby towns of Botwood and Gander. There were a couple of really cold winters when we actually skated and played hockey on the harbour. Our out-of-town games were a real treat since we would be playing indoors. In Botwood it was in an old World War II undersized building, with real ice but of course no snow clearing, while in Gander it was a regulation-sized artificial ice surface in an arena. We really had no coaches, but I recall on our out-of-town excursions our vice-principal acted as such, and I can remember him urging us in the car on our way to our game to "shoot when we got in over the blue line." I don't think we won any of those out-of-town games! Similarly, we had a few teams organized and played baseball on a makeshift diamond on the nearby field. I liked hockey, but I loved baseball. There seemed to be more strategy and planning, and I enjoyed how quickly explosive it could become.

And then there was my paper route. I delivered the weekly Grand Falls *Advertiser* every Saturday along the main street, from the United Church building almost to the end of Lewisporte West. I came to like this weekly ritual on my bike. It was the people once met who I remember most. There was an elderly Mr. Lacey who still kept his little grocery shop open, although few now frequented such an outdated place. Bigger stores had sprung up, and the little guy was soon to be no more. But it gave people like Mr. Lacey a reason to get up in the morning and a chance to chat, even to a boy like me. He was not well, and often when I would inquire about his health he would exclaim that he was "wonderful sick." One got the pulse of this part of town, from Mr. Lacey, to young adults with a second-hand motorcycle under constant repair in the yard, to the elderly lady whose generous tip at Christmas was always exhilarating, to Vatcher's auto mechanic shop, where there always seemed to be someone in the pit fixated on looking up at the underbelly of a decrepit Chevy, Ford, or Chrysler.

There was a touch of the political at this stage of my life. I remember an incident involving the then-Premier, Mr. Smallwood, who on a visit to Lewisporte sought out my father, then a social worker for the area. Apparently there had been some representation made by a local citizen who had questioned through the premier a decision Father had made concerning the citizen's eligibility for assistance. The premier took the opportunity of the visit to see my father about it. From overhearing a conversation with my mother later, Father was obviously very upset by the public nature of the visit and the fact that he was bring pressured to provide assistance where the rules prevented it. Father told the premier that he would have to set up an appointment if he wished to pursue the matter. I also remember a political rally in the local theatre for a Conservative candidate in an upcoming federal election. The candidate was Ambrose Peddle, who went on to win the riding and later become the province's ombudsman. And perhaps most importantly, I remember that at our high school a number of us got together and, in talks with the principal, set up the first student council for the school, of which I became the first president. It was also during this time that I began working during the summer holidays and at Christmastime. I remember working at a clothing store one Christmas.

But my most interesting memories are of travelling to St. John's to work with the provincial government. My first summer was working as a filing clerk at the Department of Health and Welfare in a wooden building situated near the old Newfoundland Hotel. This was a great experience that gave me exposure to the capital city. I stayed with my grandparents on Carpasian Road overlooking St. Patrick's ballpark where regular baseball games were played. Given my interest in baseball, this was a dream come true, and I spent many an evening and weekend down at the ballpark learning the finer points of the game as I tried to get near the players and coaches.

My grandfather would usually stay home and watch the games from his back garden, still using cricket terms to describe the game. I saw pictures of him in his youth as part of a cricket team in St. John's. My grandparents Young were wonderful people. My grandmother was a Ross (originally from Margaree Valley, Cape Breton). These were the grandparents who owned a lot of land in what is now Pleasantville where, they operated a farm, supplied the hospitals with milk, and sold vegetables to customers door-to-door. My grandfather was originally from Greenspond, but his parents moved to St. John's when he was a young lad. He worked for fifty years with the department store named the Royal Stores, rising to become the manager of the wallpaper department. He was a hard worker and had a great memory.

I remember his many recitations of poetry, including "Horatius at the Gate" by Lord Macaulay.

> *Then out spake brave Horatius,*
> *The Captain of the Gate:*
> *"To every man upon this earth,*
> *Death cometh soon or late;*
> *And how can man die better*
> *Than facing fearful odds,*
> *For the ashes of his fathers,*
> *And the temples of his Gods.*

I remember well his geography. The largest island in Newfoundland, meaning insular Newfoundland, was Glover Island in Grand Lake, and the largest island in all of Newfoundland was Fogo Island—ninety-two square miles—with Random Island close behind at ninety square miles, and the pear-shaped island was Ceylon.

My grandmother was a great gardener and spent endless hours nurturing her flowers and raspberries. Although small in frame, she had an indomitable spirit, and travelling the stairs to the basement many times a day, feeding the coal-fired furnace, and practising her Scottish orderliness gave testament to her hardiness.

I spent one more summer in St. John's working for the same department. Being a little older, I was no longer a clerk but had been asked to act as a welfare officer at the city office in downtown St. John's. This seemed a formidable task, since it meant learning quickly a maze of regulations since I was to interview and apply these regulations to clients (all of whom would be older than I) to see whether they qualified for assistance.

I called my parents concerning this, since I felt overwhelmed by all this responsibility. My father assured me that I could do it, and so I conquered my fear and had a very busy summer learning a lot about people whose means and/or mental or physical condition saw them as clients of the department. Surprisingly, I was even allocated to be responsible for "unmarried mothers" for a while, since there was a sudden vacancy in that area. Today, of course, without a degree or two and some experience, such work by a high school student would be viewed as shocking and possibly illegal.

I interviewed a young unmarried mother who lived in squalid conditions and needed a mattress. After a full investigation, her request was found to be a valid one, whereupon I had a mattress ordered and delivered to her residence. Elated with this new addition, she called me and offered me the first night on the mattress. In appropriate bureaucratic language, I declined the offer. An increase in the unmarried caseload was a common occurrence nine months following the Portuguese fleet, which frequented St. John's harbour for supplies, or to avert nasty storms in the North Atlantic.

The year 1959–60 marked a significant departure from the normal progression of our family evolution. The provincial government had begun a program for social workers whereby they could apply and, if accepted, attend university for educational upgrading. The successful applicant would be paid the same salary for that time as if they were working their normal job, and tuition would also be paid. The Department of Welfare had developed a relationship with the School of Social Work at the University of Toronto. My father applied and was successful, and so my four brothers and my sister and my parents moved in the summer of 1958 to Toronto, a new large urban landscape, so different and puzzling, an abrupt change from our tranquil rural background.

It was a hot summer and we were not used to these high temperatures, but it was the humidity that was really unbearable, and living in a small apartment at Metcalf and Parliament in the middle of the city compounded matters. It was a modest apartment, and many immigrants were taking up residence nearby. My father obtained a temporary job at the Canadian National Exhibition while waiting for classes to begin; he worked in the music area, given his piano prowess and interest in music. We all settled in as best we could and became familiar with the neighbourhood. My older brother succeeded in getting a job with CPR and attended night school at IBM, which had recently established an office in the city. The remaining five children were school-bound, three in primary, and my brother and I were off to high school—Jarvis Collegiate.

Toronto was a big adjustment for the whole family. Except for Father, it was the first time off the island for all of us (other than my brief stint to Nova Scotia at an air cadet camp). The humid weather, the busy streets, the streetcar, subway, skyscrapers, and the impersonal nature of the place made us feel like we were in an alien land. We were saved somewhat by a nearby park and the Riverdale Zoo, which proved a welcome escape from the noise and din of urban life.

Nothing prepared my brother and me for our high school experience. Coming from a rural town in Newfoundland of 2,000 with a one-storey high school, 200 students from grade seven to eleven, to a downtown four-storey brick building of 1,400 from grade ten to thirteen, was a real culture shock. I am not sure if I had seen a basketball before this, and certainly not a school library, gym, pool, or those high and low bars. Add to this that we spoke differently than almost everyone at the school and that most of the students did not know where Newfoundland was, and those who had some notion thought we lived in igloos. We were classic outsiders. My only friend at the school was a boy who had just moved from the Ukraine. Nevertheless, we tried to fit in and abide by the rules and regulations of this complicated, confusing place. But for me it seemed the odds were stacked against me.

I played hockey, and although I was unused to artificial ice and arenas, I decided to try out for the school team. Miraculously, I made it. That meant extensive practices at Leaside Gardens. To get there you took a streetcar, subway, and bus to the arena. Of course, that meant early mornings since these practices were all on weekdays and I had to be back to school by 9:00 a.m. On one of these practice sessions the traffic back from the arena was exceptionally heavy and I arrived back to school late, by ten or fifteen minutes. Well, this automatically meant a trip to the vice-principal's office. I explained what happened, but I was subjected to what I thought was an unnecessary interrogation.

"Young man, have you ever been in trouble before?" began the vice-principal. This I automatically took to mean whether I had broken the law, that I was being treated like some common criminal.

"I do not think that unusually heavy traffic on my return from practice justifies such a question," I answered.

Wow! That went over like a lead balloon, and I was suspended from school that day. My father was contacted, and upon being questioned by the vice-principal, he more or less took my position. His son had never been in trouble before, and being late through no fault of his own did not seem to be sufficient reason for such an approach.

I now had a record!

Sometime later, two incidents in English class further soured my time at the school.

The first concerned an essay I had written. We had been asked to put ourselves in a journalist's position and compose a newspaper report on a recent incident or issue. This was during the time when, then white South African Prime Minister Hendrik Verwoerd was embroiled in controversy over his government's apartheid policy. So I composed an article concerning the issue as if I were a journalist in Johannesburg. The day the corrected papers were passed back to the students by the English teacher, Mr. McKenzie, he refrained from passing back mine. I raised my hand and asked about the whereabouts of my paper.

"Where did you get this? You did not write this," Mr. McKenzie responded.

I explained that I had constructed this myself and that none of the writing was copied. Sadly, he did not believe me and I received no mark for my work.

Then there was the poetry incident. Mr. McKenzie was introducing a new poem and he was eager for us to understand the literary term *allusion*. In the poem there was a biblical allusion and he asked whether anyone knew from what book in the Bible this allusion was taken. Several hands were raised, including mine. He acknowledged all the raised hands but mine. All the answers given had been incorrect. My arm, still partly raised, was the lone arm visible, yet he was about to proceed when one of the more inquisitive and courageous students, obviously perplexed by the teacher's lack of recognition of me, spoke up.

"Sir, Brian has his hand up!"

"Oh, yes, yes," sputtered an embarrassed Mr. McKenzie. "Yes, okay. Brian, what do you say?"

"It is from the Book of Ecclesiastes in the Old Testament," I confidently explained.

"My, my, well, Brian, that's the best you have done all year—this is incredible," exclaimed Mr. McKenzie.

"Well, sir," I retorted, "if you had asked me on those many other occasions I had my hand up, I am sure I would have been able to give other correct answers."

That was it! "To the vice-principal's office," I was so ordered by an irate English teacher.

A brief incident with the French teacher continued my unfortunate run-ins with the teachers. We were all misbehaving, according to the teacher, and for this group indiscretion we were all to remain in our places when the final bell of the day rang. We were to place our hands on our desks and remain motionless. Sitting upright at our desks, we strived valiantly not to move and not to make a whisper. Well, there are moments like this that will test a person's soul. Suddenly, one of the students lost it and burst out laughing, whereupon the teacher rushed to the student's desk, whipped his arm around, and struck the student solidly and viciously across the face. He was about to administer an additional blow when—totally shocked by this—I called out: "Stop, you can't do this!" In a rage, the teacher ordered me out of the room and to another visit to the office.

And then there is the final "in-class" experience concerning the geography teacher. One afternoon the teacher was talking about meteorology, and the discussion led to annual precipitation and snowfalls across the nation. Of course, the nation stopped at Nova Scotia. A sharp student pointed out (before I had time) that Newfoundland had been omitted, and she wondered what the annual snowfall would be there. The teacher responded that the amounts would be similar to Toronto—no big deal. I spoke up to indicate that I was from Newfoundland and that I was pretty sure that annual snowfall in Newfoundland would be much higher than in the Toronto area. The teacher disagreed. Amazingly, that very evening a TV weather reporter was doing the same exercise on snowfall that we had done that day in school. Of course, the snowfall in Newfoundland was indeed higher than Toronto's. The next day that sharp student raised her hand (for once I was not going to say anything) and informed the teacher of the previous night's program and that the reporter had verified that what Brian had said was indeed correct. Silence enveloped the room—and then the teacher led the class into the next lesson as if nothing had happened.

But the worst was yet to come! We had a tough, cranky ex-military man as our physical education instructor. I managed to get through the swimming (before this, my only experience with swimming had been in a pond) without any problem, and his assistants did most of the gym and basketball work. Although I was new to these activities, I adapted quickly and performed adequately.

With the coming of spring, we were to go outside and do our track and field activities. I was pretty good at track and field, and at a summer air cadet camp the year before I had won a number of events including the 100-yard dash. There were certain benchmarks set for our grade/age group so that any average student could meet them.

On the day of our 100-yard dash, the cantankerous instructor was absent and one of his younger assistants replaced him. We were to line up in small groups of four and run the 100-yard dash to a previously marked area. The assistant had a stopwatch and called from the finish line for us to start. I won my race against the other three but was not told my time or that of the others. On the next day of physical education we were again outside to complete the other track and field tests in high jump, broad jump, and so on. Our cranky main instructor was back in action, and we were lined up in military formation in our shorts and T-shirts. We were lectured about our appearance and punctuality, and then he looked down at his clipboard to review the results from the previous day. A few moments passed, and then he scowled.

"Peckford!"

"Yes, sir," I responded.

"What do I have here? You did the 100-yard dash in eleven seconds? You can't do that! Our top football star can barely do that! Did you do this?"

"Yes, sir," I responded respectfully. "Your assistant supervised the race."

"Yes, yes, I know that," he shouted, "but I just can't believe it. You will have to do it again!"

I protested: "Sir, if the times of everyone else are good, why isn't mine? And running by myself, without competition, is much more difficult."

"Get up there, now," he shouted.

So I proceeded to the starting line. The assistant had a starter gun and the instructor was at the finish line with the stopwatch.

Bang!

I never ran so hard in all my life. Across the finish line the stopwatch clicked—eleven seconds!

An unamused instructor passed the clipboard and stopwatch to his assistant and shouted to us all, "Let's get on to the high jump."

Although school was not going as well as it should have, I had to be mindful that I was expected to work after school and generate revenue for home. My father was working hard at the university and spent caseload time at different social services offices across Toronto, and my older brother was working for CPR in the daytime and going to school at night at IBM. My mother was managing the small apartment for the other seven: meals, clothes, groceries. She was doing the work of two or three people. I was the only other person in the family old enough to get a job, though part-time it would be. It was not easy getting a job. There were a fair number of Italian and Greek immigrants in the area and they were competing for any employment. And, of course, the hours I could work were restricted by my school time. I got a job at a nearby corner store for a few hours after school, but this was not enough.

I went to the Power Supermarket, several blocks down Parliament Street from where we lived. This was a fairly large supermarket that employed a lot of temporary workers. I completed an application form and was queried by the assistant manager, Mr. Pettis—a short, rotund, bald-headed man who looked like this is where he belonged—and the manager, a Mr. Mueller, well-dressed, tall, and businesslike.

I believed they could tell where I was from by my accent, but they asked anyway. I found out later that there was already a Newfoundlander working there who after six months was still only making his starting wage. They told me that there was no opening right now but that if a vacancy arose they would contact me. I told them that I really needed a job and I would work for nothing for a week just to show them that I could work hard. Pettis looked at Mueller, and Mueller at Pettis.

Pettis said, "We have never had anyone make that proposal before. I guess that if you want to work for nothing, we could put you on the soap aisle."

And so, unknown to anyone else, I worked for nothing for a week: Wednesday, Thursday, Friday, 4:00 p.m. to midnight, and on Saturday and Sunday from 8:00 a.m. to midnight. I worked like a dog and sweated my heart out. The next week Mr. Pettis called and told my mother that I had a job and I could come to work on Wednesday. Wow—was I proud—forty-five cents an hour!

Late Sunday evening, before we went home, the workers would pick up their cheques at the office. Mr. Pettis called out to me while I was mopping up the floor.

"Come to the office, Brian." He passed me an envelope. "Open it," he said.

I tore open the envelope and looked at the cheque. "Mr. Pettis, you have made a mistake—this looks like it is too much," I exclaimed.

"My boy," said Pettis, "you sure can work, and we have decided to break our deal. We want to pay you for last week."

I was shocked—it had never entered my mind, I was so consumed with trying to get that job.

"Thank you, Mr. Pettis," I said.

"Back to the floor," Pettis responded.

In four weeks I was the highest-paid temporary worker in the store. And my countryman was still at the bottom of the pay scale.

Much later, when I became a teacher, I would tell this story to my students many, many times. And it remains one of my most precious memories. There is no replacement for hard work.

Of course, this lower area of Parliament Street had its own problems, like many inner-city areas. I experienced this first-hand. I almost lost one of my first paycheques.

Walking home on Parliament Street after twelve one night, I encountered a surprise attack from three boys around my own age. Two of them jumped out from an alleyway and threw me to the ground, savagely kicking me in the groin. Somehow I got to my feet and struck one of them to the ground and began to hit the second one. A third boy sprang from the alleyway, and I caught him leaping and struck at him. He staggered backwards—the first boy was still on the ground, being helped by the second—and as quick as the incident started, the boys fled. They were good with their feet, and as I stumbled home I felt the pain from my waist to my knees. I was at home a few days to recuperate, but I was content that the scoundrels did not get my cheque.

The months passed, the family adjusted as best it could, Father was doing well, my older brother was relatively happy at his work and night school, the younger siblings were happy, and Mother shouldered her responsibilities with stoic determination. But I think we were all relieved when the time came to return home. I had to stay on a little while longer to do my school exams.

So I was back in Lewisporte, Newfoundland, for the summer of 1960. I needed a job before school began in the fall, but few were available. I managed to get a few weeks at the new vocational school that had just been constructed. Some students were needed to check inventory on the new equipment that was arriving. But this only got me to the end of July. I then parked myself at a plumbing and heating store that was also involved in subcontracting, installing plumbing and heating in new buildings. I would get up early in the morning and go to the premises before it opened so that I would create the right impression—that I had no problem getting up in the morning and that I was really serious about getting a job. The first few mornings the answer was no, we have no opportunities right now. I kept going each morning. I knew the owner of the business; his son was a friend of mine. A few mornings later, the company won a contract to install the plumbing in a new school that was being constructed in a nearby town. I was there early in the morning when the chief plumber was talking to the owner about the contract. He suggested to the owner that he would need a helper for the job. Given that I was the only person who had presented himself each morning, and here I was again, the job was mine. The days were sunny and warm that August, and my boss (Mr. Val Tucker) was an excellent worker and teacher. I learned a lot from him in just thirty days. It's funny that I clearly remember this brief thirty-day job forty-nine years later. I remember mentioning this man's name at a political rally in Lewisporte over twenty-five years later—I was quickly told from the floor that he was in the audience.

The school system in Toronto went to grade thirteen. In Newfoundland it went to grade eleven. So there were many courses that I took in Toronto that did not qualify for high school graduation (junior matriculation) in Newfoundland. Hence, I was back in school in the fall. That year spun by and I tried hard to concentrate and pursue my studies, which were made more enjoyable by our main teacher, Mr. Paddock.

One of the courses, taught by another teacher, was Algebra. During these years mathematics was split among the three components of Algebra, Trigonometry, and Geometry. The class was having great difficulty understanding this subject and following the teacher's lessons. At Christmas, I think only three out of forty-two passed the exam. After the break at Christmas, a number of students approached the teacher and explained the dilemma, which of course should have been clear to him, yet he seemed oblivious to our plight and was just soldiering on as if all was well with the Algebra world. Things still did not improve, and given that he was also the principal of the school, there was little else we thought we could do. Luckily for me, my parents had just completed a room "upstairs" in our one-storey house. This became my place for study, and I would spend hours there pouring over the Algebra book trying to understand the material. I still remember the names of the authors written on the cover of that infamous book—Hall and Knight—and they were not my favourite people. Sometime during that period from January to June, I figured it out and understood enough to pass the province-wide exams. I passed the other subjects and now had to decide—where do I go from here?

I remember that my father had mentioned university, and Mr. Paddock had also mentioned it. There were not many from my class interested, and I didn't know how interested I really was. The thing was, I really was not mechanical at all, and just getting involved in the jobs like I had in the summertime would be low-paying and uninteresting as careers. And I still remembered Mr. Paddock's question—what are you going to do with the rest of your life? And of course I had heard that a brand new campus was about to open and that there was money available if you were studying to be a teacher.

Well, I applied and was accepted. Off to St. John's and a boarding house.

Mr. Paddock passed away a few years ago. When his family informed me of this, I wrote his son the following:

> Thank you for calling me and informing me of the passing of your father. I was unaware of his illness and, of course, like you, the news came as a shock.
>
> I feel obligated to write this note to you because your father was a very special person in my life.
>
> In everyone's life there are many people who influence you. And in my case that is also true. But two people tower over the rest. One is my father and the other is your father.
>
> Your father taught me in high school in Lewisporte in the early sixties. He instilled in us the necessity to think and to think logically and more importantly to think critically—and to assemble the facts before forming an opinion. These lessons were the most important I have ever learned and were and are of immeasurable value to me. There was

another great idea that I learned from him that has guided almost everything I do and that is fairness. I saw this in how he treated others and in how he taught. It was wonderful to behold. In one subtle move on his part when I was in grade 11 (I told him about this later and he said he didn't remember—I doubt that) he changed the course of my life, forcing me to reflect on who I was and what, if anything, I should be doing with my life.

You may know that I had cause to call on him when I was premier. And his help and counsel were invaluable to me—from fisheries matters to the Constitution. It was so good to know that I could call on someone like him at that time.

Shelley said of Wordsworth and I say of Brose Paddock:

"Thou hast like to a rock-built refuge stood
Above the blind and battling multitude."

CHAPTER 2: A "HIGHER" EDUCATION

"A university should be a place of light, of liberty and of learning."
—Benjamin Disraeli

IT WAS ALL A new experience. Exciting and sometimes puzzling. Everyone was swept up in the new campus celebrations. The opening of the new modern Memorial University campus, replacing an old and worn-out campus on Parade Street, took place in October, 1961.

Mr. Smallwood, the premier, had all these famous people visit, and I remember being part of the parade celebration, marching with hundreds of others along Elizabeth Avenue parallel to the new campus. There were bands and marching groups, schools and various organizations, and people representing electoral districts from all over the province. There was the prime minister of Canada, Mr. Diefenbaker, the new Chancellor Lord Thomson, and the distinguished American, Eleanor Roosevelt, wife of President Franklin Delano Roosevelt. It was a glorious time for the province, and it launched me and many others on our educational and life careers.

There was lots to learn and courses to choose from and my first exposure to lineups. Just registering at the university meant a lineup, and choosing subjects and books all involved lineups. Being a bayman, this did not come easy. We quickly became aware that this new place was very much a townie place, and we baymen were the outsiders. It was changing with the large influx of baymen registered in the Education faculty, but there was still a big swagger to those townies that did not sit well with many of us. This became even more grating when one of our own numbers tried to act like a townie.

However, perhaps the most surprising early experience of the bayman's place was a particular policy at the university. We were informed that we would all have to take a speech test. And if we did not speak "properly," we would have to take special speech lessons. Wow! This was a bit of a shocker. And so we were all given times when we would have to appear before two professors in a room and read a prose passage, the reading of which would determine whether we would have to take the special speech course or be exempted. This was perhaps the first time since my experiences in high school in Toronto that I felt I was being hard done by, as we say.

So I was ready with my own approach to the situation. On entering the room I was asked to sit, which I refused, interrupting the two professors to propose that I remain standing and recite a piece of work that I had chosen. Somewhat taken aback, the professors agreed, and I proceeded to recite from Tennyson's *Ulysses*: "It little profits that an idle king, by this still hearth, among these barren crags, match'd with an aged wife . . ."

I don't remember the exact number of lines I recited, but it was not many before I was interrupted by one of the professors and told that that was just fine—there would be no need to recite more, and I could go.

There was no speech class for me.

But the whole thing was disgraceful. This procedure did not last for many years, thankfully. Ironically, it wasn't long before there was a Folklore Department and valiant efforts made to preserve the many dialects (that we were encouraged to "eliminate") throughout the province. There was this attitude throughout the land that we had to modernize, as exemplified by the new campus, and that meant for some strange reason that our language and customs would have to undergo major surgery. I was later to realize that this was largely the Smallwood prescription for a "better" province.

Perhaps equally memorable was the initiative by the Smallwood government to provide generous assistance to us students in the form of grants and salaries. This was announced with great fanfare by Premier Smallwood with his full Cabinet in tow at a special assembly held in the Physical Education Building. There was great jubilation among the students and it seemed to be received positively by the population at large. However, a number of us thought that these measures were going too far. Personally, I felt that the present $600 per year grant to Education students, which would be forgiven with two years teaching in the province, was adequate and that we needed to get more qualified teachers in the classroom as quickly as possible. And even this should have a sunset provision at some point. Further, I felt that loans rather than grants would be the better approach to take and that salaries were just too much of a good thing. I began to recognize the politics of it all and was somewhat affronted as I watched the premier and his Cabinet so lavishly dispense with money that I was sure could be used for more worthy things.

These were negative experiences that have stayed with me, but there were many more numerous positive experiences.

I took to the university right away, notwithstanding the long walks to and from my boarding houses in rain and snow. It was exhilarating rubbing shoulders with all these bright people and listening to the more senior students discuss and debate the great ideas of the world. I was captured by it all and spent an inordinate amount of time in the Arts Building common room engaged in debate that seemed at the time more important than classes, or anything else that was happening around me.

The university faculty and administration were conservative and still maintained some sort of dress code. I remember being called to the dean's office one day to be questioned about an alleged infraction, from some days before, of the dress rules. It was all news to me and I said so to the Dean. He was a little taken back by my mildly aggressive response and confessed to me that someone connected with the Education Society had reported me and that he didn't know the facts of the matter. This was one of my first encounters with raw politics and ego-dominated organizations. At the time a number of us Education students were agitating for a more open and aggressive Education Society. The leaders were well-entrenched and seemed to want a closed shop and maintenance of the status quo. Being one of the ringleaders of the dissenting group, I guess, I was singled out to be reported to the administration.

This new, more aggressive temperament among the Education

students was really a new phenomenon, as they had been known in the past as a passive lot who did not rock the establishment boat. But a new day was beginning to dawn, and even this stodgy bunch was awakening from a long slumber. Perhaps this best manifested itself in a major undertaking by a number of us concerning teacher salaries. Looking to our eventual graduation, we began to investigate the level of remuneration that we would receive on becoming a teacher. We were astounded to find that the wages of teachers then were much lower than what graduates from other faculties would receive in their chosen fields.

So we began to make noise about this—appearing on the local TV newscast evening news (with Don Jamieson, who would later be my adversary in my first election as premier) and finally presenting a brief to the government. This proved to be a little difficult at the time, so a number of us went to the premier's office at the Confederation Building to give our brief to the premier's parliamentary assistant, Mr. Edward Roberts, who would be an Opposition Member/Leader in the legislature during my time and, later, become an effective lieutenant-governor.

The university introduced me to ideas and the necessity to think analytically. It introduced me to poetry, history, and philosophy—and most importantly I was introduced to Wordsworth and Shakespeare, Milton, Donne, and Tennyson, and a real library. I remember one day Professor Pitt revealing that if he had to live on a desolate island for the rest of his life and could take only one book with him, it would be Wordsworth's *Prelude*.

The breadth and depth of Shakespeare's understanding of human nature was so remarkable that it was difficult to credit that all the plays and sonnets were all composed by the same person. While the early comedies delight, the later ones had real characters like Malvolio and Shylock, and the histories brought into focus power and intrigue and introduced that over-the-top fellow, Falstaff. The tragedies are explorations of man's highs and lows. One can often hear the echo of Wordsworth's phrase "the still sad music of humanity" as one reads them. No other English writer surpasses Shakespeare. I was later to be introduced to American literature: Whitman, Frost, Hawthorne, Faulkner, Wolf, and America's greatest poet, Emily Dickinson.

I remember Professor Schwartz in History class making the case for the large part economics played in man's development. I had never thought about this before, so used to viewing history as an isolated list of events and personages was I. The broad sweep of discoveries and inventions through the Renaissance and Reformation—art and music opened up a world for a lifetime of reading and appreciation. I still have the wonderful book *Religion and the Rise of Capitalism* by R.H. Tawney and David Thomson's *Europe Since Napoleon*. I remember Professor Bruce and his review of Greek and Roman history. He urged me to do a paper on the influence of the Athenian navy upon the success of the Athenian state, which I did. Professor David Freemen led us through the metaphysical poets of Donne, Herrick, Herbert, and Marvell, and who can forget Milton? Sister Nolasco gave the course in Philosophy for Education students, and this was my first brush with Socrates, Plato, and Aristotle, with St. Augustine, Aquinas, Bacon, Voltaire, and Chardin. Unfortunately, it was the only stimulating course offered by the Faculty of Education.

In my third or fourth year I got involved in running for student council. I am unsure, now, how this came about, but I think it had to do with my continuous debates and discussions in the common room and my involvement in the Debating Society and a fraternity called Mu Upsilon Nu. However, I was not well-known outside of these groups, and hence seeking a seat on the council was really a bit of a long shot. Well, a small group of students—probably fired up more by the high risks and my bayman roots than anything else—swept into action to assist me and, from posters to candidate debates, we made a positive impression. To our surprise, I polled third in the balloting and took a position on the council for that year. I was responsible to council for overseeing the various clubs and societies on campus. Rex Murphy headed the polls and became president. I remember one of the first speeches he gave to some organization in the city. He contacted me for assistance, and I remember one night sweating with him over the text of the speech he should give. The council was a real debating society then, with all of the members taking many a long while to say very little. It was the nature of young, naive politicians to be so wordy, I suppose, yet I have learned that even more mature politicians don't seem to be much better.

I was drawn to the Debating Society, a fledgling organization at the time. A number of debates were sponsored by the society and I willingly participated. One I clearly remember was a debate over the statement: "Labrador belongs to Quebec." I was on the negative team with Bob (Robert) Crocker, and I remember Rex Murphy was on the affirmative team. It was memorable because of the topic (one sure way to get a Newfoundlander's dander up) and also because Rex, in an effort no doubt to intimidate his opposition and perhaps try and impress the judges, entered the theatre in dramatic fashion after everyone was seated, burdened down by a pile of books which he placed next to his lectern on the stage. Notwithstanding the flourish, Bob and I won the debate.

After my first year at university, I spent a year teaching grade six at Lewisporte Central School. It was a funny arrangement. Central school meant from grade seven to eleven in those days. But apparently there was some problem with housing the grade sixes at the elementary schools in town, and so grade six (all eighty-five of them) ended up in a section/extension of the central school with its own entrance/exit, thereby, I suppose, still keeping within the silly guidelines of maintaining the central school idea. I think my reasoning at this stage for taking a year from university was to see whether I liked teaching, since I was having some ideas about switching to law at that time.

This was a wonderful experience and solidified my original decision to go into teaching, although originally it was as much financial as it was a career choice. The provincial government at the time was offering a $600 grant for first-year Education students. The only incentive was that you had to commit to teach for two years in the province. In any case, this one year teaching was very rewarding, notwithstanding the crammed quarters and two large classes of forty and forty-two, respectively. There were two of us teachers—Jack Bussey and myself—and we had six courses: I taught three and Jack, of course, taught the other three, switching classes as appropriate.

Grade six is a great grade—the students no longer need personal help and are inquisitive without the teenage issues. We had a large number of very bright students, which in itself was a challenge, but it also presented the larger challenge of ensuring that the average student and those with difficulties were not ignored. The existing English course seemed inadequate, and so I received grudging permission to replace some of the program with materials that I had discovered from the United States. This would be a direct cost to the parents, so I wrote all the parents and received overwhelming support from them to get the new materials and bill them. This proved to be very successful and of significant benefit to students who were having some difficulty in reading and comprehension.

As I said, I enjoyed the classes immensely—they were lively and often spontaneous. After we got used to one another and a few ground rules were established, it was surprising how cohesive the classes became. Each morning there was a short period of fifteen minutes where there would be general discussion, usually about the hockey games of the day or weekend before. I remember one occasion when we were discussing a certain local hockey game in which I had played; it became obvious that I had incurred an injury above my eye—it required stitches and I was wearing a patch. The kids were eager to know what had happened. So an animated discussion ensued as to whether the opposing team was to blame, if it was an accident, or whether in fact I was a little too aggressive. In the midst of this serious debate, Wayne, eager to speak, interjected and exclaimed that he knew exactly what had happened. The other students questioned him, and with a sly grin he evaded a direct answer.

I stepped in and said: "Wayne, you owe it to the class to provide the answer. You said you really knew what happened to my eye—so stand in your place and tell the class."

Wayne slowly got to his feet and, still with that impish grin, declared, "She kisses too high."

It was this same Wayne who, in a discussion of where the moon gets its light, declared in dramatic fashion after first being reluctant to provide an answer: "Ah, it's the man in the moon with a flashlight."

Then there was Aubrey, a fifteen-year-old who for many reasons (home issues and falling through the cracks in the formal school setting) was a student in our grade six class. He was almost as tall as me, and having no other way to get attention, the first day school opened he began bullying a lot of the male students and making an overall disruptive scene. Of course, having only one year of training (I doubt whether more of the kind I got would have helped anyway), I quickly resorted to some basic common sense. First, I had to see to it that I was in total control of the class. That meant, one day after some serious disruption, taking Aubrey by the scruff of the neck and leading him out of the classroom. He quickly saw that while he was almost as tall as me he was not yet as strong, as I quickly rendered him physically helpless. However, I realized that this was just a temporary measure and that I could not do this every week and hope for a permanent fix.

I had been planning to try and get an empty classroom in the main part of the school on Friday afternoons to do some physical exercise with the students. And sure enough, I was able to get an hour that afternoon, and with the principal's permission I was about to implement it. Additionally, I had secured a basketball that we could throw around and do some basic dribbling. Of course, then students would have to wear, when possible, sneakers or other appropriate footwear. I had told the class to expect an exciting announcement. So I was before the class announcing this addition to their school activity when it suddenly dawned on me that here was my chance to reach Aubrey, and so in the course of my announcement I said that I was going to need someone to help me on Friday afternoons, looking after the basketballs, getting everyone over to the other classroom and lined up, and that I had appointed Aubrey to do this work with me. The class was happy with the announcement, of course, and when I further said that I was sure everyone would get along and co-operate with Aubrey, there was some hesitation, but then just about everyone agreed with the appointment. You could see among some of them that they knew what I was up to, and they nodded with a flash of understanding.

Not only was this afternoon activity a great boon to class cohesion, but Aubrey became a new person. We were all surprised—from the first Friday when Aubrey asked for permission to exit the class five minutes early to get ready for the new activity, to his organizing the students, looking after the balls and footwear—this was a new day for us all. Aubrey suddenly got interested in his other school work, began passing his tests, and behaved in class. I have often wondered whatever happened to Aubrey—at any rate, he passed grade six and was a well-adjusted young man the last time I saw him.

It was incidents like this that left no room for choosing another profession. In addition to the new stimulating environment of the university, I was blessed beyond measure to have had the good fortune during these years to work in some of the more remote parts of the province.

I already had experience working for the Department of Public Welfare. It seemed natural for me to see if I could get another job with them. There was a need for students in the summer months to relieve the permanent welfare officers around the province. So I visited the department, picked up an application form, completed it, and submitted it to the department. No answer. I went to the department and was able to set up a meeting a few days hence with the Director of Field Services, a Mr. Hollett. (As I write, I have been informed that he passed away at the age of eighty-five.) He explained to me the role of temporary welfare officers: they were to conduct the basics while the permanent officer was on holidays, and mainly do the annual reviews of those people who were on some kind of permanent assistance. In the larger centres there would not be a problem since there would be other permanent officers in those offices to guide the temporary people, but for those temporaries going to the more remote regions it would be a little more difficult, so there would be a couple of days training (reviewing The Welfare Act and Regulations), and off you went. Sometimes, if you were lucky, you would get a few days with the permanent officer before they left.

One surviving letter of the department's acceptance of me for one of these temporary jobs is still in my possession.

Department of Public Welfare
St. John's, Nfld

April 16, 1964

Mr. Brian Peckford
Lewisporte, Nfld

Dear Mr. Peckford:

I am pleased to advise you that your application for temporary employment with this Department has been approved.

Your salary, during your period of employment with us, will be at the rate of $200.00 per month. In addition, the Department will accept responsibility for your board and lodging up to the amount of $60.00 per month providing you are not posted to an area where it will be possible to reside in your own home. Any charge in excess of $60.00 per month, however, will be your own responsibility.

This Department gives no undertaking to employ you for any specific period of time. However, if there is no reason to feel dissatisfied with your performance it is anticipated your service will be required until late August next.

Will you please arrange to report to the undersigned at the Confederation Building on Monday, May 4, 1964, at 9:00 a.m.

Yours truly,

C.S. Knight
Director of Field Services

"BUT, MR. PECKFORD, I am sorry that there are no openings in the larger centres," announced Mr. Hollett.

"You mean there isn't a job available?" I hesitantly replied.

"No, I'm sorry. You're a little late applying and all the openings in the major centres are taken."

"Well, perhaps I could go to one of the other places," I muttered.

A surprised expression crossed Mr. Hollett's face. "You mean, you would go to a smaller place, perhaps an isolated place?"

"Yes," I said, not really fully comprehending the implications.

"Well, you're a little young and you have no experience managing an office by yourself in an isolated area. We usually persuade some older students who have had a year in a larger centre to go to one of the smaller remote offices," Mr. Hollett explained. "But we are having trouble this year, so perhaps something might become available. I will let you know if we have an opening in one of the smaller offices, and if you're still interested we'll see what we can do."

I left the office a little dejected but with a glimmer of hope that I would get a call telling me of a vacancy. Meanwhile, I began thinking about my answer. Did I really want to take a job that saw me in some isolated place for the whole summer? I needed the money so I could go back to university in the fall, and there was this tinge of adventure about the idea. So I let my proposal stand.

Luck was with me. A call came from Mr. Hollett to come and see him.

"We have an opening at La Scie," he said. "It is on the northeast coast—no doubt you have heard of it. It is isolated but not real small; there is a fish plant and a road to a couple of communities, although they are not linked to the main road system. The welfare officer will be there when you arrive and you'll have a few days with him before you're left on your own. Most of the communities in that welfare district you will have to visit by boat."

It was March and final exams were around the corner. Now that I had secured a job I could concentrate on some of the study I had failed to do for most of the year. I got through the next few weeks thinking about the summer and trying to concentrate on final exams.

It wasn't easy and my exams were all packed together in a couple of days. This was still the time when the final exam was worth 100% of the final mark—so if you blew it in those three hours, that was that.

I struggled through—studying in some cases through the night—and then went straight to the exam room. I was afraid someone was going to speak to me along the way or just outside the door to the exam room, because I felt so mentally full that if I responded, everything I had stuffed in my head the night before would suddenly spill out and leave me empty of any knowledge to answer the questions on the exam.

With exams out of the way, I contacted Mr. Hollett and began a two-day orientation, learning about the legislation and various programs and how to complete the various forms.

"There's a coastal boat leaving next week," Mr. Hollett informed me, "and we would like you to be on it to La Scie. We have secured a boarding house for you and the welfare officer will be there for a week or so to help you adjust."

Just like that, I was off the next week on the *Northern Ranger* to La Scie.

CHAPTER 3: A PRACTICAL EDUCATION

"I am a part of all that I have met."
—Tennyson

IT WAS LATE APRIL and almost miraculously the ice along the east and northeast coast had stayed several miles offshore, making possible a very early start to the coastal boat season to northern Newfoundland and Labrador. And so, unlike the harrowing experiences of my mother and her five children crossing Placentia Bay in a snowstorm in 1951, I had a relatively easy time as the boat made its way along the east coast of the island, stopping first at Twillingate and then on to La Scie.

La Scie was the easternmost point of land on the Baie Verte Peninsula, nestled under Cape John with a U-shaped harbour, and every inch a fishing community. This was the proud home of trap fishing crews and a large fish plant. The news here was all to do with fishing, the wind, the ice in the spring, and the price of fish. Sammy Thoms's general store was where the old fellers hung out, and if you wanted to get a real quick lesson of trap fishing on the northeast coast of Newfoundland, this was the place to visit. Not that it all came easy when you entered the place; it was a bustle, and after a hardy welcome from Sammy, who was otherwise too busy to talk to you, you settled on a box or barrel and waited for the conversation to slowly evolve. However, change was in the air—a contractor (friendly to Premier Smallwood's party) was busy digging and blasting as they were installing a water and sewer system in the community (completely financed by the provincial government), and the first highway to the town was under construction by another company friendly to Smallwood. There was already a crude road system from La Scie to a number of nearby communities, including the mining town of Tilt Cove. These communities all formed a part of the welfare district I was to administer—the rest of the district would be communities on the north side of Green Bay, southwest of La Scie and accessible only by boat.

The permanent welfare officer was with me for a week or so and we took one quick visit by boat to Snook's Arm and Round Harbour to give me a taste of what was in store. Well, of course, the actual experience of being on your own is always quite a shock, notwithstanding the advice given to you and the things you read. New, unique, and strange experiences await and test your youth and inexperience.

The office was a one-room (plus a small waiting room), stand-alone building with a desk, a couple of chairs, a small oil heater, a typewriter, and a filing cabinet. My being new and young, it was natural that my first week or so was to field a large influx of potential clients who wished to test my mettle. This was truly a baptism by fire, and though I began to get my footing, there were a number of incidents which, during my stay there, reflect what today would be complex social and emotional problems.

The first to arise concerned a family in Harbour Round, a nearby community accessible by road. One of the children of a family there had a serious and, as yet, undetected disease. The local nurse and doctor who visited from Baie Verte recommended that the child go to St. John's for further diagnosis and assessment. The family could not afford to pay for such a trip and I was brought into the situation by the father visiting my office to ask for help. After examining the man's circumstance, it was obvious that the department would have to pay for this matter. In the subsequent days I contacted the nurse, and arrangements were made for the child to be seen by a specialist at a hospital in St. John's. The appointment date was set for a few weeks hence, and I began the transportation and accommodation planning.

I remember reading a play in high school that told of the chief character having scrupulously planned a crime scene, but one variable was still in play and thwarted the master plan, to which he exclaimed, "I did not foresee it."

Such was the case with me when the father appeared at my office very early one morning, distraught and frightened.

"Mr. Peckford, sir, you never told me," the father stuttered.

"Told you what?" I queried.

"That you or the nurse will not be taking my daughter to St. John's to the hospital. I don't understand," the nervous father replied.

"Oh, sorry, I just assumed you would know that the family would have to take her. You see, you and your wife are available. You're not working, and while your wife is working at home, if she goes, you can look after the other children."

The man broke down. "We can't go. We have never been anywhere . . ."

I will never forget the look of fright on that man's face. He was truly afraid and became almost incomprehensible.

An hour or more passed, and although the father had come early, it was now after nine o'clock and other people were in the little waiting room, no doubt able to hear scraps of the conversation coming from the office.

"Listen," I whispered, "there are others outside there now. I don't want them to hear our talk. Tell you what I will do. I will come to Harbour Round tomorrow and visit with you and your wife. We'll have a good chat about this. Don't worry, we will solve this."

Slowly, the father gathered his composure as I continued to reassure him that everything would work out. I hurriedly escorted him from the office and past the growing number of people in the waiting room and those waiting outside the building.

The next morning I rented a car from a local merchant and travelled the ten miles to Harbour Round, which, like La Scie, was at first a French fishing station since it formed part of what was known as the French Shore. There were then a couple hundred people living there. I found the house, parked the car nearby, and walked up to the front door. Although it was around 11:00 a.m. the community was quiet—no doubt aware of my arrival.

It was a one-storey clapboard house of moderate size for the time. I knocked on the porch door and was greeted by the mother. She was of medium height, with reddish hair, and a round reddish face. I introduced myself and was led into the kitchen where the father was sitting at the chrome kitchen table. I sat next to him, and the mother across from me.

"Now, a nice cup of tea would be all right," I said, as I looked at a steaming teapot on the wood stove.

A nervous smile emerged on the mother's face as she got up to fetch the tea.

"And how are you this morning?" I inquired of the father.

"Not good, sir, I hardly slept last night."

"And I, too," exclaimed the missus.

"Let's get right down to it, then," I replied.

I went on to explain that it just would not be possible for the nurse or myself to accompany the child to St. John's, that we were needed here to help other people who had problems just as big as this one, and that there would be people to assist them along the way. I indicated that the route was to take the coastal boat from La Scie to Lewisporte; he could stay in a hotel there and then take the train to St. John's. I also made it clear that their child desperately needed to be examined by a specialist and that not to do so could endanger the child's long-term health.

The mother spoke up. "We have never even travelled on the coastal boat; we have never seen a train or been in a hospital. We are scared."

The father added, "What is it like to ride a train? Are there elevators in the hospital?"

I realized I had a lot of explaining to do, so I began by describing the coastal boat trip, where they would stay in Lewisporte, the hotel there, the train ride, and the arrangements in St. John's. I said we would make extra arrangements so that there would be someone to meet them on every step of the journey, and explained all the other details to try to increase their confidence. But the questions kept coming from the very frightened couple, so much so that I decided further conversations were needed. I met with the father and mother a few more times, involved other people, and finally, about a week later, the father agreed.

The day for the father and daughter to leave on the coastal boat finally arrived, and with the help of the mother a fond farewell ensued. We watched as the boat pulled away from the government wharf and then as it navigated between the headlands that helped form the harbour. I was relieved; the mother, however, was in tears, comforted by family and friends.

I went to the office early one morning three or four weeks later, and who should be waiting for me but the father. As I unlocked the door to the office, he rushed in, all smiles, as he hurriedly began describing his unbelievable experiences, from the screeching wheels of the trains, to his absolute certainty that as the train came to a curve it would jump the tracks, to the big hospital with its elevator that he learned to use, to the wonderful doctors and nurses that attended to him, and most particularly to his daughter.

"She is going to be all right," he exclaimed. "The doctors said she had a rare disease but it could be treated."

"And you and your wife will be all right now too," I said.

"Yes," he said, "we will be all right now. We want to thank you . . . for making us see."

That was a very pleasant experience. There were others not so pleasant. For example, one time I went to one of the isolated communities on my regular visit. My main function was to fill in for the permanent welfare office, and that was supposed to mean travelling to the various communities and updating information for those who were permanent clients of the department, such as widows, widowers, disabled, and elderly people. Of course, things are never as they seem. There were things that just happened. At this community a number of men came seeking temporary assistance. I was new and the test was on. I had discovered some days before that many men in the community had been working on a government project near the community. And the money was pretty good. When I arrived at the wharf there were several men already waiting to see me. Jack Budgell, the owner and operator of the boat I had hired, was a little nervous.

As we were tying up he said to me, "You know, these fellows seem a little nervous."

"Nervous about what?" I questioned.

"I don't know, me son, but they are acting strange to me." Jack was not new to the area and so when he gave an opinion about the area you'd better listen.

Anyway, I asked Jack to tell the men that I would see them individually in my little room in the stern of the boat. This is where I slept—it had a couple of bunks, a small wooden table a foot or so off the floor, and a tiny wood stove. There was really only room for two persons. And so the procession commenced as the men, one by one, came down, sought assistance, were refused, and, mumbling their dissatisfaction, left the boat and wharf.

"Do you mean to tell me you turned them all down?" Jack exclaimed.

"Yes," I said. "They were the fellows who were working on the government project for the last few months and do not qualify for assistance. I'd say that was why they seemed to act strange to you. They really knew that this was wrong, what they were going to do."

Of course, the word got around the harbour that this new, young relieving officer had turned down all the men. It wasn't long before there appeared on the wharf one very angry woman. Dashing up to the edge of the wharf she shouted out, "Jack, Jack, where are you?"

Jack appeared from the wheelhouse. "Yes, my dear, this is Jack!"

"Jack, where is that young relieving officer? I got to see him right away."

Jack moved swiftly to the stern of the boat, opened the doors to the stern section, and began whispering. "We've got a pretty mad woman who wants to see you right now. Man is she mad."

I climbed up the few stairs to Jack. "What—an angry woman?"

And before Jack could speak, there she was. "Are you the relieving officer?" she growled, looking at me.

"Yes, ma'am. I am."

As she pointed her finger and came toward me, she shouted, "I have to talk to you right now!"

"All right, come on down and we can have a private conversation."

She stumbled down the few stairs, fuming under her breath, and finally settled across from me on one of the bunks. In retrospect, I became a little too official, taking out my daily worksheet on which I recorded time and date and name of all who came to see me.

"Your name, please?"

"My name, my name!" she shouted. "Listen, I'm the wife of George who came to see you a couple of hours ago. You turned him down! You wouldn't give him a food order."

I lowered my head to write the date on the worksheet, my eye no longer on my client. In an instant she swooped, grabbed a large piece of firewood from the bucket by the stove, and leaning across the small expanse between us, clobbered me over the head!

I fell back on the other bunk, surprised and more than a little dazed. Seconds later, when I came to my senses, she was up over the stairs on the deck of the boat, cursing as she made her way to the wharf.

Jack thought he heard a commotion and came out of the wheelhouse in time to see the woman scampering up to the wharf deck and then on to shore.

I was climbing the stairs when Jack met me. "What happened?"

"I was knocked out by a very angry woman. She picked up a junk of wood in the bucket and let me have it."

Jack had a wicked sense of humour—a slight smile crossed his face, then a wider grin, and then a full laugh. He bent over laughing. "How will you write this one in your daily worksheet?"

IN 1966, I WAS teaching in Springdale. In 1972, I won the Progressive Conservative Party nomination for the district of Green Bay. I was campaigning in a community on the North Shore and did not realize that many of the people whose doors I had just knocked on were sort of following me down the pathway to this certain house. As I entered the property, a woman came screaming out the doorway.

"Don't you dare come on our property, we want nothing to do with those dirty Tories. I remember you, Mr. Peckford!"

My wood assailant strikes again! As we say in the political business, I marked her down as doubtful.

PERHAPS THE MOST UNUSUAL yet rewarding experience of that year was the case of the witch and my supervisor, which ended with more than a little irony.

One slow afternoon in July, I was working away in the office and was about to close a little early when I heard someone enter. Before I had a chance to open the door from the office to the waiting room, this middle-aged woman of medium height did it for me. She abruptly entered the office and began chattering on about her neighbours. I took my seat behind the desk and tried to make some sense of what the lady was saying.

"Just slow down a bit, missus," I said. "I can't pick out what you're saying. What is your name?"

She told me her name was Rosy. "I lives over there," pointing out the window, "around the harbour, in old Skipper Thoms's garden. Of course he's dead, been dead for years. But his relatives are there."

"And why did you come and see me today?"

"I come to see you because I knows you will help me. See, those relatives thinks I'm a witch."

Taken aback, I responded, "Why do you say that?"

"I told Charlie I had a dream, and he was going to drown in a few weeks. Charlie did not like that. And his wife, she will get a visit from a stranger, I told him."

"Well, don't you think telling them about such tragedies was pretty unusual?"

"But I dreamt it and it is real. But you—you are favoured. You are favoured."

"Favoured?"

"Yes, the Satan man told me."

I realized that this was not going to be easy. I figured that I should just go along and see where this would take me.

"But these are really only dreams, Rosy," I quietly replied. "They are not real."

"Oh, oh you are wrong, Mr. Peck—my dreams come true, and the Satan man? He visited me in my kitchen yesterday."

"I would say that this Satan man was really a dream too—a waking dream."

This stalled Rosy. She paused and seemed to be trying to process this twist to the conversation. She mumbled, "Waking dream, waking dream."

I thought this was a good time to pose some down-to-earth questions that might take her out of her spell.

"Rosy, are you married?"

"I was; he's gone now. Jack's gone now."

"What happened, Rosy?"

"He drowned. I told him that it was too rough out there. I told him to leave his trap until tomorrow, but he wouldn't listen. He's gone and I am alone."

"I am really sorry to hear that, Rosy. That must have been quite a shock. I had a friend who drowned."

"You did? You had a friend who drowned?"

"Yes, I did. And I was pretty sad for a long time."

"For a long time," she repeated.

"And Rosy, you have been sad for a long time, too."

"Yes, four years is a long time," she said, almost under her breath.

"Well, now you know someone who has had an experience something like yours."

"Yes, Mr. Peck. I am glad I met you. But the people in the garden, Charlie and his wife and friends, are tormenting me—they say I am a witch . . . "

"Well, I will go over to your place with you and talk to Charlie and his wife and his friends."

"You will come over with me now!" she exclaimed.

"Yes. I will, right now."

And so we left and walked around the harbour. She was now in good spirits and pointed out where her late parents had lived, where her father's stage was, where she had played tiddlywinks, and the dilapidated building that used to be her school. We finally arrived at her place.

"Rosy, if you would go and get a steaming pot of hot tea, I will go talk to Charlie."

Rosy glanced at me—a half-questioning look—but then exclaimed, "Okay, I will get us some tea."

I knocked on Charlie's door; it was early suppertime. A slightly balding man, tall and muscular, appeared in the doorway.

Of course, Charlie recognized me at once, and I could see his surprise at seeing me. Quickly, I explained the situation.

Charlie and his wife were receptive and realized immediately the reason for my visit once I mentioned Rosy. So we exchanged experiences. They confirmed to me that Rosy's husband had in fact drowned four years ago. He had fished with Charlie on many occasions. And they described how devastated Rosy was when it happened, how she had gradually withdrawn from the community and become a real loner, and that lately she was telling people tragic things that would soon befall them. It was the children and teenagers who called her a witch. No doubt a word used by their parents. I proposed a little agreement with them—try to be friendly to her and say positive things and try and get the young people to stop verbally jabbing her. In return I would keep talking to Rosy and try to get her to look outward and be more positive. We would see if this stopped the dreams, and if they detected any deterioration in her behaviour they should contact me. They were very happy to help and so I took a quick exit, explaining to them that I had a cup of tea waiting next door.

Rosy was overjoyed to see me—it was as if it had been weeks rather than minutes since I last saw her. The tea was hot and some bread buns and partridgeberry jam made for a perfect mug-up.

"Rosy," I said. "I have spoken to Charlie and Mabel and they told me that they will talk to the children and tell them to stop calling you names. They also miss your husband. They said he was a really good man."

"Yes," Rosy said, "a really, really good man!"

"And Rosy, Mabel told me you are a top-notch knitter and her boys need some new mittens."

"It's been so long I almost forget how to knit. Yes. I will get back at it and knit some mittens. That's a good idea, Mr. Peck."

We passed the rest of the mug-up in small talk. There was no more mention of witch words and seeing things.

"Okay, Rosy," I said, "I have to go, but I want you to promise me that you will come see me every Monday morning at eleven o'clock. You can fill me in on how those mittens are doing and what else you have been doing."

"Mr. Peck, I was going to ask you if I could come and see you again. Every Monday at eleven o'clock—I like these chats."

And so for the next couple of weeks, Rosy was punctual and we had some great chats. I found out all about her family and her growing up.

The Monday of the third week, Rosy did not appear, and it was that Monday that my supervisor arrived. I forgot about Rosy. The supervisor asked me to come to the office very early the next morning so that he could review administrative things with me before the office opened to the public. That night I got to wondering about the supervisor's abrupt visit. Of course, I quickly realized that my recent refusal to provide transportation to a family (even when I was instructed to provide it) and the subsequent telexes to the supervisor and the department had probably prompted this extraordinary visit.

It was all business the next morning at seven o'clock. The supervisor was unfriendly and aloof. His only interest, it seemed, was to find some fault with my work. To that end he examined the inside of every file to see whether I had cross-referenced every name from the daily worksheet. After more than an hour he found one omission and highlighted it in very strong terms and was then going to quit the scrutiny. I was not taking this very well and insisted that every name on the daily worksheets since my time there should be checked to see just how many other such mistakes I had made, pretty confident that there were no such other mistakes. Reluctantly, he continued the examination. There were no other mistakes. In the filing area, all the filing had been done and I had full reports on all the travels I had done to that point. Nevertheless, the supervisor reiterated the one omission to the exclusion of all the other things that had been completed comprehensively and correctly.

This examination continued after nine o'clock and clients were beginning to gather in the waiting room and outside the little building.

"Perhaps I should show you how to interview clients," the

supervisor explained. "You sit here at the side of the desk. I will get in behind the desk."

He went to the door of the waiting room to call in the first client he was to interview, and at that very moment the outside door of the waiting room flew open and in ran Rosy.

"Mr. Peck, Mr. Peck, where are you?" she shouted.

She bumped right into the supervisor.

"Now, now, my dear, keep your voice down and sit down here in the waiting room and wait your turn," the supervisor said.

"No. Who are you? Where is Mr. Peck?" she said.

She rushed on into the office, saw me, and began to cry and shout in an incomprehensible way.

In rushed the supervisor. He sat her down on the client chair, went around the desk, and in officialdom's most bureaucratic tone said, "Your name, please?"

And so began a series of unfortunate verbal exchanges, with Rosy completely confused and scared. The supervisor continued his cold interviewing style.

Finally, realizing that he was at sea in this particular setting, with Rosy simply looking at me and refusing to answer his questions, sobbing and calling out her husband's name, the supervisor relented and requested that I step in.

I quickly put my arms around Rosy, telling her everything would be all right. Her sobs began to subside. The supervisor, seeing this, grabbed his coat and said he was going to the boarding house.

There were about seven people in the waiting room. I immediately asked them all to leave and come back in the afternoon. They all quickly agreed, given the circumstances. With everyone gone, Rosy became more stable, trembling and quietly sobbing.

There had been a drowning overnight just outside the harbour. A child had come up near Rosy's place that morning shouting and announcing the drowning. Someone uttered, "It sounds just like when Jack drowned."

Rosy, of course, overheard it all and the terrible events of four years ago came sweeping back, fresh, as if it were today's tragedy.

"Rosy, let's go back to your house," I whispered.

As we walked around the harbour we saw Charlie and Mabel rushing toward us. They had been down at the government wharf where rescue efforts were under way; returning home, they realized that Rosy was gone and they made their way to my office.

Mabel ran toward us. "Thank God she is with you, Mr. Peckford," exclaimed Mabel.

"Let's go back to our place," Charlie said.

And so we went back to Mabel and Charlie's place. They were wonderful, consoling and recounting Jack's last days with Rosy and wishing these things didn't happen anymore. It was lunchtime now and Mabel quickly prepared the meal; before long Rosy was feeling a whole lot better.

"I am sorry I didn't turn up yesterday, Mr. Peck. I forgot."

"Well, Rosy, if you forgot I think that is a good sign. But perhaps we could get together tomorrow."

"Yes, tomorrow."

There was a knock at Charlie's door. A young man stood there with a note for Mr. Peckford. It was from the supervisor. "I will be leaving this afternoon. I can get a helicopter from the road construction camp a few miles from here."

"Who was that stranger in your office, Mr. Peck," Rosy inquired.

"Never mind, Rosy. I don't think he will be back anytime soon."

THREE MORE SUMMERS OF my temporary social work followed, engendering many intense experiences.

I was posted to Mary's Harbour on the Labrador Coast, a small community in the bottom of St. Lewis Bay, named after the river that flowed into the harbour. I boarded with the Coish family, a truly wonderful experience, with the father/husband, Bert, my hired captain with his twenty-seven-foot boat, as we plied the coastal communities as part of my job. His wife, a remarkable woman in her own right, kept a small retail store and oversaw the upbringing of seven children.

I was informed by a young woman last year that her great-grandmother had passed away. Memories of that wonderful lady came rushing to the fore, prompting me to write a little tribute to be read at the funeral.

A TRIBUTE

EVA COISH. MRS. COISH, that's how I knew her.

Life is so strange since only a few weeks ago I began an effort (I am writing a book on my life) to track down some of the people who formed part of my memories from early school through my university years. I inquired of my brother whether he remembered telling me about meeting "one of the Coish boys" I knew when I was in Mary's Harbour years ago.

And then last evening arriving home I retrieved a phone message from Charmaine telling me of the passing of her great-grandmother, Eva Coish!

I said in my book *The Past in the Present* that my time on the Labrador Coast was "magnificent" and I meant it, for I met and lived with people like Mrs. Coish and Bert. It was always Mrs. Coish to me, the confident matriarch overseeing her family, always in control.

I arrived in Mary's Harbour in April in Bert's boat. He had come to pick me up in Fox Harbour where I had been sort of marooned because of a four-day nor'easter and ice.

But from the moment I crossed the threshold of the Coish household, I became one of them, ah, but not before, however, appropriate questioning (ha!) by the missus.

What do I remember most about Mrs. Coish?

The meals—unbelievable—and being really the oldest "son" I had to always clean the plate.

She tricked me once. She put on this great supper with all the trimmings: vegetables and meat and gravy and as I was busy gulping down the food, she posed the question: "Do you know what meat you are eating?" Of course, I mumbled that it was meat, perhaps moose, rabbit, etc., trying to come up with the right answer. And with a laugh she said, "No, you're wrong—it's porcupine." It took me a while to get over that. But I came to love it.

Her diplomacy—yes she had some of that when it was necessary. A young RCMP officer who was then stationed in Battle Harbour was invited for dinner, and the missus put on quite the scoff! However, unknown to us at the time, our young Prairie officer was having a hard time adjusting to this strange place. He apparently had asked for the water jug on a couple of occasions and no one heard him. When finally he received it, he flipped. He cleared the table in one gigantic thrust of the arm, and water and food scattered across the room. Like a UN diplomat, the steady hand of the missus brought peace to what otherwise would have been an ugly incident as the rest of us were ready for a more physical response.

Her authority—she tended over us all and never missed a beat, and most particularly she was a good adviser on the goings-on. Once she had to console me after I was tricked into providing assistance to an ineligible elderly gentleman who saw it as his goal to embarrass this young gaffer from the island whom he was sure was disguised as a welfare officer. And she had warned me and I still got taken.

In another time and place she would have been the president or manager of some big operation. As it was, she influenced us all and we are all the better for it.

God bless Eva—my Mrs. Coish.

AND THEN MY EXPERIENCES with Bert, Mr. Coish. One such experience sticks in my mind.

We were chugging along on the southern coast of Labrador in August on our way to Square Islands, the northern part of my welfare district and the summer fishing place for the people of Charlottetown.

"Bert, boy, this is the final leg of our trip," I said.

"Yes, we've had quite a trip so far, Pecky, my boy," Bert responded. "You've seen a lot of new places and met a lot of people. Remember that young fellow in George's Cove who had the same birthday as you and he was just a few years older? Too bad he is so sick. And our trip in to Port Hope Simpson—what a brilliant day that was—and going in that narrow passage you exclaimed, 'Wow, it's like the Everglades.'"

"And you're still laughing at that, Bert," I retorted. "It sure was a special time going in that narrow passageway—the sun glistening on the placid water, the boat gliding slowly as we listened to the silence."

"Now, boy, that's getting just a bit too poetic." Bert laughed. "Who was it you said you studied in St. John's at the university? Some William Something, wasn't it?"

"William Wordsworth," I replied. "He was quite the poet, Bert."

"So you keep saying! I'll have to look him up in one of my big books when we get back home," Bert said.

It was about three o'clock. We had spent the previous night in Sandy Hook with Bert's old friends. We were late getting away because I went out early in the morning hauling the cod trap with the local fishermen.

"So, how long a steam to Square Islands, Bert?"

"We will be there by suppertime. I was thinking that we should stay at Ches Campbell's place when we arrive. I have known Ches and his family for a long time. They have a two-storey house, extra bedrooms, and two beds with feather mattresses—a good sleep for sure."

Around six o'clock we came around the point forming the little harbour where the Campbells lived and tied up to the stage. Ches rushed down to greet us. "Well, I thought it was you from the boat. It's good to see you, Bert. I missed seeing you last year."

"I did not get down here last year. The welfare officer got sick and was unable to travel overnight."

"Well, I am glad you could get here this year," Ches said. He was a short, stumpy man with a full weather-beaten face and large but short arms and he was sporting a sou'wester. "This must be the new relieving officer that is with you, Bert."

"Yes, this is Brian Peckford from the island. He's going to university in St. John's."

"Boy, I think they gets younger every year, Bert. But sir, I am sure you knows what you're doing, with all that university stuff."

"Well, I don't know about that, Mr. Campbell, but I will do my best," I said.

We climbed up the stage and walked into the shed onshore.

"Boy, that is a lot of fish under salt," I said. "Must be well over two hundred quintal."

"Good guess, there. Close to three hundred, I reckon."

"It has been a good season; we started in early July and it has been good every week since. This morning we had ten to fifteen barrels and this afternoon we got another seven."

"Good," said Bert. "Mr. Peckford here was out this morning in Sandy Hook with the fishermen. They had ten barrels. So the fishing has been good at most places along the coast."

"I don't know if the missus has anything on the stove. Bert, me son, if we had known you were coming, we could have had something in the pot," Ches said.

"Ah, not to worry, Ches. Peckford and I have eaten well on this trip and we had a late breakfast at Sandy Hook."

"Well, I am sure the missus could scrounge up something. We got a few early mackerel this morning."

We entered the house and Edna was there to greet us. She was taller than Ches, plump with a beaming face and sandy hair.

"Good to see you again, Bert. How are Eva and the family?"

"Everyone is doing just fine," Bert said. "And Eva is busy with the children and her little shop. We have had a good spring. There were lots of seals in the bay once the ice left, and I got more than my share."

"Edna, put the pan on the stove and fry those fresh mackerel I got this morning," Ches interjected.

"No, no, that's okay," Bert said. "We are sorry we are late. I know you guys have had your supper."

"Now, now, Bert," Edna said, "I know you won't turn down some fresh mackerel and vegetables. What about you, mister—do you like mackerel?"

"I must confess, I love mackerel," I conceded.

We washed up and Ches went back to the stage to supervise the unloading of the fish and Edna got our supper.

Of course, what is better than fresh mackerel, small potatoes, and turnip? We stuffed ourselves and went to the stage to see Ches and the sharemen head and gut the fish and carry it to the shed for packing and salting.

Ches looked up at me from the cutting table. "Have you ever been a few miles off the coast in the nighttime?"

"No," I responded. "Usually we are looking for harbour and a place to stay before dusk. Why do you ask?"

"Well, you got to see those foreigners out there. It is like a city, all lit up. They are taking a lot of fish, and although we are having a good season now, I think it will soon end. They have those trawlers that scrape the bottom. Bert, you will have to take him out," Ches said.

"Yes," said Bert. "I have mentioned this to Mr. Peckford. Some calm night we shall look for ourselves. I think you're right; there will be trouble in a few years. You can't catch the same fish twice."

"That sounds like a big problem," I surmised.

"Those European treaties are not good for our fishery, and Canada does not seem to want to do anything about them."

The men finished their work, and as the sun set, spreading its gold and orange rays across the harbour, we sauntered back to the house. Ches, a couple of sharemen, Bert, and I gathered around the kitchen table.

"It's not every day we have guests like this," Ches exclaimed. "So I guess a little libation is in order." He went to the cupboard and got a bottle of dark rum.

Great chatter ensued in which we all participated in telling stories. Ches revealed his encounter with a polar bear on the ice a few winters prior; Bert told of his sealing exploits this past spring, when in one day he shot forty seals; and the sharemen, after some persuasion and another drink, told of their porcupine hunting experiences. I could not match these interesting and heroic tales, and so I told the story of a harrowing encounter with a female client on the French Shore a year earlier when the client and her equally deranged daughter made me run for my life as they threatened me with a large kitchen knife.

Edna, who up to now was busy in the kitchen, piped up. "With all these stories, perhaps it is time to tell of a strange true story about a couple right across here in the other cove."

"What are you talking about, Edna? That's none of our business, you knows that!" Ches said, startled.

"Well, I think it is our business, and we have all been ignoring it for too long. We got Mr. Peckford here right now, and given his stories he seems like a man who could help here."

Ches was visibly upset and began to chastise Edna for raising this undisclosed matter. The sharemen remained silent.

Bert spoke up. "Edna, I think you're talking about that couple who live in the cove just over the other side of the point. They don't mix with any other people in Charlottetown, and fish by themselves when they come out here for the summer. I heard the story, but I don't know if it's true. But perhaps it's time to find out."

Ches, now feeling outnumbered, relented. "Okay. Perhaps it is time to do something. Look, Mr. Peckford, the couple that Edna and Bert are talking about spend all their time alone, as Bert says. They never get together with other people. The only time I see George is when we are out fishing, and then his talk is short—about the weather or the fish—and then he's gone.

"The story is that about fourteen or fifteen years ago, Mabel, George's wife, is supposed to have had a baby. But no one has ever seen the child. There are lots of signs that there are more than two people. They move out here to the island in cover of darkness and it is like there is an extra person being loaded aboard the boat. Tom, who has the local store, says that the food they buy is more than one would buy for two people, and he remembers that years ago they would buy a lot of canned milk." Ches concluded these remarks with a heavy sigh. "There, I have told it."

"Well, there you have it, Mr. Peckford. Do you think you can help?" Edna asked.

This was a long way from a few minutes ago when we were freely relating our experiences, exaggerating our many exploits, and enjoying one another's company. But there it was. A stark reminder that on remote coasts like this, the unusual lurked nearby.

I cleared my throat. "Well, this is a pretty unusual story. First, at this point it is all rumours, hearsay, although the signs you relate do indicate some very unusual behaviour. Second, of course, I am not sure whether we have the right to interfere, and given that I am not a permanent employee of the government, I'm unsure what I should do, if anything. But let me sleep on it."

"Thank you," Edna said. "I will say no more."

With a little mug-up of tea and molasses bread, we all agreed it was time to sleep, especially given that Ches and the sharemen would be "on deck" at three in the morning.

As we undressed upstairs, Bert inquired, "What are you going to do tomorrow about George and Mabel?"

"I don't know," I replied. "Do you know George at all, Bert?"

"Well, I met him once when he was in Tub Harbour getting some salt from the Wentzel boys. I think he was getting a loan of salt from the Wentzels because the merchant refused him. But that's all."

"I'll decide in the morning."

The night proved to be a long one despite the Campbells' featherbed. The other cove and George and Mabel kept recurring in my mind—half awake, half asleep. Around three o'clock I woke with a start. I heard Ches get up. I tried to review the situation.

There was the point that this was second-hand information and that it was really none of my business. Why should I act on such scanty information? Then there was the idea that Ches and Edna were honest people who were not making something up. Edna felt that there was an obligation on government to investigate. Most people in the area, it seemed, felt something odd was in play. Was this sufficient for me to investigate? Did a social worker have an obligation to investigate in such circumstances?

We awoke to a glorious summer morning. The fishing crews were already at their traps, unloading and resetting them. Any minute we would hear the boats enter the cove.

Edna was up and had breakfast ready—fish and beans, homemade bread, and tea. We ate well. I confided in Edna that Bert and I would go over to George's place, but if there was any resentment I would not push the matter and I would move on. Edna understood and thanked me for being interested and at least making an effort.

"I have my fingers crossed," she shouted as we walked down the pathway to the stage. I turned and waved goodbye.

The putt-putt of Acadian and Atlantic four- and six-cylinder engines could be heard, and when we saw Ches's skiff come into view we waited at the edge of the stagehead.

"It was good to see you again, Bert, and it was nice to meet you, Mr. Peckford. Hope you enjoyed last evening," said Ches.

"I think we both enjoyed it," I said. "I had a confidential word with Edna about what I am going to do this morning. She can fill you in." We pulled away from the wharf and Bert waved a final goodbye.

"Where are we going, Pecky?" Bert asked, as if he hadn't already surmised.

"If you don't disagree, I think we shall pay a visit to George and Mabel."

The slightest of grins crossed Bert's face. "I figured that is what you had decided. And I agree."

"Now, if there's a lot of hostility we'll move on. Let's just play it by ear," I said.

Slowly we cruised over to the cove. The sun's rays slanted across our bow, while distant putt-putts cracked the morning silence. It was one of those special days on the Labrador Coast.

We approached the stagehead of George and Mabel's place. Their house was located on a hill, a couple hundred yards' climb from the stage. As we touched the stage, George was there to catch the painter and tie up the boat.

"What brings you fellows here today?" George inquired nervously.

Bert learned fast. "Well, I wanted you to meet the new welfare officer."

"You're Bert Coish, aren't you, from Mary's Harbour? You were over to the Campbells' last night. I saw your boat come in. What would I want with the welfare officer anyway?" George exclaimed, raising his voice.

I decided it was time to go into action. "George, boy, I was just in the area and figured I would come over and say hello," I said, looking up from the boat. "There aren't many government men in the area, so I thought a hello would be in order." With that I climbed quickly to the top of the stage and put my hand out to George, who slowly reached out his hand.

"Well, we don't need nothing here. We are all right."

"Oh, yes, I figured that, George. It is just a visit. I should go up and say hello to your wife and then we will be off."

I quickly passed him, moving off the stage to the pathway, and began climbing the hill. Bert had climbed up the stage and began to engage George in conversation. George was looking at Bert and calling out to me.

"There is no need going up there—my wife doesn't want to see you—stop, come on back." Bert was trying to engage George in more conversation and blunt the anger that he could see rising up in the man. I continued walking to the house.

I reached the house and the door was ajar. It was a small, makeshift, wood-frame house, typical of the houses in the various temporary fishing stations then existing along the coast of St. Michaels Bay and Hawke's Bay—usually two rooms, a large kitchen, and a bedroom.

I pushed open the door and passed over the threshold into the kitchen. I almost bumped into Mary, standing agitated in front of me. She was thirty-six, tall and slim, with a pretty but drawn face and clear blue eyes and brown hair.

"Who are you?" she stuttered nervously. "I saw you coming up the path through the window."

"I'm the temporary welfare officer. I am stationed in Mary's Harbour. I am making my rounds around the district and thought I would drop in and say hello since I was just across the bay at the Campbells'. I see you have the teapot on—any chance of a cup of tea?"

As she moved toward the stove she muttered, "I see, but no welfare officer ever came before. Why you?"

"Well, I can't really answer that. It was such a lovely day and I'm not that busy, with just a couple of older people to see, so I felt really good. So I said to Bert, 'Let's go over and say hello.'"

Mary found a mug on a small counter. I sat down at the wooden kitchen table and she put a mug of tea and a can of Carnation milk before me.

"Mary, get yourself a mug of tea and come sit at the table so we can have a chat," I implored.

"A chat," Mary repeated, bewildered. "A chat about what?"

As she got herself some tea, I responded, "Just a chat—that's all."

I knew I was now pushing my luck. I really hadn't thought I would get this far. I could hear Bert and George coming up the path; there was a lot of heated conversation as Bert tried to delay George's arrival. George's voice was rising. Mary sat down with her tea.

"So, Mary, it's just you and George in the house? Is that right?"

Mary gave me a haunted look, her face strained, eyes flitting to and fro, waiting, no doubt, for George to arrive any second. "We got married fourteen years ago," she stuttered. "We have been fishing in this cove every year since then."

George burst through the doorway with Bert close behind. Standing in the middle of the kitchen, George fumed. "Now, get out of here! You have said hello to Mary and me, so go—go now!" He was almost spitting as he spoke, looking both angry and confused.

"Now, George, I am just having a cup of tea with Mary, that's all—and then I will be gone."

"George, sit down," Bert said. "Mr. Peckford is not here to cause trouble."

George grabbed a chair and sat down.

"George, boy, Mary tells me you have been here for fourteen summers. It's a nice place—nice and peaceful."

"Yeah," George growled. "We works hard and we have never had anything to do with the government."

"Yes, that's something to be proud of, George. My grandfather was a fisherman for fifty years and he was proud like you. Nothing to do with government, nothing. And he went to the front, seal fishing for forty-nine years," I said.

Mary put a mug of tea by George. "Would you like a cup of tea . . . Bert, is that your name?"

"Well, I will in a little while, Mary, but I better go check on the boat. I think I put her on the wrong side of the stage. A little breeze is coming up, so I better check."

What's Bert doing, I asked myself, *leaving me here alone with this fragile situation? He can't be thinking.* And then like a flash, I knew:

Bert was taking a calculated risk; he figured if George and Mary were going to talk, it would likely be when they were alone with me. Bert crossed the kitchen and went out the door.

I had to make the best of it. I looked at George straight in his eyes, holding his gaze for a few seconds, then Mary's. "Listen. I am only here for the summer. I am going to university in St. John's and it is almost for sure I will never see you again. So I started thinking, perhaps I can help . . ."

"Help, what do you mean help?" George sputtered. "The fish is good—we work hard. We don't need no help." He started to get up.

"No," Mary said, water forming in her eyes. "Wait, George. Let the man finish."

"Listen, George." I lowered my voice to almost a whisper. "I don't mean help the way you mean it. You don't need a food order. But the government can help in other ways—when people are sick or disabled or with other problems. It is not like it used to be, George. It is different now."

Mary, still sitting, trembled as tears flowed down her strained face. George began to stutter under his breath. With every ounce of compassion I could muster, I whispered to George with my hand on his arm. "Are there three people in this house, George?"

George looked at Mary, at me, back at Mary. She sobbed. "Yes, George, we have to tell . . ."

With a gush of emotion, trembling in his chair and his head in his hands, George mumbled, "Yes, there are three of us!"

The emotion was intense, the crying almost unbearable—and all three of us sobbed together for a long time. Finally, George got up and took Mary's hand. "Come with us," he said.

We walked through their bedroom, and in the farthest wall was a narrow doorway leading to another room, long and narrow. One crude, wooden bunk was all the room contained, and on that bunk lay a lanky, thin boy, blind and deaf. This was Jake: the third member of the family. The strain and secrecy now lifted, George and Mary sighed.

A little after noon we pushed away from George's stage. Mary and George were standing there huddled together, expressing their thanks, knowing I would get help for them.

As we sailed out the cove, Bert mused, "Well, me son, I think you've done a whole season's work right there."

"No, we have done a whole season's work, you and me. We are a good team, Bert."

THEN THERE WAS THE trip I took with Bert to Cape Charles, where we learned how the weather can play tricks on you. It was to be a short trip. Just a short hop out the bay from Mary's Harbour to Cape Charles. It was June 24 and the ice was gone from the strong westerly winds of the past several days—the signs of fish were good and everyone on the southern Labrador Coast was in a positive mood and looking forward to a good year. So, in our open twenty-seven-foot skiff with the eight-horsepower Stewart, Bert Coish and I embarked.

I enjoyed steaming out St. Lewis Bay, whether it was to the southern or northern side. On this southern side we had to pass by Indian Harbour (the place in the song "Where me father fished before"). Although not the fishing community it once was, there were still a couple of dozen families making a living from cod fishing on the historically lucrative fishing grounds not far from the community. After steaming past Indian Harbour, we had to pass through a tickle that separated an island and the mainland, and then on to Cape Charles on the coast.

Cape Charles was the summer coastal fishing station for most of the people of Lodge Bay. The fishing grounds were right off the shelf in the open ocean, and Lodge Bay meant the community at the bottom of the bay, sheltered from the ocean and the fierce winter winds and storms. Even hardy Labrador fishermen realized that it was better to be as far inland as possible in the winter. And, of course, you were closer to wood for building houses and boats and for catching animals to eat. Anyway, Bert and I were making this fast trip to see a couple of clients—an older person and a widow—and that would be that. There was also Skipper Ken Pye, an old friend of Bert's who we had to visit.

When we arrived in the harbour (with fishing rooms on both

sides of the tickle), we sensed the hustle and bustle: everyone who was able-bodied was busy inspecting nets on the stageheads, or on a piece of beach nearby; newly painted and caulked skiffs had their engines checked; and a couple of skiffs unloaded some of the first fish of the year. It felt good being there witnessing all the activity, even though we were mere bystanders to all the commotion.

Well, it did not take long to complete the necessary forms of the clients I had to see, and then we were off to visit Skipper Ken. Ken was an old friend of Bert's who had fished for many years on the coast. He was of average height, and I think at that time he was in his mid-seventies. It was a large head and a weather-beaten face that greeted us with a great smile as he opened the door of his yellow, faded two-storey house.

"Oh my God, Bert, my son, Bert Coish, what a surprise. It is so good to see you. I did not see you come in the harbour."

"Skipper Ken," Bert said, "for once we arrived without your keen eyes watching us."

"And who is this young man you has in tow?"

"This is the new relieving officer. He had a few people he had to see, and given that it was a short trip we thought we would do it today. We got a long trip down the coast in a few weeks, so we wanted to get this done now—and of course to see you."

"Well, well, this is a great pleasure for me, to have you fellers come and see me today. Everyone is so busy since we moved out from the bay that no one is very interested in spending time with an old feller like me. There's a real good sign of fish. The boys were out yesterday, and in a few hours with a makeshift trap got seven or eight barrels, and big fish, too."

"This has always been a good place for fish," Bert said.

"I looked at the records about this place since my arrival," I noted. "This is an industrious place. No welfare here."

"Oh no," said the skipper. "We got good fishing grounds and good fish killers."

"I am getting a little thirsty," Bert said. "Have you got a bottle of homebrew around?"

"I was about to ask," the skipper said with a sly look in his eye, "whether you would like a little libation, but I was holding off a bit because when you got a government man around, you got to be careful."

We all laughed, and realizing (a little late perhaps) that this was really a question directed at me, I hastily exclaimed, "No problem! I would love a drink right now. Man cannot live by bread alone!"

"I have some 'controllers' liquor left from last year's final coastal boat run," the skipper said. "Some good dark rum!"

Our eyes told it all, and soon we were sipping the good stuff and animated discussion ensued. And the lies that were told . . . I suppose the right question would be, What questions or issues *didn't* we cover? There was the weather, which meant at this time of year the wind, since this factor largely controlled whether you could get out fishing or not; there was Smallwood—no one talked of the government—it was all Smallwood and that he never visited (well, he didn't have to, what with old-age pensions, family allowances, widow's allowances, disabled allowance, and that was it); and the fishery, where on the coast there was a good sign of fish and where there was no sign at all—and this was all cloaked in second- and third-hand accounts. There was one piece of news making the rounds that both Bert and the skipper had heard about recently: there was a new net—a nylon gillnet, known to catch lots of fish and not to deteriorate like the other nets—and it was getting a lot of talk around the fishermen. Some saw it as a godsend while others figured over time it would hurt the fishery, given that many nets would get lost in storms and would continue netting fish that were never brought ashore.

Well, before we knew it, it was evening and now too late to get back to Mary's Harbour. In any case, we were in no condition to navigate at dusk and after dark. Skipper was overjoyed that we had stayed so long, and scraping around the kitchen in Aladdin lamplight, we helped him find some bread and some salt fish. A few dry pieces of wood in the stove (we had let the thing go out hours before) and a kettle of water and some black tea, and we were in business for a good mug-up. We laughed at our situation as we staggered about, each telling the other two of similar circumstances like this that we had all experienced.

Sleep came easy in the featherbed in Skipper's upstairs bedroom. When we awoke at six the next morning, the skipper was up and the fire crackling downstairs. Peering out the window, we saw that the weather was ugly with a cold nor'easter blowing mist and fog. Down the narrow, squeaky staircase we stumbled into the warm kitchen. The kettle was boiled, the teapot was heating, and some leftover fish and brewis in the pan on the stove told us breakfast was being served.

"There's a nice wind blowing," the skipper said. "No one got out this morning."

"No," Bert said. "I figure the fish are safe for a few more hours, but it looks a bit ugly, all right. We have got to get back. I told the missus we'd be back this morning for sure. Sort of thought we might get away late last night once we had a few and got yarnin'. So we will have to get out in it."

"Well, you're going in the bay, and after a bit of crosswind for the first while you'll be able to go with it for the better part of the stream, I think," the skipper commented.

"Yes, it shouldn't be too bad," said Bert. "It might be too rough to get a seal or duck, though."

And so the conversation went. We finished our breakfast after a second cup of strong tea and got ready to leave.

"Well, boys, thanks ever so much for coming, and it was nice meeting you, Mr. Peckford. You have a few good stories of your own, for a young feller. The best to you!"

So down to the stagehead we went, and climbed aboard the boat. It was cold and the fog was settling in, and some "slop" snow was coming across the cove. But we were determined to continue. Bert started the engine, I pushed her off from the stage, and we were off. We had to head to the west, go around a few islands, and then due west into St. Lewis Bay to Mary's Harbour. Bert was at the tiller and I went up to the bow so that I could have a good look as we steamed along. We had only steamed for five minutes and the wet snow and fog had already enveloped us. Suddenly, there was no land to be seen. We were going to follow the land to our south until we found the tickle, crossed the cove, then went through the tickle and out in St. Lewis Bay. And home.

"I'll slow her down a bit," Bert shouted.

"That's a good idea," I shouted back.

With the boat now crawling along, Bert called out again. "Do you see anything?"

"Nope," I said.

We knew that normal steam time to the tickle would be about fifteen minutes. We chugged along just off from the rocks, the land intermittently coming into view.

I moved back toward Bert. "No, boy, that fog is right down on us, Bert. I can't see the land at all."

"The wind has died down but the fog has got thicker," said Bert. "Perhaps we should cross over and see if we hit the tickle."

So, gingerly we crossed the cove and I went back to the bow to see if I could see land and the tickle. A few minutes passed.

"Oops," I shouted, "there's land—we're going to ram into it!"

Bert did a reverse and we nudged the rocks. I eased the blow with the gaff in three feet of water.

We had to figure out if the tickle was to the right of us or to the left—we thought it might be to our left, or west—so we veered the boat over to port and crawled farther along, with the rocks of the shore in view. The fog still hung to the shore and the wet snow increased.

"We missed it, Pecky boy, we missed it—that damn fog and snow makes a bad combination. We're headed in Lodge Bay!" Bert exclaimed. He stopped the engine and I gently helped bring the boat to a stop, nudging the gaff along the bottom.

We were now getting wet—we really hadn't dressed for this—as we both were wearing only a windbreaker and pants. We had some rain gear in the cuddy, but that was it.

"Well," said Bert, "I guess we have a choice—we can continue to look for that tickle or we can just go on up Lodge Bay to the settlement, go in one of the houses, and wait this out."

"I like that latter idea," I said. "We are getting wet. We might miss the tickle going the other way and get confused around those islands and have to pull in where there is no shelter."

"I think you're right, Pecky, as much as I would like to give it another try."

So we began our slow journey up Lodge Bay nudging next to the rocks. We couldn't go very fast, and so it was an hour or more before we could make out a stage and pull up to it and see a few houses on the shore. The fog just would not lift and the wet snow kept coming.

Most of the houses were unlocked, and we just looked for one that had some dry wood in the porch or in the woodshed. We had some matches (we both liked a smoke).

"Now look there," I said. "That's a pretty nice place, and the woodshed has lots of wood."

"Okay," Bert said.

With a few armfuls of wood we entered the house and started up a big fire in the kitchen stove. It wasn't long before it was sheer comfort in that house and we began drying out.

"You know, I've seen this weather before and I would not be surprised if this stuff lifted later this afternoon and we could make a dash for Mary's Harbour," said Bert.

"Well, it sure doesn't look like it now," I replied. "But with the weather, who knows?"

Bert rummaged around the pantry and found a couple of cans of Vienna sausage. We opened them and gulped the down. We had some smokes left, so we both sat at the kitchen table drawing on them and slowly took stock of our situation.

"Boy, that was quite a mistake I made there," Bert said. "I have not made many like that in my day. I could have sworn we would hit the tickle, but we must have moved along faster than I thought. The fog makes things tricky, doesn't it?"

"Yes, Bert me son, 'tis tricky all right, but I'm glad the wind dropped, otherwise that little bump on the shore back there would have been a big problem. The gaff and a late reverse in the engine would not have been enough."

"Dammit," said Bert.

"Bert boy," I began with some reluctance, "I guess one of these days you'll have to get a compass."

Bert snickered. "It wasn't that we didn't have a compass—we didn't time it right. That's all."

I realized this was a bad time to raise such things. Bert had been plying the coast for years, and he had a good record, so I abruptly dropped it. "Yeah, you're right; it was the timing."

It was now around midday, and we thought if the weather was to change it would be in the next few hours, so we just busied ourselves splitting some wood in the woodshed and entering some other houses to see if there was any canned food about. We found a can of bully beef and a small can of beans. Not bad.

As we walked down to the stagehead together, Bert said, "Have you ever been in this situation before? I don't suppose you have."

"No, Bert. I haven't. Although last year in Green Bay we struck some bad weather, but it wasn't an open boat and we had a more powerful engine."

"Well, welcome to the Labrador Coast," Bert replied.

We got down and checked the boat at the stage and looked out the bay.

"There seems to be some light," Bert announced. The snow had almost stopped. "My son, give it another hour and we'll be able to see all the way out the bay. The wind's coming round to western—good sign."

And, yes, it seemed to be clearing.

"Let's go up to the house and have that bully beef and beans. Then we can come down and take another look," I interjected.

"Yes, let's do that," Bert said.

On our way to the house, Bert seemed a little worried.

"You got a bit of a frown there," I remarked.

"Just thinking, the missus would expect us home by now. I expect she will be checking with Battle Harbour and Cape Charles . . ."

There was a radio telephone available for use by the general public in each of the communities. It was always in some person's home, but the public could request its use.

"Yeah, I dare say Cape Charles has let everyone know we left there this morning," I rejoined.

We opened our bully beef and beans, found a bent-up saucepan good enough to heat the food, and found a few old forks in a drawer. Boy, it wasn't a bad lunch at all.

"How much gas do we have, Bert?"

"We're all right. We've got a half-tank and another full one," Bert responded. He looked out the kitchen window. "Yes, my son, she's clearing up, just look."

We went out on the bridge and noticed what was happening. The bright sky was now more in evidence, the snow had completely stopped, and we could sense a new front passing through with cool air from the west.

"Let's get the boat ready," Bert said, showing a new burst of energy. Down to the stage we went and got ready to leave.

"I wonder if I should see if we can find some more canned food to take with us, Bert," I asked.

"Yeah. Go up and check a few more houses. I'll get everything ready. I'll get the rain gear out. At least it will keep us warmer going out the bay."

By the time I untied the painter from the stagehead, you could see halfway out the bay.

"Did you find any more canned stuff?" Bert shouted as we steamed away from the stage.

"No," I said, "I didn't find a tin. I guess we were lucky in finding the sausages, beef, and beans."

Although the clearing was well under way, we still stuck fairly close to shore as we steamed along the north side. Was it ever good to see land again! In the fog, the land seemed so different, and loomed, seeming larger than it really was as it came into view. A westerly breeze of ten miles per hour was bringing the clearing, and we were a happy couple as we chugged along.

When we reached the tickle we smiled at how easy it all seemed now. How could one miss it? We made the turn to the north through the tickle and into St. Lewis Bay.

We had no sooner turned west in the bay when I heard Bert's shout. "Look to the starboard, quick!" Flying past was a small flock of ducks. Bert jumped from the tiller and grabbed the shotgun. I leaped back to control the tiller and slow the engine.

Gunshots rang out.

Bert was known up and down the shore as a good shot. Well, given that he had to move very quickly, and the boat was still moving, I figured it would be impossible to knock down a bird.

"Swing her around," he shouted. "Swing her around, move the boat to the port, swiftly!" I followed his instructions, and there floating in the water were two dead ducks. Bert passed me the gaff and I leaned over the boat and hauled the birds to the boat.

"Won't need any canned stuff now. What a shot, Skipper!" I shouted.

A sly grin crossed Bert's face. "But I only got two."

"Only two. It's a miracle to me we got any," I stammered.

I turned the boat around and headed back in the bay. Bert came back by the tiller.

"Bert, what about the missus and the others back in Mary's Har—"

"Ah! They're all right. We'll be home in a few hours for sure, and they know we'll be birding and sealing as we come in the bay. I figure they have us in some cove until it cleared up."

"Remember I was telling you about the bay seals? Well, the ice has just gone," I said.

"Slow her down—stop her and let us float for a spell. We have to make this a good trip after all our troubles today," Bert exclaimed. "There should be some beaters in the bay. Looks like a good price this year. Now, you have to look very closely—the seals are swimming just below the water. Sometimes you will only see their snout. I'll get in the middle of the boat—that's where she is most steady—and get my gun ready."

"Off to the starboard, two o'clock," I shouted. Bert steadied and shot. Blood spurted. I grabbed the gaff, sculled toward the blood, grabbed the seal before it submerged in the water, then hauled it in the boat.

"To the port, ten o'clock," Bert shouted. I lunged toward the tiller and repositioned the boat.

More gunshots. More blood and our second beater. We were floating out the bay with the westerly wind, and away from Mary's Harbour.

"Another five minutes," Bert said, "and we will start the motor."

We scanned the water.

"Dammit," growled Bert. "Can't see anymore."

"Well, we got something, and I never saw a shot like that before, Bert. That was fantastic!"

Bert grinned. "Well, I used to be a good shot, but this past year or so I've slipped a little. Not enough seals and I haven't practised like I used to. Years ago we would get out in the harbour and throw these spin tops in the water and see who could hit them."

We started steaming in the bay. We could see a few boats out from Indian Harbour looking for beaters. We passed by and waved.

Everybody older than ten in a community knew a boat when it came over the horizon toward the harbour—it was either because of the design or colour of the boat or, when in hearing range, the sound of the engine. So as we approached Mary's Harbour and as our identity became known, we could see people moving toward the wharf to greet us.

Someone called out as we approached. "Are you fellas all right?"

"We're just fine," I shouted from the bow.

And someone else asked, "Are there any beaters in the bay?"

I CANNOT FORGET CROQUE, on the French Shore, the wind and the ice, Ben Fillier, and other interesting people.

It was well past midday. Saturday, I think, perhaps two o'clock. We thought we would leave Croque, having been there for four days because of lousy weather—wind, rain, and slop snow. It was spring, and anything was possible. And the ice was just off the coast, shifting its location with every new draft of wind.

Everyone had an opinion concerning the wind and ice. Would we get a good nor'easter and drive the ice tight to the rocks like this past week? Skipper George thought so. And some of the younger guys said there wasn't going to be much to it; the wind would veer around to the west and in a few hours there would be nothing left of it. And the last Almanac predicted an early spring.

I wanted to move on. So did Ben, the owner and operator of the boat I had rented and now a good friend. We were getting close to wearing out our welcome. Not that we didn't like the place. We did, what with the homebrew and moonshine. But being a welfare officer, even a temporary one like me (some called my position a relieving officer), you can stay too long, and people being people, they could— yes, would—cook up new ways to see what else they could get from this young gaffer sent down from St. John's for the spring and summer.

As I said, I enjoyed the place, and through my work meeting people and visiting their homes, it was a short few days.

This is a part of the French Shore, a part of the Newfoundland coast to which the French had a right to fish right up to the Anglo-French Convention of 1904. In Croque, there was a French cemetery, and during this time (1964) a French frigate would visit every year or so and care for the graves. It was a well-protected harbour a good ways in from the coast. I remember entering the arm (an elongated body of water) heading in a northwesterly direction for several miles; it looked as if there was just a dead end up ahead, when suddenly the arm turned abruptly to the southeast and we entered a tickle. On ahead there was Croque, tucked away from the lashing sea and tireless wind of the coast. Ben smiled at me for not noticing there would be an opening, since only a few days earlier I was recounting to him my time on the Labrador Coast the previous year and how you couldn't tell sometimes that there would be a cove just around this head or that point of land. I was fooled again!

Given its seclusion it was hard to tell from Croque harbour just what was happening "on the outside." So, with our impatience leading us on, we decided to leave and have a look for ourselves to determine what our chances were of getting around Windy Point and back home to Englee by nightfall. Off we went in our forty-foot boat, which had been our home now for almost two weeks.

"What do you think?" Ben shouted from the wheelhouse as I was reeling up the painter on the bow of the boat.

"It's hard to say. We're too far in from the coast. The boys who were out yesterday said the ice was off to the Grey Islands and seemed to be moving farther off."

"Yes," said Ben. "We will know soon enough."

Ben knew this well. He was born and bred on this shore, and this was the usual situation every April and May. He had seen it all before, for over forty years now. But he liked it no better now than when, as a boy one mid-May, he was with his uncle and almost drowned off Hooping Harbour, just south of Englee.

We moseyed out the harbour and around the point to the arm. It was overcast with the temperature hovering around freezing. We were both in the wheelhouse scanning the horizon.

"Bit of a breeze, Ben boy," I said as we completed the turn around Harbour Point.

"Yeah, I think so. Hard to tell its direction. It's coming from all over," Ben replied.

We were now heading across the arm to Windy Point and then to open ocean. As we crossed the arm, we began to see the open sea and the Grey Islands.

"The ice is just off the Grey Islands, Ben," I shouted over the noise of the engine. "Do you see it?"

"Yes, you're right. That's about five or six miles, I figure. But which way is it headed now?"

That was the real question, because the way the wind was shifting around, there was no way to tell about the ice.

"What are we going to do, Ben?" I asked as we began to move around Windy Point and then to open ocean. "Will we go on or will we go back to Croque?"

"Well, we don't have to go all the way to Englee if we hit trouble. We can put in to Conche, can't we?"

"Yes, boy, we can do that, and that's only a little over half the steam to Englee."

So around the point we went, and headed south to Conche, a course that seemed possible.

There are stories on top of stories about the sea and the weather.

Newfoundlanders have all heard of them. Our history is clogged with this or that disaster, from the seal fishery to the Banks fishery and a lot of harrowing experiences in between. Every family can tell a story of a loved one of some generation who felt the tragic ferocity and unpredictability of the North Atlantic. It helped make a hardy people and at one time a self-reliant people. My own grandfather was master watch on the SS *Greenland* when disaster struck, and saw only thirty-seven of eighty-five men survive a furious winter storm on the ice floes in 1898.

Fifteen minutes past Windy Point we felt the wind rising. I stuck my head out the wheelhouse. "Ben, boy, I think it's starting to come up, and I think it's coming from the northeast. She's settled around to the northeast, boy."

"Shit, can't be true!" Ben shouted. "What luck! Take the wheel and let me have a look."

Ben got out on deck and held onto the door of the wheelhouse, sniffed the biting air, and peered out toward the Grey Islands.

"You're right. A good wind has come up and right this way. The ice will move like lightning now." Scattering wet snow began howling around us. As the wind increased, our progress slowed. And the race was on. Could we get inside Fox Head, the headland before Conche, before the ice?

We were punching broadside to the waves. We tried to zigzag and shoot straight into the waves, then coast in and repeat, but the wind was making that difficult.

With the boat heaving, I asked Ben, "You told me about the time with your uncle. Have you been out in many storms in recent times?"

"No, boy, I have not. We've had a few good years of just a little ice and no storm winds. But it looks like we're getting back to an old-fashioned spring. Christ, look!" he shouted suddenly, looking out on deck. "I think we're losing the water barrel! Can you get out there and fasten it down?"

"I can try," I shouted back.

I opened the wheelhouse door. With the wind coming broadside, the only way I could possibly survive on the now slippery deck was to crawl. On all fours, I ventured outside, the wind slamming the door shut behind me. Jesus, it was getting cold, and the water on the deck was forming tiny pebbles of ice. The boat heaved dangerously.

The water barrel was fastened to the outside wall of the wheelhouse by ring bolts. Straps of leather were wrapped around the barrel and then fastened to the ringbolts. I was to try to tighten the leather so that the barrel was closer to the bolts, thus reducing the shaking of the barrel with the rocking of the boat.

It was too slippery to stay in a crawling position, so I quickly found myself on my stomach shimmying gingerly, army-like, toward the barrel. With a little timing and the appropriate rocking of the boat, I was able to reach my arm toward the leather strap and clasp my hand on it. But with such a motion of the boat, my body flung across the deck, with my feet almost dangling over the gunnels. I grabbed the other strap with my left hand, hauling my legs from the edge, and with my chin banging against the barrel, I looked up to see if I could tighten the straps.

Ben, realizing my precarious position through the half-misty wheelhouse window, opened the door and howled to me, "For Christ's sake, get out of there!" The rest was drowned by nature's ferocity.

I was in deep trouble. Somehow I had to shimmy back to the wheelhouse door. Forget the bloody barrel—it's not like we would have died of thirst. Why did we take such chances over a friggin' old barrel? We can't lose anything regardless of risk, was our motto. How silly!

I had to pick my chance. Get my body ready, look to see the movement of the waves and wind and how it would affect the boat, and slide back to the starboard and the door when there was the least movement. But what would I grab hold of when I let go of the barrel straps? There was nothing.

Moving my face away from the barrel, I glanced out to sea. There were bits of ice not a mile from the boat, and as I looked farther out toward the Grey Islands, there was only white to see.

Ben opened the wheelhouse door and threw a heavy rope around the corner of the wheelhouse toward me. He was holding on to the other end of the rope with one hand and trying to steer with the other, with the door swinging frantically back and forth. There wasn't much time for me to make a move. Ben couldn't stay long in his position, nor could I hold mine for more than a few minutes. As the boat heaved, I lunged back toward the rope, gliding on the icy deck, grasping the rope with my left hand and then with my right. Ben hauled on the rope and I swung around the wheelhouse with my legs hanging out over the boat. He kept hauling on the rope to pull me closer and I kept clasping the rope. With both hands now, Ben pulled as the boat crashed aimlessly against the ice-laden waves. I was near the edge of the door, and with one desperate attempt I hauled on the rope and succeeded in getting my right hand on the raised step under the door. I was almost there. With one more haul from Ben, I was dragged over the step into the wheelhouse.

Ben leapt for the wheel, and getting to my knees I went for the door, grabbed the door knob, and slammed the door shut!

"Holy Jesus, that was close!" I gasped.

"I thought you were gone," Ben uttered breathlessly. "That deck froze in a few minutes. Just look at that ice—the tide's coming in and the wind coming with it. There will be pieces of ice around any minute, and then we'll have to slow down even more. Are you all right?"

"Yeah, I'm okay. Shoulder is paining a bit and one of my elbows is bleeding, but nothing serious. I never saw anything move like that ice—the devil himself must be in charge," I said.

"My grandfather used to tell stories about this when we were boys," Ben said. "In the wintertime, when everyone had more time, he would be there in the stage loft with his buddies spinning yarns about dangerous situations when he was still fishing. We used to laugh and figured that Pop was blowing up a real story to get us interested. We soon found out that Pop was telling the truth. Where are we now?"

"We're just coming up on Pyramid Head, I think. Boy, it's slow going!" I said.

"Yeah, you can say that again. We have to get beyond Rough Harbour, then Crouse Head, and then a nice steam before Fox Head and Conche."

The wind was still howling, slop snow interfering with visibility, and the ice was no more than half a mile away.

"It's close to six o'clock. We only got a couple of hours of light left, Ben," I said.

"We can't make it to Conche at this rate," Ben grunted. "And the ice has moved closer to shore back there."

Small bits of ice were almost to the boat. We cut the motor and began the slow, laborious process of watching for every bit of ice that came so that we could manoeuvre through them. We were now moving very slowly.

"I'd say the wind will die with the light, Ben."

"It might, but it's still strong and that tide will continue to bring the ice," Ben said.

As daylight faded and the wind subsided, we found ourselves moving ever closer to shore as we gingerly moved among the ice pans.

"Get the gaff and the oars that are strapped to the wheelhouse," Ben ordered. I noticed his face taking a distinctive worried look.

"Right away," I shouted back.

Although the boat was still rocking, it was far easier on the deck than it had been earlier. Opening the wheelhouse door, I moved cautiously around the back to the gaff and oars. Behind here, sheltered a little from the elements, my feet found purchase on the deck. I got the oars and gaff and made my way back.

"We've got to keep moving and we have to watch for the bigger pans now. So you will have to take the gaff and go up to the bow and be ready to steer some of the pans away, and keep letting me know what's coming," Ben explained, shouting to be heard.

"Okay," I shouted back as I left the wheelhouse. With gaff in hand I moved up to the bow and started my watch and steering the pans of ice.

A sudden flash of memory and I am in Marystown in the fifties, in the harbour as a boy of ten or twelve. The harbour ice is breaking up and all the boys are frantic with excitement as we leave shore to begin our copying across the harbour. But the ice moves this way and that, all over the place, and Kevin slips and falls, dragging me back on the pan. Tom slips and catches himself. I'm on my arse and soaking wet. This was in the harbour one fine day. Just harbour ice!

Several large pans broke me from my reverie. "Cut the engine, Ben, some big ones are coming." There were some real ice pans now.

With the gaff I started to nudge a pan off the bow on the port side and then another to the starboard, calling to Ben as the situation warranted.

I got this sudden empty feeling in my gut. We were in a bloody dangerous situation—the boat was barely moving. Crouse Head was a couple of miles away. We nudged along in a sea of ice. I started to think of us and the boat. *How long can we go on like this?* The wind was almost gone and a small swell was the only thing left of the turbulence of an hour ago.

Ever so slowly we moved through ever thicker ice. "We're not going to get past Crouse Head with the ice packing like this," Ben shouted as he leaned out the wheelhouse door.

I just waved to him from the bow, acknowledging what was now obvious. We would not be able to continue forward movement much longer. Darkness was now upon us—the ice providing the only bit of light—and we were only half a mile from shore.

For a moment I could only think of the boat, Ben's boat. He'd had it for almost fifteen years, and now, after all its previous trips up and down the French Shore, it was in danger of smashing to bits. Not going to bottom like most ships, but a far worse fate.

I was jolted out of this thought as the boat bumped into one of the larger pans that I could no longer steer away with the gaff. The ice was just too thick.

Ben cut the motor completely. We were almost abreast of Crouse Head. I made my way back to the wheelhouse. It was no use trying to go on anymore.

"Well, my son, what do you think of this?" Ben asked, as I slid toward the door, a look of resignation on his face.

"We're in a bad way," I said with great understatement.

In times like these, something natural clicks in; you do not dramatize the situation. You know the gravity of the circumstance and you deal with it—clearly, survival is now the main preoccupation. You are not cold.

We could hear the ice beginning to grind against our wooden craft. "We got two bottles of homebrew left," Ben said with a courageous grin.

"Let's click the caps and have them," I responded brazenly.

As we took the first swigs of beer, our eyes met—we were no more than a few feet apart—and there was fear, but controlled fear, as we both considered our predicament.

"How tight is the ice packed now?" Ben asked. His voice was strong.

"It's packed pretty tight," I responded, trying to sound equally strong.

"Let's take a good look," he said.

We went out on deck and took a gaff and an oar and began to try to push the ice pans. There was still a swell and the ice was packing real tight.

"Your sight is better than mine. Do you think it's tight like this along shore?" Ben shouted.

"It's hard to tell for sure, but it looks tight to me," I answered.

"That's Crouse Head, I think."

"Yes, I think that's right," I exclaimed. "I remember it from the chart."

"Well, we're going to have to leave her," Ben uttered in frustration. "Take the gaff and I'll take the oar. If we can reach shore, there's an old path in there that should take us to Crouse—perhaps three miles from the Head."

"Our rubber logans are not going to be good on that ice," I lamented. "We'll slip all over the place. Did you ever hear tell of those baseball players in America? They got steel stuff in the bottom of their shoes that grabs real good."

"No," said Ben, "and we haven't got time to discuss it. If we only had some running shoes, that would satisfy me."

"Now, me son, have you got your mitts and the matches? We will be off this thing and on the ice. Christ, where's the axe? We got one somewhere."

"It's there in the corner of the wheelhouse, right behind the extra twine that we took. I'll get it," Ben said.

With these meagre additions, we climbed over the starboard side of the boat onto the ice. Slippery logans and all. The visibility was pretty good and just a slight breeze blowing. It was now eleven o'clock.

For the first hundred yards, the pans were close together, and by sliding our boots along the ice we moved at a nice pace. Then we encountered looser ice and had to be nimble and watch our chance to copy from one pan to the other. This was the way it was until we reached shore—some packed ice, some looser ice. The ice was loose at the shore and we were forced into the water up to our knees. That, we thought, was not too bad.

Now we were on landwash: rocks, ground, solid. Did that feel good!

We sat on a large rock and hauled off our boots. We dumped out the water, removed our socks, wrung them out, and put both back on. We stood up and looked out to the boat. There, looming up against the ice, was *Jennifer Dawn*, Ben's boat of fifteen years, now left to itself in the uncertain wind and ice of northeastern Newfoundland.

Ben mused about how his two daughters would feel if they could see what was happening now to their namesake. Then the silence. I was sure we both mused as to whether we would see it again.

As we turned and moved up off the landwash, I remembered the flashlight. "Ben, we don't have the light. How stunned are we?"

"It's broken. Bulb broke when it fell in the wheelhouse when I was hauling you in from the deck. I didn't have the heart to tell you then." Ben sighed.

"It'll be a job to find the path without that, given the light goes as one gets away from the ice, won't it, Ben?" I asked.

"We'll get used to the dark in a minute," Ben said. "The problem is remembering where it starts. It's years since I travelled it."

Ben had a good nose, and in no time we found the entry to the partly overgrown path and began our short trek of two or three miles. We were wet and hungry.

It was after midnight when we approached the first house in Crouse. Joe Kearney was an old buddy of Ben's, so when he opened the door of his porch and saw us standing there, his surprise quickly turned to recognition and we were heartily received.

As we sat down and began taking off our boots and soaked socks, Joe exclaimed, "Blessed Jesus, Ben, what have you fellers been up to? Where did you come from? The ice is tight to the land. It's been blowin' a storm up to a couple of hours ago!"

"Just had to leave the boat off the head," Ben replied. "Left Croque after midday and thought we could make it to Englee. The ice was off the Grey Islands then, but as we came along Windy Point the wind come round to the northeast and, of course, with the tide coming in, she's all packed now."

"You left the *Jennifer Dawn*? I never thought I'd see the day! Is she gone?" Joe implored.

"Not when we left her almost an hour ago," Ben said. "The wind has gone down, there's a small swell, but that shouldn't be enough to crush her. If the wind doesn't come back up from the northeast, she should be okay for a few hours anyway. And if the wind comes round to the west or northwest, we could retrieve her—it's a long shot, but you never know."

"Ben, you're just as crazy as you were years ago when we got caught snowshoeing out from the logging camp in a snowstorm," said Joe. "We thought we had to see those girls that night. Now, my son, you don't think you can get back on your boat, do you? That's a long shot, all right, 'cause when that ice starts to move off, it will be gone in a flash."

"We'll have to watch for the wind, that's all, and watch closely," Ben responded.

"You guys must be starved," said Joe. "I'll put a few junks in the stove; fire is almost gone out. I had just turned in when you guys knocked on the door." And, looking at me, Joe asked, "You must be the new relieving officer."

"Yes, Joe," I said, "I am here for the summer."

"Well, you got a good man there in Ben. He knows the water, like his father before him. But that ice, there's no way to gauge that—'tis like the cod some years: one day the fish is in the cove, and the next day there isn't one for the pot. They named it right, I say."

"Got any beer?" Ben asked. "A beer would go down pretty good right now."

"I just put a brew in yesterday, but George got some bought beer he got in Conche a few days ago. But you will have to get him out of bed to get it. Do you remember George? He lost his missus last fall. He was a scaler in the woods with us."

Ben took off down the path, got George out of bed, and returned in no time with a couple dozen Red Label and, of course, with George in tow.

"Now, boys, before we starts, we got to have a system to watch the wind," Ben said with some authority. "I'm going to try and save that boat, if I can. The wife and kids would never forgive me if I didn't do everything possible to save her. If the wind veers around at all, we are going to try and get back on that boat. So we got to have someone outside all the time."

"Christ, you're gone crazy," said George. "You're lucky to have gotten off her—trying to get back is pushing it. You got the government man here. If anything goes wrong, my son, you'll be finished. It's one thing to try and cheat me on the wood you cut; it's quite another thing to fool with Mother Nature! She won't like that!"

Joe cut in. "This is not to be fooled with, Ben. 'Tis like that movie we saw in the hall the other night, when John Wayne told some of the boys at the bar, 'You're rolling the dice!'"

As the beer was passed around, I realized I should say something, since I hired the boat and that this would be partly my decision. Of course, if I said I wouldn't go any farther, the boat would no longer be under hire. But Ben was determined to save the boat, and he would do that, hire or no hire. Would I then abandon him and say the hire was no longer in place? That would get any potential problem for me and the government out of the way. I would be washing my hands of the thing and I would stay there with Joe and George until the ice was gone later that day or the next day. Neither Joe nor George seemed in that good of shape, and getting them involved would only complicate matters.

Ben and I had been together now for a few weeks, and we had become buddies. We understood one another, we worked well together, and I was developing a liking for the old craft. Although I was supposed to be a big shot—albeit young—I didn't feel that way and I respected those who confronted the elements, like Ben. And I already knew in my bones that you never let your buddy down, and Ben was my buddy.

"She's still under hire, Ben," I exclaimed. "If you want to try it, I'm with you all the way."

"Well, look at that, Joe," George said. "Ben's got him converted! Ben must be like that preacher up in Roddickton last Sunday. They say he saved more than twenty; they got up dancing and going off in tongues."

"I'm not saved," I responded, "but I am staying with Ben."

"That's it, then. Let's alternate outside, half an hour each time," Ben said.

"I'll go first," I interjected, "and you guys can yarn awhile. I'll sniff out the wind on the path to the point. Give me an extra beer and a flashlight."

It was around 1:30 a.m., perhaps two or three below zero. The night was dark, but as you looked to the harbour it lightened up with the ice close to Joe's stage. I took the path for half a mile until I came to a little rise so I could detect if there was any wind. There wasn't a draft. I headed back to Joe's.

As I entered the kitchen, the boys were in a big discussion on the fishery.

"No wind, boys," I said. "Who's next?"

"I'll take the next turn," Joe said and put on his jacket. As Joe headed for the door, he turned to me. "Mr. Peckford, I know you're not with the fishery, but you're a government man. We were just talking about the fishery. We want you to give a message to those fellers in St. John's and up in Canada. The foreigners are taking our fish—we can see them out there on a clear night—you can't catch a fish twice, and that new gillnet, well, there's the ruination for sure."

"Yes, I've heard a lot about those two issues since I have been on the French Shore, and I also heard it last year when I was in southern Labrador. Boys, it doesn't seem to me that anyone's listening. But I will pass it along nevertheless. I know it's a big issue, but a lot of people want to ignore it, and I don't know if those people up in Ottawa understand. They don't live near the ocean."

Joe proceeded out the door on to his shift and George, Ben, and I continued our discussion on the fishery and the logging business. And so with the beer and some food and lively conversation, the shifts to check the wind continued as the morning slipped by.

It seemed almost too still outside, a sure sign that a new wind was coming. Soon enough, around five o'clock, George rushed back from his watch. "She's veering round, Ben my son. I dare say it has already picked up on the point."

Ben scravelled for his jacket and boots. I did the same. We were out on the trail with a few beers in our pockets and an extra gaff from Joe while shouting back our thanks to the boys.

We broke into a run as we sensed that time might not be on our side. Ben was in the lead and I was some ways back; both of us were trying to keep from hitting each other with the gaffs. A scrawny old stump tripped me up, and down I went. One of the beer cracked open in my pocket. I picked myself up and sprinted hard to catch up with Ben.

He shouted back, "Are you there?"

"Yeah, I'm coming," I cried.

That last half-mile seemed like going around the world. George's words to Ben—*you're crazy*—kept humming in my ears. We left Croque and got into trouble, and now we were leaving Crouse? Suddenly, we broke clear on the landwash. The sky was starting to lighten.

"The ice is starting to move already," Ben gasped as he rushed down to the edge of the ice and water, slipping and stumbling on the rocks and using the gaff to right himself. He looked around and I was almost falling on him. Here we were again, looking squarely at one another, not inches apart.

"We can do it, Ben," I shouted with brash determination, looking straight into his eyes.

The *Jennifer Dawn* was a little farther out from where we had left her, but not a lot, so we had a real chance. She seemed like she was waiting for us; she was calling us now!

"You're damn right," exclaimed Ben. "We got to reach her, that's it! She is waiting for us, no time to lose."

He stopped and looked at me. "How did you get wet? The water is dripping from your coat."

"That's beer. I fell back there, broke one of the bottles in my pocket."

"Well, get the glass out before we get on the ice," Ben ordered with some impatience.

I hurriedly got the glass out.

"The ice is not as tight as last night," Ben commented, "so we'll have to copy real careful and stay close in case one of us gets into trouble. Use that gaff carefully—let's go."

Onto the ice we went, copying from pan to pan in as straight a line to the boat as we could go. The pans were fairly large and we could copy to one, pause, get a good footing, and move to the next.

"Not so fast! You're not copying in the harbour or walking on Water Street now," Ben howled at me.

Slowly, we got closer to the boat. Each minute felt like an hour. The wind was picking up, blowing westerly from the land, but still not very strong.

"The last hundred yards is the hardest," Ben said as he turned to me on one of the larger pans. "I don't think we'll be able to be together on the pans closer to the boat. They're smaller—some of the larger ones have broken up."

Ben went ahead on one of the first smaller pans. They were no more than three or four feet across. Ben stepped off one. I waited for the pan to right itself from Ben's weight, then stepped on it.

Very gingerly we got to within a few feet of the boat; Ben reached his gaff to the gunnels, hauled himself broadside, and shimmied up to the deck of the boat. "I told you I would be back. I heard you calling to me!" Ben said to his boat.

I had only a couple of pans to go. "Ben," I shouted, "talk to me."

"Yes, boy, yes boy, sorry, I got carried away."

In that split second looking up on deck for Ben, I slipped. Flailing in the icy water between the pans, I held up my gaff for Ben to reach.

Quick as a flash, he grabbed it and plucked me up over the side of the boat. I collapsed like a sack of flour on the deck.

"Blessed Lord, we made it," shouted Ben at the top of his voice. "We saved her, we saved her—hallelujah!"

I struggled to my feet. We hugged and danced in the frigid air.

"You go to the fo'c'sle and start the fire. Change your clothes and get warm. I'll start the engine," Ben instructed.

And so we moved, slowly, the ice slid by us out to sea—I, up on the bow with my gaff steering away the floes, taking instructions from Ben shouting from the door of the wheelhouse.

As we went around Fox Head, the wind was getting stronger, the ice now looser and of little real danger.

"I think we've taken enough risks," shouted Ben. "We'll go into Conche until the wind goes down again."

We glided up to the government wharf—it was Sunday around 8:00 a.m. The bells of the local church were ringing for early mass.

"We're not Catholic, but I think we should go and give thanks," said Ben. "It's been a tough eighteen hours. I figure the Fella upstairs must have been on our side. What do you say?"

"Good idea."

CHAPTER 4: TO TEACH, AND MY FIRST REAL TASTE OF POLITICS

"Under every stone lurks a politician."
—Aristophanes

IN 1966, I GRADUATED from Memorial University. During that spring I was busy investigating possible teaching positions in the province. Given my experiences as a temporary social worker I was amenable to going to almost any place, at least for a few years. I remember that there was a vacancy in Bonavista and I applied and was offered a position. At the same time I was approached by Roger Simmons, the principal of a new high school in Springdale called Grant Collegiate. I was offered a job teaching English, which was my preference. Given that I was getting to teach my subject and that the new school seemed progressive, I accepted the offer.

Springdale was a bustling town in 1966, what with three small operating copper mines in the area and it being the service centre for several nearby communities. There was a highly motivated staff at the school and this made for a lively and creative experience. I suppose the highlight was when Eric Abbott (I think Roger Simmons, the principal, being of the Salvation Army persuasion, like Eric, assisted in capturing him), a well-known Newfoundland music teacher, was attracted to the school. This bubbly, eccentric, lovable guy proceeded to establish a school band, which excelled in a few short years and became something of a provincial phenomenon.

It became obvious that advancement in the school system would be difficult. Those who came before me were well-ensconced in the administrative positions, and being still relatively young they had many years left, and short of some unlikely tragedy or gross misdemeanour, few vacancies for advancement were likely.

It was during this time that my interest in politics arose as I listened to Premier Smallwood announcing the formation of an organized Liberal Party that would be democratic and to which he would look for advice and counsel. The party would be—like all things Smallwoodian—a great new movement in democracy, establishing associations in each provincial electoral district in the province. Of course, this was really not brought on by some "road to Damascus" conversion on Smallwood's part, but more by a growing new younger group that he was attracting to the party, personified by two lawyers: John Crosbie and Clyde Wells. And so a new party emerged.

The local district association was to be formed for Green Bay, the district in which Springdale was located, and Mr. Smallwood himself would be attending, as would John Crosbie, who was now seen as vying for the leadership of the new party. On the afternoon of the event, I suddenly decided that I would attend the organizational meeting, and furthermore, run for president of the new entity.

Don't ask me how this all came about, because I don't know. I was immediately seized with this, and I was intent on following it to the end. I hurriedly composed a short biography and had it copied on the school's copying machine. At the door of the hall where the event was taking place, I stood at the appointed hour distributing my biography and introducing myself. Of course, I was met with great surprise since it had already been decided, sort of, that the long-serving Smallwood contact in the area would be the new president and that others already associated with Smallwood would fill in the other positions on the executive. So you might say I threw a bit of a monkey wrench into the "planned" gathering. Mr. Smallwood and Mr. Crosbie arrived and, finally, after some confusion by the organizers, the meeting was called to order.

Sitting near the back, I realized that my urgent business was to get someone to nominate me for president. A sudden shiver went through my body as I realized that in this sham of a meeting, getting someone to nominate me might not be that easy. Why hadn't I thought of this before the meeting? Anyway, I hurriedly whispered to a person in front of me, "Will you nominate me for president?" To my surprise the answer was yes. I do not remember who that person was. With the meeting's pleasantries out of the way, nominations were called for the position of president. And, of course, right on cue a person rose in their place and nominated the Smallwood crony. The chair was about to close nominations when I whispered desperately to my agreed nominator to stand and nominate me. Quickly to his feet, he made the nomination. There were no other nominations, and nominations were duly closed.

Knowing that my competitor was not a good speaker and that his last name began with "C," I quickly rose to my feet and made a motion. "Be it resolved that the two persons nominated for president address the gathering and that this be done in alphabetical order." There was some mild shuffling of feet and some grumbling could be heard. I proceeded to address the motion saying that I thought since Mr. Smallwood was championing a democratic party, as he had said in his announcement, I was sure he would endorse, in this first meeting to establish a district association in Green Bay, an open forum for the candidates for president to lay out their credentials and plans. Well, the chair was a little taken back, but there did not seem to be any real opposition. The question was called and passed.

My competitor addressed the gathering, citing his long association with Mr. Smallwood and his residency in the district and that he thought he could do the job.

I took my turn and stressed the importance of having young people involved, that this was the future and I knew that this is what the premier wanted, since he spoke of a new and vibrant party. I then spoke of my knowledge of the province, having worked for several summers in Labrador, northeast and northwest, as well as southern Newfoundland. I think I went on a little too long. After the initial few nervous moments, I was enjoying it.

I had no sooner taken my seat when Mr. Smallwood rose in his place. He had sensed the meeting getting away from its planned outcome. He stressed how youth could be frivolous and immature, that we needed experience and maturity, and so on. In other words, he made it clear what he expected to occur once the so-called free vote was taken.

I almost did it—I was beaten 54 to 50. Now here was a real taste of politics!

Smallwood was quick to his feet after the vote was announced, and proposed that someone should immediately nominate me for the vice-president position. I was nominated and won by acclamation, along with the other positions on the executive. I never did discover who the planned nominee for vice-president was supposed to be.

Of course, the whole thing was just a Smallwood exercise to give the appearance of an organized democratic party, when in reality he was organizing for the eventual Leadership Convention against John Crosbie. He could then claim his democratic bona fides.

Of course, it was not long before the leadership of the new party became the central feature of politics in the province, and, finally, Smallwood announced a Leadership Convention for the fall of 1969. John Crosbie was, of course, the major opposition to Smallwood, even though, early on, Smallwood had implied that he was stepping down, a pledge that few people believed. He said he changed his mind because he was afraid the party would fall in "the wrong hands." A contest between the new up-and-comer and the only living father, Smallwood, ensued.

In early 1969, Crosbie contacted me as he was organizing his leadership campaign and seeking to get people on his organizing team. I was teaching at the time, and after a number of trips to St. John's I finalized a deal with Crosbie, whereby I would come to work for the campaign as soon as school finished in June and work until the convention in October. There was one hitch: What was I to do if Crosbie lost? I would have relinquished my teaching job and would be out of work. On a verbal promise from Crosbie, I would be paid for the rest of the year the same monthly remuneration as if I was teaching, that being the same income I would get during the campaign plus expenses and a car. My job was to organize Crosbie supporters in the districts from Baie Verte to Clarenville, to try to get as many people to the nominating meetings as possible so that we could elect delegates who would vote for Crosbie at the convention.

Although John and his leadership team had some idea of the Smallwood strength, I do not think they realized the depth of that strength—how Smallwood, in electing a new grassroots party, had ensured that the vast majority of district executives, who are automatic delegates to the convention, were his supporters. They did not realize that in rural Newfoundland, generally, Smallwood support was still very strong and he could get his old cronies in many communities to organize to have the right people elected at all the delegate election meetings. And, of course, that is exactly what happened. Travelling around the area, it was difficult to mobilize a group to campaign openly for Crosbie. Even those people who had written Crosbie expressing their support for his leadership bid proved to be reluctant to do anything more. Essentially, most people were afraid. Such people would be ostracized in their community since, almost without exception, the leaders in the community were pro-Smallwood. To be anything else at that time was suicidal. There was no public tendering act and the government highway services were completely partisan, as were taxi licenses, beer outlet licenses, and the list goes on.

The other problem that people today do not realize is that at that time John Crosbie was a terrible public speaker. I know this is hard to believe for those who have seen Crosbie speak in the House of Commons or at other political events. But this is all a learned art, if you will. I remember when the leadership organizers brought in mainland speech people to help Crosbie hone up his speaking prowess. One of the big problems we organizers had was getting Crosbie to be more passionate and emotional when we had him attend various rallies. His family history was one of businessmen and not orators.

I remember well a particular Crosbie meeting we had organized for Glovertown. We were pretty sure we would get out a couple hundred people. But it was essential that Crosbie be seen as personal and articulate. Many had already known of his lack of warmth since some had met him when he was minister of Municipal Affairs and minister of Health. He had this habit of closing his eyes when he spoke!

It was necessary for the organizers to try to get him roused up before the speech. That afternoon we all met at Caleb Acreman's house. Knowing the Crosbie family's love for rum, we ensured that a number of full dark rum bottles were available and that Crosbie had a few good swigs before the meeting. Well, lo and behold, he was animated and the crowd loved it. Unfortunately, this was not replicated that often in the campaign, so this one promising event was not a prelude to the rest of the campaign. The Botwood region was one area where Crosbie was strong mainly due to courageous citizens and the brave support of a small businessman, Ben Elliot, and his wife, Jean, who was a local town councillor and teacher.

Of course, Smallwood easily won the convention. However, it was at a cost. He had first talked of stepping down and the convention would choose a new leader, only to change his mind. He had helped to get a whole new generation of young people involved in politics, which later became instrumental in the PC victory and defeat of Smallwood only three years later. I thoroughly enjoyed my time visiting the many communities and meeting new people interested in the politics of our province.

We all went away and licked our wounds the first few days following the convention. A week or so later, I returned to St. John's to see John Crosbie and determine what he wanted me to do for him for the next several months. His campaign had an office on New Gower Street, and that is where I was to see him.

I was in for a shock. John had no recollection of our talk in which he had promised to continue my compensation until June of the next year if I stayed with him until the convention. I had arranged, therefore, for someone else to take my teaching position for the year.

I was devastated. I could hardly speak. I just looked at him. And then, suddenly, I became angry. I told him that I found this forgetfulness was not a characteristic of his, rather he had an excellent memory and that I had arranged, on his promise, to have someone take my teaching position for the year and that I had no intention of breaking my agreement with that teacher. I said he had to keep his word. I was recently married and needed an income. Furthermore, if this promise was not kept, I would have no recourse but to make it public.

He was taken back with the ferocity of my reaction and seemed visibly uneasy. He backed away from his earlier position and indicated he would have to see what he could do. Though somewhat relieved, I reiterated my point that it was absolutely necessary for him to keep his promise, no ifs, ands, or buts.

It was a couple of days before things were arranged; I was to be paid out of the Crosbie Empire. And so I worked out of the New Gower Street office assisting Crosbie and his Liberal Reform Group, the loose association of Crosbie (as chair), Clyde Wells, and Bonne Bay MHA Gerry Murden. Most of my time was spent keeping in contact with the many Crosbie supporters around the province, and from time to time doing research for his work in the House of Assembly.

The next year saw me back in South Brook, teaching that fall at Grant Collegiate. Of course, I was now much more a political animal than I had been when I first ran for the presidency of the Liberal District Association. In 1970, I wrote a letter to the St. John's *Evening Telegram* in which I said the following:

> As a new decade approaches can we say that we shall have a province whose politics will be one of involvement, a province where two political parties shall present leaders and policies so that a true democratic, two-party system can function?

The new Liberal Party had not changed since the Leadership Convention. It was still the same. I began to realize that my days as a Liberal were numbered. This realization, buttressed by what I had witnessed on the leadership campaign, convinced me that Mr. Smallwood had outlived his usefulness and that the Liberal Party itself needed time to change and become democratic "on the ground" and not just the fiefdom of one person still glowing from Uncle Ottawa's money. The new, younger voter wanted a more accountable political party and a province that was not just a backwater of Confederation, with an Ottawa dependency.

The year 1971 was momentous. I joined the small band of Conservatives in Springdale—just about all were small business people (Ford Rolfe, Neeta Spencer, Roy Manuel, Guy Croucher, Harold Parsons)—and got my first taste of district (Green Bay) politics. Frank Moores had become leader of the Progressive Conservative Party, and it was making headway. Smallwood called an election in the fall and I became the campaign manager for the PC candidate, local garage owner, and overall great guy, Ford Rolfe.

This was getting to be a desperate time for the Liberals, who were seeing their fortunes plummet and were trying all kinds of tactics to hang on to power. Cheques were showing up in the hands of party hacks and threats were everywhere. Out of the blue I got a call from Mr. Smallwood's campaign manager in St. John's, Mr. Andrew Crosbie, telling me that the premier wanted me to get to Gander as soon as possible—*"Forget the teaching, just tell me how much you want!"*—to manage the campaign for the Liberal candidate, the local mayor, Doug Sheppard. I refused, saying I was already with another party and going to manage the campaign in Green Bay District for the PC candidate. This was met with a barrage of comments on how silly I was to leave the Liberals and that I should rethink that decision immediately. "I mean, do you know what you are doing? Think about it." The phone went silent.

The next day another phone call, this one from a Mr. Barron McDonald, Andrew Crosbie's right-hand man in business: "You are not left for Gander yet? The premier wants you there immediately. Get your bags together and get out there now. Money is no object!"

Once again the big explanation and the same feedback: How much do you want? You must obey the premier, etc. The phone went dead!

The final call, a few hours later from the premier himself: "I want you out to Gander now. We cannot allow this province to be taken over by those Tories. It would be a disaster!"

I don't know if I realized the import of it all, and that I was taking a pretty big chance, but I just kept saying no, no, no. And that was that—at least for a few months.

Anyway, we were on the campaign trail in Green Bay. Ford Rolfe had no political experience and wasn't a speaker who could move the crowds, but he learned quickly. Near the end of the campaign, he was handling himself really well and his speeches were much better. But he was up against a formidable foe, the minister of Highways, Harold Starkes, originally from Nippers Harbour on the north shore of the district. Starkes was a big name, having been associated with the district and the Liberal Party for generations. Harold's father had been elected for the Liberals in the 1932 election, when only one other district elected a Liberal in the whole country (we were a country then). We mounted a good campaign—which, as it turned out, was a great trial run for the big one in the spring of the next year—but we lost by over 700 votes.

An interesting story that tells a lot about politics concerns Ford Rolfe. A few months after the fall campaign, five men from Snook's Arm, a small community on the north shore of the district, arrived in Ford's showroom seeking prices on his new Ski-Doo line. Of course, they were all apologetic about Ford's recent electoral loss and indicated how they had all voted for him. Ford waited for a few seconds and then exclaimed: "Boys, at least one of you guys is lying, because I only got four votes in your community in the election!" Ironically, I got the same number in March, 1972, no doubt the same four real old Tories.

I was becoming vocal during this time and obviously ruffling the feathers of the "powers that be" just a little bit. With my new position as president of the Green Bay PC Association, I found myself giving comments on public policy matters that affected the district to a Grand Falls radio station (the most listened-to station in our area) aggressively looking for local comment.

One such topic was how the government was arbitrarily allocating sections of forest for wood harvesting. Hence, only certain friends or supporters were getting allocations. One was the chairman of the school board, under whose jurisdiction I was teaching. Add to that the fact that the loggers working for this contractor became embroiled in a dispute in the woods, which led to a stoppage of work and the real possibility of violence. The loggers requested that I help resolve the matter with them and the contractor. The aggrieved loggers left the woods camp and came to see me. I then accompanied them back to the woods camp and held talks with the foreman for the contractor and then the loggers. I was able to resolve the issue to the loggers' satisfaction, and work resumed.

The fall election was inconclusive, and it seemed only a matter of time before there would have to be a second one. The tide was going out for the Liberals, and now one could hear new voices expressing, without fear, views contrary to the premier's. Smallwood was finally losing his grip. The fear of losing one's taxi license, beer license, or being blackballed from getting government work was beginning to ease, and all kinds of people started to speak of change. But the old order dies hard. I was subjected to a phone threat from one school board leader (my job could be in jeopardy—I had better watch what I was saying—this on New Year's Eve night), and a personal home visit by another education official early in the New Year. But I refused to give in.

And so the politics of the province were turbulent and uncertain as the year 1972 began. Smallwood finally resigned in late January, and Frank Moores became premier. Lacking a reasonable majority, a provincial election was called for March and I became one of the candidates to represent the PCs in Green Bay District. Unfortunately, Green Bay District was not considered to be a winnable seat by the revitalized PC Party, and hence it was late before a duly constituted nomination meeting was held. I was busy campaigning to get people to come to the nomination meeting, there being two other candidates running as well. Finally, ten days before election day, the meeting was held. The turnout surprised everyone. Another building had to be found to accommodate the overflow crowds in the original building. And many of the female students at my school got involved and came to the meeting, putting on a demonstration when I was introduced to speak. I suspect this was the first political demonstration for a candidate at a nomination meeting in Green Bay District, ever. Times they were a-changing. My hard work had paid off, and many who I had cajoled actually came to the meeting and ensured my victory. It was a glorious night. But then the reality: I had nine days to campaign, and, of course, I was way behind. The minister of Highways, Mr. Starkes, was running again.

Early the next morning I went to the bank. The manager was busy, but I barged into his office.

"I won the PC nomination last night. I have only nine days to campaign. I will be writing cheques. Cover them!" I exclaimed.

The manager was taken back and began getting into banking legalese. I had no time for niceties now. "Listen," I said. "If I win I will have an income and we can set up a loan for whatever monies I have spent. And if I lose I will have an income; I will be back teaching and the loan can be set up. Don't bounce any cheques."

I don't remember whether I signed a form or not. I was out the door and off to the Superintendent of Education's office. Here I would have to get permission to leave my teaching job for the duration of the campaign, or perhaps forever, if I won—and I had a teacher to fill in for me.

Well, the superintendent, who in earlier years had been my principal and had originally hired me, was a Liberal. I went to his office. I was in a hurry, and cooling my heels didn't sit well with me.

I just opened the door and walked into his office, related my victory of the night before, and requested leave. There was this hesitation, and his wanting to discuss more.

"No, no, no," I said. "There is no time for discussion. The board allows this type of thing, so I am off to the campaign trail. I have a teacher to replace me." And out I went.

Two wonderful ladies "manned" my little campaign office: Queen Matthews and Madeline Peters. And then Marg Wheeler and Davis Hull and many others joined the fray as the days unfolded. And good that they did take care of things—raising money, getting the polls set up, dealing with PC headquarters in St. John's, and a multitude of things that I just did not have time to attend to.

And then another older person joined the campaign: Arthur

Burton of South Brook, where I lived, wanted to accompany me, and he was a great help giving me history that I didn't know and humour to keep me going.

I was off the next day to Shoe Cove and Tilt Cove, the farthest communities from Springdale in the district, on the north shore of Green Bay on the Baie Verte Peninsula. And the door-to-door began. This whole north shore of communities was solidly Liberal—I mean 90% or more. But I was determined to knock on every door and show them a Tory who hopefully made sense. There was reluctance to talk, but most were respectful and that got me through my first day. On to Snook's Arm and Round Harbour; I may have picked up one vote in Round Harbour. Then I was on to Nippers Harbour, the home of my opponent, a solid Liberal place if ever there was one.

Obviously, the reception was a little cool, but I was saved by a simply wonderful couple, the Proles, the only known PCs in the community. They were independent fisher people from Indian Burying Place, a community just a few miles out the bay, which had been earlier resettled. George and his wife sought me out as I was knocking on doors near their house, which led to a wonderful lunch and a confession of his Tory roots stretching back before Confederation. He never liked Joey Smallwood and he thought he would die without seeing a Tory elected in the district.

"But, by God," he said, "I haves this feeling you will make it, not here but in the south of the bay and Springdale."

I had no such optimism, but he sure lifted my spirits. He was an indefatigable campaigner; from that day on he was busy putting up PC signs and my picture. It was he who on election day made an unusual request of our headquarters.

"I wants a couple of dozen signs," he said.

Of course headquarters staff were reluctant to hire a car and ship off the last of our signs to a hopeless part of the district. I had just called in (as I did many times each day of the campaign, as I gave orders to the loyal campaigners while on the run) to hear part of the discussion concerning George's request.

"Listen," I said, "if you can spare him a dozen, get them down to him."

The office thought I had lost my mind, and not for the first time on these many call-ins. Of course they obliged.

You see, George was my only contact in Nippers Harbour, and all the signs we had sent him had been torn down each night by the Liberals. But George was out to have the last laugh. Convinced that I would win, he boldly requested the signs on polling day. That night as the results came in that I had won, George paraded around Nippers Harbour erecting the signs.

The Liberal tide had gone out and with a new blue tide approaching—even in Green Bay, this hotbed of Newfoundland liberalism and all things Smallwood.

The new signs were left up, and George's premonition became a reality. After decades of derision, failed hopes and dreams, George had his day in the sun, signs and all!

But I am ahead of my story. I continued on going door-to-door throughout the remainder of the north shore: Smith's Harbour, Burlington, and Middle Arm. Except for a few brave souls in Burlington, it was tough sledding, climaxed by the lady who had knocked me unconscious years before when I was a welfare officer in the area. I had completely forgotten the earlier incident and was going full throttle, knocking on every door and introducing myself and asking for their support. Being so engaged I failed to notice that as I got nearer the infamous lady's door, the neighbours, whose houses I had just visited, remained outside as I continued my knocking along this particular road, all eagerly awaiting my fateful knock.

"You dirty Tory. You get out of here, get out of my garden; you was no good when you was here as a welfare officer and you're no better now. Get, get, get." And so, like a scalded cat, I retreated to the safety of the public road. And so ended my campaigning on the north shore of Green Bay!

In the bottom of Green Bay, and not far from Springdale by road, were the communities of King's Point and Rattling Brook. There was a smattering of Conservatives here (Guy Bartlett and his wife and family, true conservatives who, despite this known political affiliation, had a successful grocery business, and he was renowned for his honesty and fair play) and some indication that we were gaining some additional political ground. Farther out the other side of the bay were the communities of Jackson's Cove, Silverdale, and Harry's Harbour (and two smaller places: Langdon's Cove and Nick's Nose Cove). Once again there seemed to be some political change in the air and I was feeling a little better.

Closer to Springdale were the small communities of Beachside, Little Bay, and St. Patrick's, the last two the only Catholic communities in the whole district, and they were almost 100% Catholic. Because I was teaching then at what was called the Integrated School (Protestant without the Pentecostals) and there were insufficient high school students to warrant their own school, the Catholic parents sent their children to the school where I taught in Springdale. Therefore, I knew a lot of the parents in these communities. Many of the Catholics were Conservatives, a real holdover from the early Confederation battles of the 1940s when the Catholic Church, along with the Conservatives, opposed Confederation. The door-to-door campaign here provided a welcome relief from the negativism of the north shore and further lifted my spirits. Beachside was a Pentecostal community, and though it looked like I was making some inroads, Smallwood and the Liberals prevailed, although I had wonderful support from Sandy Young and his wife, who were true supporters and later became friends. They were small business people who understood the need for change and came to resent the demagoguery prevalent among many of the Liberal supporters.

My Springdale team was growing, and upon their advice it was decided that I should immediately go to the southeast of the district and begin campaigning there. My first stop was Sunday Cove Island and the communities of Miles Cove and Port Anson. Parenthetically, the town of South Brook where I lived (right in the bottom of Halls Bay), was bypassed on the assumption that I would win it anyway, there being a large minority of PCs there long before I came around.

Fortunately, this turned out to be an accurate forecast, since I won it handily. I was always of the view—and still am—that if those who know you best do not support you without campaign pressure, there is little hope of success in more unfamiliar places.

Sunday Cove Island was not much more than a stone's throw from the Newfoundland mainland, and every election the people had been promised by Mr. Smallwood's son, Bill (who had been the MHA from 1949 to 1971), that a causeway was to be built during the next term. It never happened in all the twenty-two years of Liberal rule. Nevertheless, it was strongly Liberal.

This is one of the most puzzling aspects of political affairs. Here were two small communities still religiously Liberal in spite of all the broken promises of their most important issue, delivered repeatedly by the son of the only living father and on one occasion by the "living father" himself. The people there were most respectful of my presence and somewhat surprised that I would "waste" my time there. I knocked on every single door, perhaps 100 to 150 in total. I remember that I lost Miles Cove in that first election, but won it big in the second election of 1975 by a whopping 47 to 2. It was a bit of a puzzle to the locals who those two holdout Liberals were, and on a subsequent visit after the second election, I was walking on the landwash to get to a nearby home when I suddenly saw an elderly gentleman picking up shells on the beach. Of course, I hailed a hello and approached him.

"Good day, sir," I said. "It's a nice one."

"Yes," he responded, "a large one indeed."

He did not recognize me. I introduced myself.

"Yes, yes, of course. I wasn't home when you knocked on my door a few years ago. Well, it is nice to meet you, sir. You've done well, and you've got our causeway for us."

"Yes, I did," I said proudly. "I can count on your vote next time?" I inquired.

"Well, I don't know about that. I haven't voted for you yet. But you seem like a good fellow. I guess I will have to think about it next time. But, Joey was a good man!"

So here was one of the two holdouts, now identified. Loyalties remained.

"Well sir, your vote is secret and that is your choice. Nice meeting you," I said as I proceeded on the beach.

There were two other islands in the district: Little Bay Islands and Long Island. I went to Little Bay Islands (very Liberal) late one evening and began a furious door-to-door the next day. I got people up out of bed in the morning, and that evening, on my final door, I got an elderly couple out of bed. I don't know if that helped or hindered my prospects, but I was determined that this young Tory could never be accused of not trying to make contact with everyone and that the old fish merchant label of decades past no longer was a relevant characteristic of today's Progressive Conservatives.

I remember a middle-aged widow who lived "down near the water" from the local road. There was a bit of a flat, not much but enough to keep a cow and a few chickens. What struck me was the independence and resilience of this woman—her optimism was a stark contrast to others I had met that day who were almost blaming me for the fact that there was little fish, or that the road was unfit, or that the ferry was late. I don't know how she voted, but it was people like her who kept me going, knowing that my project was a pretty minimal one compared to her project of just making ends meet.

Long Island was not far from Little Bay Islands and was linked to it by ferry and to the mainland by the one provincial ferry system. Unlike Little Bay Islands, there were a number of individual communities set in the many coves that dotted the island: Beaumont South and North and Beaumont Central and Lushes Bight. Here delightful old English was spoken; the Beaumont communities were more Liberal, while Lushes Bight seemed ready for change. The rallying cry was that of wanting their own ferry. Later they got their own ferry, but as I write I have people from the island emailing me telling me that it is about to be lost. It is a symbol of what has happened to rural Newfoundland as the ground fishery has failed and larger centres draw the young for education and work.

The last places I visited (Robert's Arm, Pilley's Island, and Triton) were those that seemed to be conducive to change and where people had already begun organizing with the help of the campaign office in Springdale. Two earlier events had already given traction for this area to move away from the Liberal Party. One was the earlier Liberal leadership campaign and the other was the IWA—the International Woodworkers of America.

I had campaigned especially in this area of the district for John Crosbie's leadership and many people had got involved. There were a number of active Liberals who witnessed some of the unusual tactics of the Smallwood loyalists and were not impressed. So there was fertile ground for a resurgent PC Party in the Robert's Arm area.

Farther along the shore were Triton and Brighton. The people of this area were renowned for their hard work and determination. Many here were highliner fishermen, top loggers for the paper mill in Grand Falls, or foremen and excellent tradesmen for provincial construction companies. I came to learn that few communities in the province could match the initiative and drive of these people. When I did campaign there, I was told by the newly minted poll captains that I did not need to spend much time there, that they had everything under control, that the people here would vote for me, and I should spend my time in the other part of the bay, where I needed to get new votes. And the IWA issue of the late fifties was not forgotten.

The loggers of the province were eager to be more organized. At that time they had what the loggers considered to be an ineffective group to represent them called the Newfoundland Loggers Association. The International Woodworkers of America were invited by the loggers to represent them and the IWA obliged. It was not long before an impasse occurred with the Anglo-Newfoundland Development (A.N.D.) Company, the owners and operators of the Grand Falls mill, ancillary wood camps, and the new union, the IWA, which led to a strike by the loggers for better wages and living conditions. Meanwhile, the old Loggers Association and much of the media opposed the IWA's intrusion into the Newfoundland forest industry and its fiery leader, H. Landon Ladd.

The strike reached its sixth week when Premier Smallwood, sensing a populace that was negative toward the new union, intervened and passed legislation stripping the IWA of bargaining rights in the province and established a new organization that the loggers would have to represent them. Public support was hardened against the IWA when, in a confrontation on the picket line, a policeman was killed. Through all of this, most loggers supported the IWA, none more staunchly than the loggers in the Triton area. I was now the recipient of fertile ground that had been partly tilled earlier, and the loggers and other independent people had had enough of an intrusive and partisan government. I gained a lot of inspiration from the people of this whole area, both in the last days of the campaign and during all my years in government. They were and are a fair people, eager to work and strong contributors to their respective communities.

Two Triton stories that symbolize their zeal for work and craftiness need to be told.

My first portfolio as a Cabinet Member was Minister of Municipal Affairs. The council of Triton decided they should visit me at my office in St. John's. I mean, it was good to have your MHA, the minister of the very department to which all municipal councils reported. And so they arrived in the capital and, in addition to the regular meetings, I invited them to dinner. Of course we hashed over the results of the departmental meetings and other matters of mutual importance, including fish or the lack thereof.

And then one of the councillors looked at the mayor and uttered: "Well, we better tell him, your Worship."

"Tell him what?" responded a surprised mayor.

"Well, you know . . ." said the now-subdued councillor.

"I thought we had agreed that we would not mention it," said the mayor.

"Well, I have had a change of mind," the councillor retorted.

"Well, Brian, it's like this," the mayor began. "We have this piece of land, the only decent piece of land to economically make into a subdivision. So we divided it into lots and put in a road and services. And we have been selling the lots. I think we got them sold now."

I intervened. "I think that is fine."

"Yes," said the mayor, "but we were rather careful about who got the lots."

"What do you mean?" I said, puzzled.

"There are some people who would not be an asset to the town, who don't work that much, who would bring the town down. We refused a couple of lots to people like that."

And then on another occasion the council told me of their very legal but unusual financing. When the council was started, first the councillors were told that they could expect certain monies from the province. They would get a dollar from the province for each dollar the town raised, up to a certain amount, then seventy-five cents for each dollar to another amount and then fifty cents . . .

Well, the council got to thinking. If they could get all their taxes paid really early in the year, instead of having it spread over the whole year, the province would have to provide the matching funds and the council would have a sizable amount of money, most of which it could deposit in the bank and make interest. No other municipality did this.

But I digress from the campaign . . .

My last day of the campaign was in Springdale, where the campaign office over the previous week was beginning to balloon with new people who wanted to help. The poll captains and their helpers blanketed the town and taught the new poll captains in the other communities around the district to identify those who were definitely going to vote for us, those who were definitely opposed, and those who were truly undecided, and then on polling day to get those for us out by noon, those undecided by suppertime, and any of these two groups who were out of town or busy earlier, out before the polls closed. What a day.

And then about ten minutes before the polls closed I noticed that there was a decided for us that had not voted. I shouted, "What happened here? Margaret Warr hasn't voted. Who slipped up?"

"Well, no one, boss," Davis Hull exclaimed. "Marg is nine months pregnant, can go any time, you know."

"No, I did not know," I retorted. I knew we were closing in. I could not lose by one vote! "Who has a car? Let's go."

We made a mad dash for Marg's door. She opened the door wearing her housecoat.

"Sorry, Marg, needs that vote. Let's go."

We made the polling booth with a minute to spare! "Oh, what a night it was, it really was," sang Elvis.

We won that night, a real upset, by the grand sum of 51 votes. The next day we increased it to 135 votes with the special polls from around the province. It marked the first time that Green Bay had voted Conservative in its history, and the last district to elect a Conservative in the province.

My political career was launched. Two former English students to whom I introduced Shakespeare in grade seven sent me a telegram: "Madness in great ones must not unwatched go." Hamlet. Congratulations from Alvin and Dave.

LEARNING AND LEGISLATING

OF COURSE, IT WAS only a day or so and the phone calls and letters began to pour in. One elderly lady nearby called requesting that I see her immediately, since she had voted for me, so she said. I obliged and was confronted with the demand that I purchase a new furnace for her as soon as possible, since her present one was in deplorable condition. There was no easy way to approach this situation, so I bluntly informed the lady that this kind of gift did not come with the job. If she was receiving government assistance, then I could make representation to the social service authorities to have her condition assessed to see if she qualified.

I don't know if it was deliberate or not (even then I was becoming a little wary of the federal government), but there was this spike in incidents of alleged income tax evasion and threatening letters from Revenue Canada to small business people in the Green Bay area. There was a forest contractor, a service station owner, and a fisherman. So, suddenly, I became a bit of a lawyer, representing these people at appeals I launched on their behalf. One was simply a bookkeeping mistake that could have been handled in a phone call; another was a mix-up in correspondence; and the last one, the fisherman, was a Revenue

Canada mistake. The fisherman was distraught, frightened, and felt like he had committed some hideous crime. What was common in all three cases was how a government department could move in such a heavy-handed fashion and trample on a person's dignity.

One of my biggest problems in those early days was to respond promptly to the letters I received. Since I was without a secretary or typewriter, I went to a local store and purchased several writing tablets—carbon sheets and all—and began responding to the letters in longhand. Many of the letter writers were surprised to get such a quick answer and often called me to express their appreciation. Then it was off to St. John's to get an office and some secretarial help.

Outside the Confederation Building there were parking spaces for all the members of the House of Assembly. And so I parked dutifully in the place marked Green Bay. I was still driving my first car, a standard shift, four-door 1967 Chevelle. It had seen better days. It was then carrying over 100,000 miles, what with carrying basketball teams around the province and travelling many gravel byways; it was not in good shape. I think it was my first week in St. John's. I left my new office lunchtime and went to get my car to go to a meeting downtown. But there was no car in my Green Bay space. I was puzzled. Surely no one would steal the car in such a public spot in the middle of the day! And anyway, who would want to steal such an old, unattractive car as mine? Retreating to my office, I mentioned my problem to one of the experienced secretaries, who immediately got on the phone to the Public Works Department.

"George, this is Peggy from the Member's office."

"Yes, Peggy, what's up?"

"Well, Mr. Peckford, the new Member for Green Bay, went to get his car in the Green Bay parking space out front and it was gone. He suspects it has been stolen."

"What kind of car is it?"

"It's a dark tan 1967 Chevelle."

"With some rust on it?"

Peggy looked at me. "Is there rust on your car?"

"Well, yes, a little bit."

"Yes," Peggy said to George.

"Oh, we made a mistake. We just towed it away. We figured such an old thing would not belong to a Member."

Apologies all around, my car was returned.

I was eagerly anticipating the opening of the House of Assembly because I knew I would enjoy the cut and thrust of debate, and I thought that over time I could be effective in this forum, perhaps catch the attention of the senior parliamentarians, and also impress our House Leader and the premier. Therefore, I spent a fair amount of time in those first weeks reading the parliamentary authorities, Arthur Beauchesne and Thomas Erskine May.

On April 25, 1972, I made my inaugural speech in the House of Assembly. It began with the following: "Mr. Speaker, may I say at the outset that I am very proud to stand in the House of Assembly today and represent a district, the district of Green Bay, which for the last century or so has not seen a representative from the Progressive Conservative Party."

From that day forward until my retirement in March, 1989, I enjoyed every minute of my time in the legislature.

Of course, even with my previous experience with the Department of Welfare as a student, there was still a lot to learn about the government, the workings of the departments, and getting to know who in those departments were the key people, the workings of the Treasury Board, the Throne Speech process, and the budget process. And most particularly to learn of the slow pace of government and how certain policies or procedures, once fixed, were very difficult to change.

This latter point was driven home to me when I first encountered the Department of Highways. Roy Foster had a carrot patch on the road from King's Point to Rattling Brook in my district. The six-mile stretch dead-ended at Rattling Brook, aptly named after a waterfall nearby. This was the farming area of my district. A lot of families grew root crops and in the fall at harvest time marketed their produce door-to-door in a wide area of Central Newfoundland.

Roy loved his carrot patch and boasted that he had the best

carrots in all the area and that he had the customers to prove it. I met Roy and his wife during my campaign—they were real supporters and were very independent—she the teacher and he the part-time farmer.

They asked for nothing and just wanted some good, old-fashioned, honest government.

Unknown to Roy or anyone else, engineers with the Department of Highways at the Regional Headquarters had their own ideas about upgrades for that stretch of road. Just after I was elected, Roy had a stranger knock on his door. This was an engineer from Highways.

"Are you Mr. Roy Foster?" queried the stranger.

"Yes," said Roy.

"I am from the Department of Highways. Do you own some land near that turn in the road going to Rattling Brook?"

"Yes, I do," Roy responded.

"That turn by your land is very dangerous. We have to make it safer. We will need to take your land, so we want to do an agreement. If you don't agree, we will have to expropriate."

Roy was shaken. "Expropriate? What does that mean?" Roy inquired.

"We would take it from you and give you some money for it."

Roy could no longer speak. His wife appeared and bailed him out of this unreal encounter. "Please go away," she said to the Highways man. "We have to think about it."

Roy was devastated. His cherished carrot patch, which had been part of the family for generations, was about to be no more. For days Roy and his wife debated the incident they had with the Highways man. What could they do? Finally she said, "We will have to call Brian and see what he thinks."

"No," Roy said. "He's just elected, and we never supported him to try and get something from him."

"Well, we are not," she said. "We didn't know about this when Brian was running for election. I'm sure he would help us." Roy would not relent.

However, the Fosters had a son, Mervyn, who had just been hired for a teaching position at the school where I had taught. I had met him.

One day, I got a call from Mervyn, explaining his parents' predicament and inquiring whether I would go visit his parents to review their situation. Of course, I remembered the Fosters and was only too happy to go visit them.

The next week, back in my district, I visited the Fosters. After a big chat about the problem, Roy took me to the site. He wanted me to see the patch. Down below the turn in the road was this scenic level piece of land that tumbled at its edge to the beach and the salt water. A more idyllic setting would be hard to find.

"Simply beautiful," I exclaimed to Roy.

"Yes, boy, it's pretty, isn't it? Brian, I got one of my buddies to look at this turn. He knows about road building; he builds forest access roads. He says that it isn't necessary to come out from the present turn to cut down on the steep angle. He says the hill that causes the turn is not hard rock, that it looks like shale rock that would crumble easily, and the cost would be less than building that big turn."

Well, back to St. John's the next week, and a meeting with the deputy minister to explain the situation and how this problem of mine could be easily rectified.

"No doubt the engineers in Grand Falls have already looked at your alternative and found it doesn't work," said the deputy minister.

"Do you know that to be the case?" I responded.

"No, but it makes sense that they would have looked at this."

"Can we call Grand Falls?"

Reluctantly, the DM called Grand Falls, and to his surprise the engineers had not considered the alternate plan. After some persuasion, I convinced the DM to have the engineer revisit the site with me and Mr. Foster.

The big day arrived, and by now the engineer was not a pleased man, what with having his project questioned and having to come back to the scene on orders from the DM to examine some silly alternate way to do the project.

Roy and I both had a go, but the engineer was adamant that his way to build was the best and only way.

"What about we get a backhoe or tractor to just test that bank," I proposed. "Then we will know if the alternative makes any sense."

Roy thought this a good compromise and readily agreed to put his idea to a test. The engineer remained unconvinced. "Let me think about it," he uttered. "I will call you tomorrow."

The next morning the call came and the engineer agreed to the test. A local backhoe was brought to site the next day and the engineer oversaw the operation; with a few strikes in the bank the shale rock was loosened, and gravel and rock almost blocked the road!

Roy was overjoyed. The engineer got out of his truck and approached Roy. "You were right," he said. "This looks like a much better method."

The project was estimated to cost $110,000. The new approach was less than $90,000 and safety was assured. But of most importance, Roy's carrot patch was saved!

The rest of 1972 saw me dealing with district issues and learning the ropes of government. It was a lot of work but I jumped in with both feet and found it all very interesting.

With the arrival of 1973 I could claim that I was really getting to understand the legislature and the workings of government. I guess Premier Moores thought the same way, since he appointed me to work in his office as a Special Assistant. I also acted as his parliamentary assistant in the legislature. This was a great promotion because it gave me some authority to deal with government departments and agencies and to interact with senior officials and the ministers. The office was disorganized, and after a meeting with the premier, during which I questioned what all those mountains of paper were doing on his desk and how come the many letters were not answered, I had his blessing (cloaked in a sarcastic tone) to clean it up. And with the other people working in the office, we set about doing that.

It was obvious that there was a small clique of ministers who the premier trusted at that time, including Dr. Tom Farrell, William Doody, and Joseph Rousseau. They spent a lot of time together and it would not do well to cross either of these gentlemen. I tried not to. But I remember that once I must have gotten on the wrong side of Mr. Rousseau, since I was unceremoniously called to see the premier to answer to accusations that I had criticized him at a public gathering. When I questioned as to the nature of this public gathering, it so happened that I had not even attended it, since I had been out of town at the time. Once I explained this, the premier told me who his informant was: Mr. Rousseau. I learned quickly to be very, very careful.

The year 1974 was an important one. I was invited into the Cabinet to serve as minister of Municipal Affairs and Housing. I felt willing and able to jump right into the ministerial fray. And I did. It was refreshing, if not daunting. The department needed serious restructuring. With the quick resignation of the then deputy minister, I was able to begin with many of the existing people there to improve the efficiency and financial apparatus of the place. This had been the repository of some of Smallwood's appointments. There still was Mr. Harold Rowe, brother of one of Smallwood's former elected lieutenants, Frederick Rowe (then serving his reward in the Canadian Senate), receiving a salary and having the title of Special Adviser. I respected his longevity and marvelled at the stories he could tell about when he and other ministers and deputy ministers were on the receiving line of Smallwood's special intercom system and would hear Smallwood's voice, at any time, summoning them to the "great one's" office to be belittled in front of cold strangers.

Lucky for me, one of the unsung giants of the Public Service, Peter Withers, was the assistant deputy minister, who I quickly appointed deputy minister. With his advice and dedication we enlisted many of the existing employees to begin the hard work of giving credibility to the department, especially within the government central agencies of Treasury Board, Executive Council, and the Department of Finance.

First and foremost we had to get the existing staff on side. So a regular staff meeting was initiated, the first time in the department's history. Then we began working on the finance administration side of things. We persuaded the Treasury Board to approve the creation of a Finance Division in the department. Then we began to provide some regional presence of the department in Gander and Corner Brook. Most importantly, we began to get a handle on the Capital Works process. Up to now a lot of projects were approved in an ad hoc manner where politics played too large a role. We tried to assess the projects on their merit and ensure that where health and safety were involved, such projects were recommended to Cabinet on a priority basis.

I was also responsible for the Housing Corporation. This was the fiefdom of then Chairman Al Gosse, a dapper, short man exuding confidence and authority. The Housing Corporation was involved in many social housing projects around the province as well as at that time developing the major economic housing project (Newtown) that was to become a part of the City of Mount Pearl, a major bedroom community to St. John's.

At that time the federal government was involved in housing and each year there was a federal allocation to the provinces after relevant negotiations between the provincial Housing Corporation and the federal Canada and Mortgage Housing Corporation. One particular year at budget time we were informed casually by CMHC that our allocation had been drastically reduced. This came as a surprise since talks up to then had indicated that an allocation similar to the previous year was likely, and a lot of planned projects were predicated on such an allocation. When apprised of this sudden turn of events, I immediately contacted CMHC in Ottawa. However, it was impossible to speak to anyone in authority. I telexed the chairman, but received a gobbled, bureaucratic answer from some underling. I contacted other provinces and found that their Housing authorities had not received similar drastic cuts in federal housing allocations. This was indeed troubling and left me very angry. I contacted the premier and told him that, unless he disagreed, I was off to Ottawa to confront in person CMHC and have the allocation restored. Premier Moores was a little amused by it all and thought that it would be a wasted trip but told me if I thought I could do something there, go for it.

Off to Ottawa I went, and I was in the office of CMHC the next morning, having taken an early morning flight from St. John's. The president was Mr. Bill Teron, a developer friend of Prime Minister Trudeau's. Teron was to build a controversial swimming pool at the prime minister's residence, the funding of which is still a mystery. The *Vancouver Sun* of February, 2006, in doing a story on whether Prime Minister Harper should move to 24 Sussex Drive, described the history of the place:

> In 1975, Pierre Trudeau allowed a $200,000 pool house—complete with sauna and sitting area, joined to the main house by underground tunnel—to be built by Ottawa developer Bill Teron, who refused to say who paid for it. (Trudeau named Teron president of the CMHC in 1973 and deputy minister for urban affairs in the late 1970s.)

Another reference to this incident is contained in a book written by Mark Denhez in 1994 entitled *The Canadian Home: From Cave to Electronic Cocoon*. In it one finds the following:

> Journalists also immortalized Teron's little "chat" with Pierre Trudeau in 1974 concerning 24 Sussex. Gwyn [Richard Gwyn, a well-known commentator of the time] describes it: "Wouldn't an indoor swimming pool be a great idea? It would cost, Teron reckoned, about $60,000 and could be built easily and without fuss by Public Works. It was not anyone's fault, exactly, that the pool eventually cost over $200,000. Too much rock, mostly, and had to be paid by wealthy donors, in exchange for anonymity and a tax write off. What mattered about the pool was that it soon became a metaphor for breach of trust."

Of course, I had committed the cardinal sin of not having an appointment, so when I appeared at the reception desk to seek a meeting with the president for that day, I was met with surprise and an unco-operative attitude. I explained to the receptionist that I was the Housing minister for Newfoundland and had just taken an early flight to Ottawa and that I wanted to see the president on an urgent basis since I believed there was some mistake in my province's allocation of housing money for this coming year. I was quickly informed that the president was busy all day. I indicated that I was available any time from then until midnight or the next day. Still no time available!

Well, I said, "Please tell Mr. Teron's secretary to tell Mr. Teron that I shall be here until Mr. Teron sees me—either today, tomorrow, or whatever day. I will be here every day during business hours to see him. I will not be leaving until I see him."

With a frown the receptionist said, "I will let her know."

And so the morning elapsed, people coming and going, and I just sat there in the reception office.

"Oh," I said to the receptionist, "does your president have another external exit beside this front door that I used?"

Curtly, she replied, "No, sir!"

Lunch came and went—and still no action.

Around three o'clock this gentleman came to the reception room, introduced himself as a vice-president, and indicated that the president had instructed him to see me.

"Thank you," I said, "but I must see the president. No disrespect, but the issue is one for me and the president to resolve."

The hours passed, and it was now closing time. People were leaving for the day. Sometime between six-thirty and seven o'clock, the president's secretary came to the reception area and asked me to come with her—the president was going to see me.

Well, it was short.

I was ready with my arguments, and as we shook hands I had begun to explain.

"No, no," Teron exclaimed. "Your allocation has been restored. Anything else?"

Stuttering and surprised, I said, "No, no, no, that will be fine."

And Teron was out the door. Of course, I left elated and went back to my hotel. I didn't know (and still don't to this day) why I had been treated this way, and now that I had the full allocation, I don't think I spent time trying to discover the reason for this bizarre action.

Of course, on my return home I informed the premier, who was delighted, admitting, in telling my incident amusedly to Cabinet the next week, that he thought my action would be a waste of time.

Being minister of Municipal Affairs provided good experience since it allowed me to get to know many parts of the province that I did not know or had not visited, as well as dealing with municipal organizations, which meant knowing about these communities and regions at the ground level. I remember once hiring a plane out of Goose Bay and travelling the Labrador Straits area, since it was often a forgotten area of Labrador and the province.

During this period I also became aware of the inner workings of Cabinet, serving on the Social Policy Committee of Cabinet and then as chair of the committee. I became acutely aware, really for the first time, of the very poor financial position of the province, that we really did not have the money to do the things that we were now as a province expected to do. The degree to which this existed was a bit of a shock to me. Essentially, the province was cutting corners everywhere except in health and education, and the spending there on new hospitals and schools—like all capital works—was borrowed money. We had the lowest credit rating in Canada—many of our schools lacked the science labs and libraries commonplace in other parts of Canada—and trying to keep up in medical technology was almost impossible.

In my own department new capital projects would take many years to complete: a $1 million water and sewer project would be done in annual phases of $250,000. In this way we could announce more projects, although it would take years for any of them to be completed. Because of the nature of the development of the municipal movement in the province, only a handful of councils levied property tax and hence were highly dependent on the province for funds. There was never enough money even for reasonable, vital things, and often there was no money at all. It was natural now in this circumstance to see both the Smallwood era of giveaways—like the Upper Churchill and the Terms of Union, of no meaningful fisheries, say—as gigantic blunders, sentencing the province to year after year of difficult budgets and parochial infighting everywhere.

It was in this context that I began to view the new Department of Mines and Energy as a new and up-and-coming department. It seemed that there was promise here, and papers were presented to Cabinet about the possibilities of offshore oil and gas. The then minister of Mines and Energy, John Crosbie, resigned to enter federal politics, seeming always uneasy in his role having to play second fiddle.

I then did the unthinkable.

I went to the premier and told him that I wanted to be the new minister of Mines and Energy, just like that. I knew I was taking a chance, that I might come off brash and too opportunistic. But I weighed the risks: I had been given the Department of Municipal Affairs and Housing two years before. It had had many problems. I tackled those problems, kept the government and especially the premier out of trouble, and when there was trouble I did not run to the premier to solve them, but instead solved them at the department level. I had participated constructively in Cabinet and the Social Policy Committee and otherwise presented a positive image of the government through the department. I also knew that the premier liked to delegate, that he would want someone in this department who could tackle the emerging opportunities and challenges. I thought, therefore, that I was a good candidate for the job. And, frankly, I was afraid that if I did not show an interest right away the premier, on some other Cabinet colleague's recommendation or strong lobbying, might just give the appointment to someone other than me.

Thankfully, the premier agreed with me, and for that I am forever grateful. I don't remember if he hesitated or whether it took a few days or not for him to make the decision. I suspect if I hadn't received the appointment I might remember.

From the first day, I knew I was in the right place. There were a lot of ideas floating around, both on the energy and the mining side.

I knew a little about mining, representing a district that had three small copper mines in recent years. As a matter of fact, one such mine that had recently closed down, the Whalesback Mine, was reactivated by local investors and called Green Bay Mining. And two of my best friends, Fred Goudie and Joe Bomgartl, were both involved in mining in my district. And of course, on the energy side there was Newfoundland and Labrador Hydro (with whom during that period I had an uneasy relationship, given their sense of superiority and desire to deal with just the premier), and the promise of offshore oil and gas.

When you have people like Cabot Martin, Steve Millan, and John Fitzgerald around, things are going to happen, especially when they realize (contrary to their likely earlier perceptions that the premier has appointed a lightweight) that I was open and ready to learn, that I was amenable to a strong provincial position on offshore, and that I enjoyed the cut and thrust of debate around new ideas. There was many a night that I stayed late (Eastern Canada Building, Bonaventure Avenue) to read and learn the new terms dealing with offshore. I remember meeting one fellow, a cleaner, at 6:00 a.m., who was on his way to work as I was leaving after a night of study. I would return at 9:00 a.m.

So the department was a busy place. The mining side was busy with the iron ore mines in Labrador City and Wabush in Labrador, the zinc mine in Daniel's Harbour on the island, and the closing of the fluorspar mine in St. Lawrence; the energy side was busy on both the developing offshore issue and the ongoing Upper and Lower Churchill issues, as well as the development of additional hydro power on the island.

Two developments on the island—the Upper Salmon Hydro Project and the Hinds Lake Hydro Project—became very controversial. In both cases, being Energy minister, I was to take a leading role and found myself immersed in local, often vicious, personal negative reactions. It must be remembered that in the mid- to late seventies the province was mired in debt and at that time there was little on the horizon that would see an end to our economic and financial circumstance. Hence, every development of any kind or size immediately drew quick and local responses—all the way from jobs to environmental and native concerns, some legitimate and many others emotional responses to dire local conditions.

In the Upper Salmon case, this development was really an extension to the already existing large Bay D'Espoir Hydro Development on the south coast of the island and would not generate that many jobs. But the local towns of St. Alban's, Head of Bay D'Espoir, Milltown, Morrisville, and the largely Mi'kmaq town of Conne River were up in arms about jobs, the development risking caribou habitat, and local Liberals wanted to embarrass the government. This all came to a head in a demonstration at the Bay D'Espoir site when the management of Newfoundland and Labrador Hydro and I were there to announce the development. It was the first time that I saw pictures with negative statements about myself, and I was burned in effigy. I proposed a delegation to meet with me and reluctantly the crowd agreed; some semblance of reality was brought to what the development could and could not do for the area. Things proceeded after that in a relatively calm manner, the bottom line being that this was a short development with few permanent jobs and would not and could not be the answer for the more structural economic problems of the area.

In somewhat of a similar vein, the Hinds Lake development drew the ire of the people in the south central Buchans area, even though the development was some distance in the southwestern area on Grand Lake. However, Buchans had seen its large decades-old base metal mine close and hundreds had left the community. It was felt that this development should help Buchans by building a new road to the development (there was a much longer road access already available) and hence make it possible for workers from Buchans to have a better chance to get the benefit of the development. This became quite a *cause célèbre* with the local unions, who, of course, mobilized the larger union movement and the Member of Parliament, a Liberal, and no friend, therefore, of the provincial Conservative government. Even the national CBC got in on the act.

All of this culminated in a large meeting in Buchans (I think it was on a Saturday or Sunday afternoon) to protest the lack of commitment by the province and minister, in particular, with their plan for the development. I was asked to appear before this rally and explain myself. I remember my colleague, Joe Goudie, the Member from Labrador and fellow minister, accompanied me on this occasion. I drove to Buchans with Joe and arrived at the building where the protest rally was being held. We were right on time and the hall was already filled with proceedings about to start, all just waiting to see if I would attend. I walked in the building and proceeded to the front of the hall, accompanied by boos and catcalls. All the union leadership were present, and the MP—and CBC.

Of course, the only topic was the hydro development. The various speakers all took their turns criticizing the government and me for the callous way this whole thing was being handled, followed by lots of supportive applause and each speaker referring to the fact that I was now there and would have to answer. This must have gone on for an hour or more. The anticipation grew because all were now waiting to hear from the one person all the speakers were saying could do something to help. All the speakers were on the stage, including me. When finally I was introduced, I decided I would not remain on the stage. Instead, I took the few steps down from the stage and stood immediately in front of the audience.

I began very slowly and very methodically and in a subdued voice. I explained that like all such projects, this was a provincial project, not a local or regional project. It would provide electricity to the entire province. Would it be fair to charge everyone in the province higher bills just to please one group in one part of the province for a year or two? What about another project next year? Would I have to build a road or similar thing for people who protested and were having a hard time that had nothing to do with the project? The people from the Buchans area could still compete for jobs on the project and drive to the project like people all over the province. As Energy minister I could not be expected to try and solve the deep economic problems of a place or region on the back of a short-term project. That was not fair! I was not Santa Claus.

Suddenly, to a number of these points, I heard someone say in a low voice, "Yes, that's right," and another, "Yes, I understand," or words to that effect. I pointed out none too subtly that it was all right for those on the stage to criticize, but they did not have any responsibility on this matter to the taxpayers, to all the citizens of the province. I went on to describe other areas where the economy was not good, where a fish plant was closed down, where another mine had closed—three in my own district—where loggers had to drive from distant communities to the lumber woods, with others going to Labrador and others to the mainland—some who had relatives right here in this room. Miraculously, many were now applauding the things that I said. Now there seemed a very small minority in the room who were against me.

When I finished I got a standing ovation from most in the room. You see, contrary to popular myth, people understand fairness. As my campaign manager used to say, there's wisdom in the crowd, especially if the facts and the truth are presented. CBC and crew silently stole away. There was no blood this time.

Things were moving quickly in the department on the offshore file as we honed our skills on offshore matters and finalized our position on jurisdiction, introducing legislation, establishing a petroleum directorate, acquiring expertise, and, most importantly, establishing our own regulations. Likewise with the Upper and Lower Churchill, things were moving and various talks with the federal and Quebec governments occurred as well as the introduction of the Lower Churchill Development Corporation Act. Both these issues will be discussed in another section of this book.

During this time I was given the added responsibilities of the Department of Rural and Northern Development. This was an interesting and challenging task in that it provided for further extensive travels to rural Newfoundland (as if I needed further education in this regard), and more particularly Labrador, where my experience was limited. I therefore visited all the communities in Labrador and became more familiar with the Inuit and Innu peoples.

One of my more unpleasant experiences was to fire one of our workers in Davis Inlet. The province oversaw retail operations in the aboriginal communities. One summer morning I arrived by seaplane at Davis Inlet. It was around 10:00 a.m. The government store was not far from the government wharf where we disembarked from the plane. However, the store was not open. It was a regular workday and there was no reason for the store to be closed. A number of native children were nearby on the road, so I asked them where the manager for the store lived. They took me up one of the roads and on to another and pointed at the house. I went up to the door and knocked, but there was no answer. I proceeded inside only to find manager and wife still in bed. When I finally awakened the manager and he arose from the bed, I informed him that he was fired. I had already had a number of complaints against the manager, and this dereliction of duty could not be tolerated. Apparently, there had been a celebration the day before and our good manager was a willing participant to the extent that he was unable to perform his work duties the next morning.

This department was an honest attempt by the government of the day to support and encourage small business enterprise, especially in the resource sector of logging, fishing, farming, and tourism and craft development. The department supported rural development associations throughout the province and their parent body, the Rural Development Council, whose job was to identify opportunities and encourage proper business practice and leadership.

As mentioned, the offshore file was moving fast and the Petroleum and Natural Gas Act of 1977, and the accompanying regulations under this act in 1978, established the reality that Newfoundland intended to assert its ownership of the exploration and development of oil and gas on the continental shelf and margin. This gave rise to all companies having to apply to the province, for the first time, for a permit to explore offshore. Of course, the federal government maintained that the offshore was in their jurisdiction, so the companies were faced with two sets of regulations. The development and implementation of these regulations meant many meetings with the oil companies and saw myself, Cabot Martin, and Steve Millan, in particular, spending many days and hours in hotels in Calgary talking with executives of the oil companies.

This was no fun. While the companies all complied in the end, there was a lot of "weeping and gnashing of teeth." I remember one evening while in Calgary having to talk to an executive of Total Eastcan (they had federal permits off Labrador) on the phone from Paris. A heated discussion ensued in which the executive, in broken English, expressed anger and disgust with our regulations and our whole approach. I think at the end of the conversation I, too, was mad and told the executive that if he didn't like it (he could lump it), then that was just too bad. I am not sure whether any government minister had ever spoken to him in such terms and with such emotion before, since this quickly ended the conversation. Along with the new provincial regulations, the department, with the blessing of the Cabinet, developed an expensive booklet called *Heritage of the Sea*—our case on offshore mineral resources, which was sent to every householder in the province.

I was now, of course, involved in the Resource Policy Committee of Cabinet and hence had the opportunity to see the developments occurring in the other resource departments in the same way as, earlier, I was involved in the Social Policy Committee of Cabinet when I was minister of Municipal Affairs. I became chairman of the committee and also deputy chair of the Treasury Board.

Given these roles and my previous Municipal Affairs and Housing portfolio, it was becoming obvious that the present configuration of the provincial economy was such that even with our major economic levers of fishery, forestry, and mining performing at capacity, it would not generate sufficient revenue to make a significant difference in the revenues to the province. And if this was all we had, then "have not" status with the federal government (being our chief income provider) would be a permanent condition.

At this point the fishery was still seen as having real potential for growth, and various numbers were used to indicate significant increased tonnage to the TAC, total allowable catch. New fish plants were on the drawing board for places like Triton (which was built), Jackson's Arm, Lewisporte, and other places. While this optimism was encouraging at the time in that it would stabilize the rural population and help sustain the present demographic, many of the plants would be largely seasonal and the population highly dependent upon unemployment insurance. I am afraid there was a practice in some places where plants hired people on for a certain period to qualify for UIC (now called EI) and then would lay them off and hire another group, and the cycle proceeded. Certain fishing families would do this within the family unit; in the winter months, all the adult members of the family were receiving a sizable UIC cheque. The province largely ignored such practices, and therefore a real system developed whereby UIC was looked upon by many as an entitlement as opposed to insurance to be used to bridge a time between jobs. In the Economic Council of Canada Report of 1980, the following can be found in its Summary and Recommendations section, page 9:

> Because the fishery is a common property resource, there was no limit to the number of people who could enter it before the recent freeze on new licenses. Through subsidies for boats and gear, people are granted assistance to go fishing. Once in the fishery, unemployment insurance guarantees some kind of income assistance during the off season, provided they earn a weekly minimum during the initial twenty-week qualifying period. If they also work in a fish plant, they can be guaranteed even longer off-season benefits. Once on the system, the eligibility requirement drops to ten weeks and the annual cycle is set up to be repeated indefinitely. There is, of course, no limit to the number of other members in the same family who can make use of the system.

It was becoming obvious, almost day by day, the huge potential that offshore oil and gas could offer if significant quantities were found, and an even bigger potential if the province would be able to reap significant revenue and economic spinoff from any such discovery.

It was also becoming obvious to many on the inside around 1978 that Frank Moores was tiring of the job and that the difficulties of managing a political party, caucus, and Cabinet, the minutia in which a leader was forced to be involved, were not areas that kept his attention. Furthermore, there were lingering issues dealing with the Public Works department that had led to a scandal involving a local electrical contractor, which necessitated an inquiry conducted by a retired Supreme Court of Newfoundland Judge Furlong. There was also considerable suspicion concerning a late-night fire at Elizabeth Towers involving some Cabinet ministers. There were clouds forming and there was a lot of internal discussion about leadership. I remember being in the premier's office some months before his announced retirement, where he informed me that he intended to retire very soon (within months) and wondered if I was going to run. Well, Frank followed through on this and announced his retirement.

Of course, I had by then thought about the idea of challenging for the leadership, but I also realized that this would be a monumental challenge. However, I felt up to it. I decided to give it serious thought.

That next weekend I dropped in to see my parents. They lived in Gander then. My father was the administrator of Lakeside Homes. I had to drive through Gander to reach my constituency, so I was a frequent visitor. It was Friday evening. During a quick supper, I mentioned that I was considering running for the leadership now that the sitting premier had announced his intention to resign. My mother was a little shocked and urged caution, that perhaps being a minister was enough and that taking on such a big undertaking was just too much. Father said little, except for a few questions, which I dutifully answered. I indicated that I had not yet made up my mind—that I would check with my wife and friends and the district association—and would be coming back on Sunday evening, at which time, of course, I would drop in again. Sunday evening saw me back at my parents, for supper before the 200-mile drive to St. John's that night. Mother had a great supper as usual and the three of us sat down to dine. Of course, there was only one question—Are you going to run? Mother posed it, at which time Father said to my mother and me:

"Wait." He got up from the table and went to the bedroom, hauled something from a side drawer, and came back to the table. He passed an envelope to me.

"Open it," he said.

I opened it, and there was a cheque for $1,000.

"I wanted to be the first donor to your campaign," Father exclaimed.

"Ewart," said Mother, "how do you know he is going to run?"

"Allison, it was clear when he was here Friday . . . he has no choice anyway."

Of course, others had encouraged me to consider this opportunity. My later campaign manager, Frank Ryan, who was honest and super able, visited my office and suggested I seriously examine this option. Additionally, I was further encouraged by a meeting I held in Gander of supporters led by Ron and Agnes Richard. These people knew me well and I could count on them to provide frank and direct advice.

CHAPTER 5: STEPPING FORWARD

"Politics is the art of the possible."
—Otto Von Bismarck

Statement by the Honourable Brian Peckford
Minister of Mines and Energy
January 31, 1979

A New Generation of Leadership

I have decided to run for the leadership of the Newfoundland and Labrador Progressive Conservative Party at its convention to be held on March 16 and 17. This was not an easy decision. I have thought long and hard about it. I have consulted with my wife and family, friends, my district association, and supporters from around the province. There are many reasons for my decision. I shall attempt to highlight some of them:

1. Since an early age, I have been interested in public life. The same drive and ambition that brought me into politics eleven years ago still possesses me today.

2. As a people or society we have in this century "sold out" to those who would develop our resources for themselves and others without providing a fair return to the owners of the resources—the people of Newfoundland and Labrador. We are on

the threshold of having perhaps our last chance to "make it" or "break it." I think I can help us make it.

3. Since being involved in government I have seen injustice that I would like to set right: social, economic, and political injustice.

4. Reform must be the order of the day if we are to succeed; that is, a new politics based on ability and integrity. It is a strong conviction I have held for a long time.

5. People whose opinions I respect have confidence and faith that I can provide the leadership that's needed. Both my district association and a large group of people from around the province who met in Gander on Monday night endorse this view.

Perhaps the all-pervasive, underlying reason has to do with two concepts: leadership and the province's future. The two are intertwined.

Our resources—the fishery, energy and minerals, forestry, agriculture, tourism—and our people all have a great capacity for expansion, to improve the living standard of all our people. If and only if we in government representing the people use the right methods, pursue the right policies, and have clearly developed aims and objectives established after adequate public debate. It is easy to answer the question "What should we do?" It is much more difficult to answer the question "Why should we do it?" We must answer the question of why before we can be sure that the answer to the question of *what* is the right one. Sound, realistic, long-term resource development goals are the only sure way to meet the many social needs and have a healthy society. It will take strong resolve and determination—that is, leadership—to look beyond the project-oriented approach to government to one that involves the long-term good of our people, to be creative yet responsible. It is a challenge that must be met now. I am excited by such a challenge and wish to embrace it with all vigour.

The March 16–17 convention is perhaps the most important one ever held by the PC Party in its history because not only is the party choosing a leader, but at one and the same time a premier is being selected. I consider it absolutely vital, therefore, that the delegates know where I stand and what I will try to do if elected. Of course, it will not be possible to give in-depth policy statements, but I will issue specific statements which will provide clear direction on my thinking. The first statement will deal with political reform. Statements will follow over the next weeks dealing with economic development, social development, and cultural development.

My wife and I, beginning today, will visit every district in the province to meet with district associations and explain and elaborate on ideas contained in this announcement.

I challenge all those interested in better government not more government—in a new generation of leadership—to get involved to ensure a bright future for our people.

THIS WAS AN EXHILARATING time. New people were coming forward. Frank Ryan, my campaign manager, was putting together a solid team at our new campaign headquarters and, hence, I could go on the road to meet the executives of the district associations around the province. These executives were already voting delegates, so meeting and trying to get their support was crucial, for their own votes as well as their ability, given their stature, of influencing the other delegates to be elected from the riding. Three incidents stand out as I write.

The Port au Port District Association had a public meeting to which they invited all the candidates for the leadership to address the gathering and give the people of that region a chance to assess each candidate. Of course, all the main candidates attended. Given that there was no hotel on the Port au Port Peninsula, all the candidates stayed at a well-known hotel in nearby Stephenville. The night went well, with a full house at the meeting. After the formal part of the meeting a dance followed, at which time the candidates were able to mingle and meet "the people." This proved to be a late night; however, I think I was one of the first candidates to leave, when I was sure I had done all I could that night to attract support and that wine and song was to be the order for the rest of the night. I also had an ulterior motive.

I was up early the next morning and off to the peninsula to meet the executive members of that association, and I did not have a lot of time. I had found out from the locals the previous evening where the executive members lived. My first stop on the peninsula was a small house right on a curve of the road. This was the Campbells' residence; Mr. Campbell was an executive member of the association. It was all of 8:00 a.m. when I tapped on the door. No answer. I tapped again, and then a third time. Suddenly, the door opened, and standing in her nightgown was Mrs. Campbell.

"Oh!" I blurted out. "Sorry to get you up so early. My name is Brian Peckford and I am running for the PC leadership."

"Yes, yes," Mrs. Campbell said. "Well, we are just getting up, but do come in."

The wood stove had been lit and a good heat was circulating around the kitchen. A door off the kitchen opened and Mr. Campbell appeared.

"Well, well, Mr. Peckford, you are an early bird," he said.

"I am," I replied, "but if I don't start early I will never get to all the districts, and I must do that if I want to be elected."

And so the missus got us some breakfast and we had a grand chat about the upcoming convention and politics in general.

The Campbells became very strong supporters at the convention and campaigned vigorously on the floor of the convention hall. They remained strong supporters.

By late morning I had met the four executive members for the

Port au Port district and then headed back to the hotel for an early lunch. None of the other candidates had been out that morning; all of them were having a late breakfast or early lunch. I did not disclose to them my earlier campaigning. I credit this hard work as one of the major contributing factors to my success in the upcoming convention and in other subsequent electoral successes.

Sometimes your mind can play tricks on you, especially when you are remembering personal things from over thirty years ago. So, I wanted to check this Campbell story. I contacted former MHA, local Stephenville lawyer Fred Stagg. Fred responded to my inquiry with a wonderful letter, part of which described the matter of Mr. Campbell:

> ". . . John Francis Campbell. He was a World War II veteran, served in the British Isles, and may have been in the forestry section. In any event, he met a Scottish woman, Irene, and they married. They came to Newfoundland in 1945 or 1946 and set up a store in Campbell Creek. It was a prototypical store, lots of knickknacks and miscellaneous items, housed in a nondescript building which still exists.
>
> It is certainly true that John Francis Campbell was a devotee of yours. As leadership campaigns go, I was trying to recruit people for Leo Barry [a rival candidate for the leadership] and spoke to Mr. Campbell. He was kind and courteous to me, but there was no doubt who he supported. He was a disabled man who was partially crippled. I am not sure how that came about. I do know, however, that when you got elected and the night of the celebration that followed, John Francis Campbell was alert, athletic, and I am sure regarded it as one of the great victories of his life. The celebration must have taken a lot out of him because he died on the 23rd of July 1979. He did live to see your victory at the convention, and most importantly, he lived to see your victory in the June

1979 election. His nephew, John Campbell, a retired teacher (who you may remember from university), inherited the property when Irene Campbell died on September 6, 2001."

A second incident took me to Port Saunders to meet the president of the district association there. Given the distances involved in touring the Great Northern Peninsula, I was in a big hurry to ensure I visited St. Anthony, located north of Port Saunders and Roddickton, and to the east on the other side of the peninsula. And so, once again I was knocking on someone's door in the early morning as I sought out the president. Sure enough, she had just arisen and was surprised to see me at her door. But some breakfast and a good chat left me with the impression that I was likely to get her support and that of others with whom she was associated. Of course it didn't hurt that I was able to inform her of an earlier time when I served as temporary welfare officer for the month of August, 1964, in Port Saunders!

My first inclination that things were really going well was my trip to Roddickton. The mayor and council were looking for a meeting with me. Now, this was a very strong Liberal place (and riding), and for the mayor and council to be looking for a meeting with a Conservative leadership candidate told me that they thought I had a chance of succeeding. And so I met with them and we discussed their many and varied problems, and I gave suggestions on how they could resolve them. Once again, having been the welfare officer for this area (stationed in Englee nearby), I could relate to many of the issues that we discussed.

A crucial turning point came when three of the most prominent Conservatives in the party announced they were throwing their support behind me: William Marshall, then the Member for St. John's East; well-respected lawyer and parliamentarian Gerald Ottenheimer, Member for St. John's South, renowned orator, highly educated, and former leader of the Progressive Conservative Opposition during the Smallwood days; and Dr. John Collins, a highly regarded pediatrician. This support came after a thorough grilling by the three at Marshall's study one day. I guess I passed the test. All three were to become invaluable members in my Cabinet, without whom our many achievements that are now obvious would not have been possible.

The campaign was running well from the highly motivated office in St. John's. We had enlisted the services of John Lashinger of Toronto, who was of immense assistance. As Frank Ryan, my competent campaign manager, said, "He was a great help to us on all fronts, material procurement, delegate organization, and great design work. He had the necessary contacts we needed for a first-class campaign."

And we were winning our share of delegate support from the many district meetings. Yet it remained a formidable task since we were running against the establishment, given that the premier (contrary to his promise to me) was actively campaigning for Bill Doody then, also a minister in the Cabinet. Many political pundits at the time saw him as the front-runner. But there were seven other candidates who also felt they had a shot or could influence who the leader would be. So in all there were ten of us running: seven ministers, the former mayor of St. John's, a student, and a farmer from the Humber Valley.

By the day of the convention it was clear that we had the most organized team, both in the many hotel meetings, transportation, and on the floor of the convention. And the Doody camp, now seen by most as our biggest rival, was in desperation mode.

The speeches of the candidates went as expected, and the real campaigning began on the floor as the voting began. It was our objective to try and make 200 votes or better to be in the lead on the first ballot. This was seen as a real symbolic marker.

There were 736 votes cast on the first ballot. I received exactly the magic number, 200. Bill Doody had 157; Walter Carter, a veteran political warhorse, 87; and Leo Barry, a bright, ambitious lawyer, 84. The other six candidates had a total of 108, with the last two, the farmer and former mayor, taking no votes.

A second ballot ensued. This time there were only the top four competing. A total of 638 votes were cast. I increased my vote total to 272, Doody increased his to 184, Carter dropped to 83, and Barry increased to 99. I was growing more than any of the other candidates, but I still had not achieved the magic 50% plus one.

A third ballot was necessary. Obviously, it looked like a two-person race; however, Barry refused to drop out. There were 619 ballots cast. Peckford 331, Doody 208, Barry 80.

Victory—for hard work and organization!

Perhaps the passion and commitment to the cause is best summarized by my indomitable sister, Brenda:

> My memory of the March 17 leadership is as murky as the day itself. It was a windy, rain-snow mix and the parking lot of the hall was a thick layer of slush.
>
> I had had surgery only a few months before and I was not at my best. I was the only family member with a vote and I had quit my job to devote my time to the campaign. My request to my employer, a sitting MHA, for a leave of absence to help my brother's campaign was denied. He was supporting another candidate. The hall was packed with cheering supporters from all camps. The speeches were delivered and the voting began. I remember the first ballot. The fever pitch of chanting on the floor was deafening and the heat was stifling. At some point during the voting I knew trouble was afoot as I was feeling faint. My legs were wobbling and I knew I had to leave. I was quickly ushered to the trailer outside the hall by Fintan Aylward and Cabot Martin. When it became obvious that a third ballot was going to be necessary, I summoned up the strength to be escorted back to the hall, and, although my memory is vague, I cast my ballot. I couldn't even imagine what I would have gone through if I had not voted and Brian had lost by one vote. That was not an option. Years later as I recalled the eventful day, there are still bits and pieces of it I still can't quite remember. The most important part is still clear—Brian won!

Now the real work was to begin.

I was unhappy with being under the mandate of the former leader and eager to put my own stamp on the direction I wanted to see the province take. Therefore, after getting a Cabinet in place and becoming somewhat organized, I was determined to have a Throne Speech clearly articulating the goals and vision of the new administration and then call an election. And I did for June 18.

I did not foresee that a very formidable candidate was looming on the horizon. The Liberals were in disarray, and knew it, when I called the election. Within days they had persuaded the popular and long-serving MP and former minister in the federal Cabinet, Don Jamieson, to take the mantle of the Liberal leadership and to return to the province and challenge me.

It was said at the time that when Mr. Jamieson arrived at Torbay Airport in St. John's, it was the largest cavalcade of vehicles ever seen in the province. I think it was the next day that my chief of staff expressed some concern about what seemed like a Liberal renaissance and that it did not look good. There was a poll that showed us well behind.

Well, I rallied the troops and said, "This will get our juices going—let's go full steam ahead." Frank Ryan was my campaign manager again and we hired some policy and public relations people from Ontario. And away we went into the fray.

Several things stand out about that campaign.

First, we had to be relentless and travel everywhere to get our message out. Here is a press release issued on June 11 during that campaign that reflects this approach:

> Frank Ryan, campaign manager for Premier Brian Peckford, released today a summary of the past week's tour schedule for the premier. During the period Friday June 1st to Sunday June 10, the premier visited seventy-one communities in thirty-one districts.
>
> Mr. Ryan stated: "Premier Peckford has travelled over 4,000 miles by fixed wing aircraft, helicopter, and car throughout all parts of Newfoundland and

Labrador. This pace is a testimony to the energy and
drive of Brian Peckford—assets that will serve him
well as premier."

Mr. Ryan indicated that Premier Peckford will
leave for Labrador immediately after tonight's
scheduled television debate and is scheduled to visit
twenty-five districts during the final seven days.

One of these hectic days saw me helicopter to Melrose in Trinity North
District, a Conservative stronghold that we did not want to overlook.
So we were on our way. Only one problem: the fog descended on the
coast and made travelling the coastline impossible, so the pilot had
to veer inland and fly low to the ground, following the Bonavista
Highway. But we could not get close to the coast.

We asked the pilot if he could land on the highway—he circled,
looked for the electricity poles, looked for traffic, and hollered, "Yeah,
I think we could do it." Down we went on the highway. I got out and
the helicopter took off to find a fog-free place to land, likely back at
Clarenville or in St. John's.

We waited a few minutes and then heard a car coming. We
flagged it down. A middle-aged woman, a teacher, was driving home
to Bonavista. I told her my plight, that I had to make it to a rally in
Melrose, and would she turn around and take us there?

At Melrose the local hall was filled to capacity, but all were sure
we would not make it, knowing as they did that I was coming by
helicopter.

The local MHA, and later minister in my Cabinet, Charlie Brett,
described it thus:

"When temperatures are right, particularly during the summer,
heavy fog forms over Placentia Bay. It comes ashore and crosses the
isthmus of the Avalon in the Chance Cove–Random area. It then
follows the coastline of Trinity Bay, on the north side, all the way
down and flows out over the Melrose–Port Union area into Bonavista
Bay. I call it the 'three bays fog.'"

It was this wall of fog that we ran into while on our way to

Melrose by helicopter during the provincial election. The helicopter was not equipped to fly in the fog, which was too high to fly over and extended too far over the Atlantic to fly around. Thus we were forced to land about ten or fifteen miles from Melrose. I was one disappointed politician because I had promised the people of Melrose that I would visit their community during the election, and here we were stranded in the fog on the Bonavista Highway.

You can imagine the look on the face of the first person that came along driving a car. Here was the premier of the province hitchhiking a ride down over the Bonavista Highway. To make a long story short, we were soon on our way to Melrose, with the hall full of people awaiting our arrival. When the crowd saw us it seemed almost a miracle and that it was meant to be. The rally that followed gave us the uplift and welcome that only Melrose knows how to give.

From Melrose we were driven to Clarenville by car, where we spent some time meeting people at the local mall, people who had come from all over the area to meet Premier Peckford. There was overwhelming support in that area.

It was one of those days that one remembers. It looked like the "three bays fog" had shut us down, when in fact it turned out to be a very successful day.

Of course, the press the next day was full of this incident and our campaign was invigorated.

The second thing that stood out in that campaign was that we had to be responsible and prudent. Hence, when Mr. Jamieson announced that he would introduce a new, elaborate pharmacare program, we attacked it as too expensive and unaffordable for the province. I think the people knew it was too rich for our blood, and this showed that we would not try and match promises the other parties were making but that we would say and act responsibly. Contrary to popular myth, the people are often wiser than politicians think.

Thirdly, we had to provide a direction in writing. In this we wanted to be positive, hence our slogan "Step forward with Peckford," and the tag line on our policy document contained the words "The Way We Want to Grow." We spelled out direction on social and economic matters, parliamentary reform, strong leadership, and standing up for a better deal in Confederation.

We were also assisted by support coming from one of the larger newspapers in the province, the *Western Star*, which on June 12 said this:

"Premier Brian Peckford has shown in the short time that he has been in politics that he has the energy and drive that Newfoundland needs. He insisted that the province should have jurisdiction on offshore mineral resources, a stand that has been endorsed by Joe Clark. Mr. Peckford, who took over from Frank Moores in the spring, has earned the chance to lead the government for at least the next term."

As the last days of the campaign unfolded, it seemed clear we were out-hustling the Opposition and providing the kind of policy and leadership the province wanted at that time.

On Tuesday, June 19, the largest paper in the province, the *Evening Telegram*, carried the following headline: "A new day is breaking. Peckford pounds Liberals, final score 33–19."

Above: Premier Peckford and his older brother, Bruce, at Whitbourne, 1949.

Below: Premier Peckford tending his birch woodpile at his cottage, Boot Harbour, Halls Bay, 1986. (author photos)

Above: Ice fishing at Boot Harbour waters near Halls Bay, 1984.

Below: Wharf and boat at cottage, Boot Harbour, Halls Bay, 1984. Premier Peckford's wife, Carol, can be seen in the foreground picking partridgeberries. (author photos)

Above: Rabbit hunting exploits. Premier Peckford at his wildlife cabin, near Joe Glodes Pond, Central Newfoundland, 1983. (author photo)

Below: Candidate Brian Peckford at provincial Leadership Convention of Progressive Conservative Party, March 17, 1979.

Minister Brian Peckford signing papers to become Minister of Mines and Energy in the presence of Lieutenant-governor Honourable Gordon Winter, 1976.

Premier Peckford with a copy of his first book, *The Past in the Present*, 1983.

Premier Peckford at federal Progressive Conservative convention, Ottawa, 1983. (photo by Jim Merrithew)

Premier Peter Lougheed and Premier Peckford travelling by helicopter to offshore oil and gas exploration sites, 1984.

Mines and Energy Minister Brian Peckford reviewing
"Heritage of the Sea" document, 1978.

Prime Minister Brian Mulroney and Premier Brian Peckford at the press conference for the signing of the Atlantic Accord, St. John's, 1985.

Above: Federal Energy Minister Pat Carney at the press conference, St. John's, for the signing of the Atlantic Accord, 1985.

Below: Provincial Minister of Energy Bill Marshall speaking at the press conference announcing the signing of the Atlantic Accord, St. John's, 1985.

Front row L-R: Minister Bill Marshall; Premier Brian Peckford; Prime Minister Brian Mulroney; Minister Pat Carney. Back row shows Federal and Provincial Negotiating Teams and support personnel at the signing of the Atlantic Accord, St. John's, 1985. Back row L-R: Barry Lipsett; George Anderson; John Fitzgerald; Dave Vardy; Len Good; Stephen Probyn; Cabot Martin; Cyril Abery; Harry Near; Paul Tellier; Ron Wright; Barbara Knight; Ron Penney; Jim Thistle. Missing from photo is David Norris.

The signing of the Come By Chance Agreement in 1986 marked the reopening and rehabilitation of the Come By Chance refinery. L-R: Ken Brown, president of the new operating company; Premier Brian Peckford; Jim Haseotes, Cumberland Farms; Energy minister Bill Marshall.

CHAPTER 6: INTO THE FIRE

"And while I must deal with today
I must worry about tomorrow because I don't want it to be like yesterday."
—Premier Brian Peckford, October 26, 1982

I WAS EAGER TO clearly outline the administration's vision and focus. I had come to realize that with the pending constitutional talks approaching, our position should be made very clear. So the first Throne Speech said the following:

> Forty-five years ago, our people faced the greatest crisis in their history. The suspension of Dominion status, an economic and political crisis that cost them their hard-won democratic institutions and control over their social and economic destiny.
>
> Since then we have gone through a period of social and economic reconstruction and development which has seen a Commission of Government for fifteen years, our entrance into Confederation, and a thirty-year post-Confederation development period. Throughout the whole, the determination of the Newfoundland people to control their social and economic destiny has not wavered. The debate has only been about the appropriate means by which the great overriding objective is to be achieved. While it is clear that our entry into Confederation cannot be questioned, there is a growing realization that the present structure of Confederation does not allow

this province to realize the full economic benefits of its own resources or to adequately promote the enhancement of our unique cultural heritage.

The speech went on to say:

My government feels that we must go through a final but necessary stage of reconstruction. Our people are, I am sure, ready, yes, even anxious to complete the task of securing for themselves the means by which they, as a people, can assure their future as a distinct society. This objective can only be achieved if we, once again, have adequate control over our marine resources: fisheries and offshore oil and gas. If we are to move forward there must be constitutional change . . . My government will make strenuous efforts to renegotiate certain arrangements already in place, in particular the power contract at the Upper Churchill . . .

And the final quote I will reference from that Throne Speech:

A detailed five-year plan will be presented to the federal government before the end of this calendar year, which will serve as a basis for a complete rationalization (in the medium term) of the financial relationships between the Government of Canada and the Government of Newfoundland and Labrador.

I am going through some pains to quote this first Throne Speech since it marks the beginning of my time as first minister of the province, but also more particularly as it highlights the three main thrusts that I pursued, ones I thought were the most necessary for the future: first, fish, because of its historic roots and also because of the labour and demographic dimensions of the issue; second, the Upper and Lower Churchill Falls, both to try and correct the wrongs of the Upper Churchill contract—which if changed to current economics would, in one fell swoop, make us a "have" province—and to develop the Lower Churchill for future energy needs; and third, offshore oil and gas, the new frontier where we could start from the ground floor and try to reverse the resource giveaways of the past, including fish through the Terms of Union, Upper Churchill Falls through the Upper Churchill contract, forest concessions in both the Corner Brook and Grand Falls original deals, mineral concessions to John Doyle, and railway concessions to the Reid family and the Come By Chance refinery bankruptcy.

Now, it is likely forgotten just how poor we still were even thirty years after Confederation and how necessary the changes, as outlined in that speech, really were. I am unsure whether at the time the people really appreciated this circumstance. Of course, after a while negative overload kicks in, and in order to cope people must get on with managing their own lives as best they can.

The speech talked about a detailed five-year plan. It was completed and made public in October, 1980, and was called "Managing All Our Resources." As part of that, comparative economic indicators highlighted our very weak position:

- GDP per capita was $5,951; the Canadian average was $11,317.

- Average family income was $18,326; the Canadian average was $24,816.

- Earned income per capita was $4,228; for Canada it was $7,798.

- The number of people employed as a percentage of the adult population was 44.5%; the Canadian average was 58.6%.

- The unemployment rate was 15.4%; the Canadian average was 7.5%.

- Liquor taxes brought in as much money as corporate taxes.

- And tobacco taxes brought in more money than all mining taxes and royalties.

If you used 100 as Newfoundland's earned income, the next province would be Prince Edward Island at 114, 14% more; Saskatchewan at 71% more; Alberta and British Columbia were both over 200; and the Canadian average was 185—85% more. It is necessary to quote the document:

> If Newfoundland is to become a full and equal partner in Confederation, it must overcome its dependence on transfer payments and the only way to do that is to generate real wealth within the province. To create wealth Newfoundland must have the same degree of control over its resources as the other provinces already have over theirs. It must always be stressed that Newfoundland is not asking for anything special, but merely the recognition that it has equal rights with other provinces. If the federal government controlled resources in other provinces, our stance might be considered unreasonable, but such is not the case. Newfoundland lacks control because its resources happen to be in the ocean, under the ocean, or in rivers in Labrador, and are somehow perceived to be different.

It goes on to say:

> In order to understand Newfoundland's need to control its resources, it is useful to examine the relative position of Newfoundland and the rest of Canada with respect to earned incomes, which is the real indicator of wealth. Newfoundland ranks

a dismal last in Canada, and although the gap has closed slightly in the last twenty years, the average earned income in Canada is still 85% greater than in Newfoundland.

Therefore, just to reach the national average, earned incomes in Newfoundland would have to almost double to catch Ontario; to catch BC and Alberta they would have to more than double. In fact, the reality is even more onerous than this because the other provinces are growing at the same time. For example, if Ontario, Alberta, and BC grow at 3% per year in real terms over the next twenty years, then Newfoundland would have to grow 6.6% per year to catch them by the year 2000. This would be an almost four-fold increase in real earned incomes in twenty years to get up to the national average.

The budget of 1982 gives some sense of the enormity of the problem. Expenditures were $336,445,000 less than revenues on a total budget of $1.7 billion.

The budget records a 2% point rise on Personal Income Tax; Corporate Income Tax increased on large corporations from 10% to 16%; and interest on loans to fishermen, farmers, and small businesses increased from 8% to 12%. Additionally, wage restraint was announced for those receiving compensation from the province, and over the years that went from a 5% cap to 5%, 4%, and 3% (highest, middle, lowest-paid employees) to 3%, 2%, and 1%, and finally to no increase for two years.

The dependency on Ottawa was such that 48.8% of our revenues ($841,216,000 of which over $500,000,000 was equalization) came from the federal government and that debt payments were the third largest expenditure, ahead of social service expenditures.

It was obvious to me, my Cabinet colleagues, and our senior public servants that the present arrangements within the country, as it related to our province, could not see our province reach national average earned incomes. Even if everything went perfectly in our fishing, forestry, mining, agricultural, and tourism industries, we could not possibly earn sufficient revenue to attain anywhere near levels of income to approach the national average or attain "have" status.

This was the stark reality! There were some of society's leaders who never accepted this—labour leaders, fishing industry leaders, other business leaders, and politicians (municipal, provincial, and federal). There were some who more or less accepted this reality and saw the best way was just to abandon this "highfalutin notion" (some called me a rural romantic and others thought I grew up sporting a massive chip on the shoulder) of somehow reaching "have" status and just "accept what you cannot change," within the Confederation.

Our condition also manifested itself in other ways. For example, during my first election as leader of the PC Party, the nurses were on strike, and my last election the teachers were on strike. There just wasn't enough money to provide reasonable remuneration to these large groups who were paid out of the provincial treasury. Interestingly, I won both elections. Sometimes the crowd has a better sense than the elites of what can reasonably be done. Similarly, during the first election, a generous drug program was proposed by the Liberal Party but gained little traction. Once again the wisdom of the populace seemed to be there when the leadership of the province seemed too content to fight their little parochial battles.

Yet the Opposition was strong and influential in attacking and opposing the larger agenda of fish, Churchill power, and offshore resources.

On the fish matter, the Fishermen's Union never came onside and many fish companies remained ambiguous given that they were beholden to the federal government regarding quotas. Early on, the union was led by a former Liberal MP who unfortunately, at that time, took the interest of the union ahead of the province, although he possessed the ability to show leadership and take the larger view. I think he later regretted that stance. And even with the inherent conflict of interest—that is, trying to represent the offshore fishery, the inshore fishery, and the fish plant workers—the union was nevertheless a formidable force and had many friends in the federal bureaucracy. Unfortunately, there was little leadership within the fishing industry or the business community or in the populace at large to expose this conflict for what it was.

As it relates to the Churchill power situation, there was great public support, but among the elites there was simmering skepticism, and many in the business community were more interested in seeing the Lower Churchill projects of Gull Island and Muskrat Falls proceed, rather than protracted talks and court actions related to trying to change the infamous Upper Churchill contract, even though Quebec was earning more than $500 million per year from it.

The offshore was brand new, without existing constitutional impediments or unfair entrenched contracts. But from the start it was a battle royal and many voices inside and outside the province opposed our approach.

But the course was set, and from 1979 on we were determined to pursue those three actions with relentless argument and passion. That was the plan, our vision, our raison d'être on which we would never surrender.

In a speech to our annual meeting of the Progressive Conservative Party of Newfoundland on November 5, 1983, I exclaimed:

> We hold in trust the welfare of generations unborn to chart a course with the proper and prudent development of our resources so that we shall reach equality with other Canadians within this confederation.
>
> Let us step forward nurtured by the belief in Lin Jackson's words: "We must develop a new, bolder self-respect—a renewed self-confidence in ourselves and in our ability, not simply to survive (as it always was), but to take our situation in hand and become masters of it."
>
> In so doing, we will be able to exclaim from the

mountaintops—"One day the sun will shine and
have not will be no more."

However, we were only too painfully aware of the moment,
brought home every day with either people protesting, striking, or
petitions and representations from all over the province for basic
services that were taken for granted in the other provinces of the
country.

I remember well the agonizing meetings and arguments and
trade-offs in trying to come close to balancing the budget (that is,
just the operating budget). The capital budget would all have to be
borrowed. That was the brutal reality of having a credit rating, the
lowest in Canada, of Baa1.

By the time we had taken care of the health and safety priorities
of our municipal capital budget (over 90% of the municipalities could
not finance their own capital projects), there was little left to begin
new ones. The roofs on our trade schools were leaking and we would
have to prioritize the worst ones and let the rest get stopgap repairs
and hold out for another year or more for permanent repairs. Basic
health services were well below the national average, and trying to
implement some drug coverage while not balancing the budget was
a challenge.

I remember suggestions (well-intentioned) from within
government to look at our parks and Newfoundland Hydro for
changes to get savings (privatize?), and after having such suggestions
arise for a second year in a row, I blew my top and exclaimed: "Water
and parks are off limits regardless of how bad it is or gets."

The list of legitimate demands was endless. We were forced to
bargain hard with all those who were paid by the government, which
naturally led to acrimonious discourse with all union leaders, from
the teachers and nurses to the Newfoundland Association of Public
Employees and CUPE.

We introduced, and the legislature passed, Bill 59, which banned
rotating strikes and provided for additional essential workers during
a strike to protect health and safety. This of course meant harsh

criticism from inside and outside the province and even attracted a United Nations agency (that font of all wisdom) to wade into the fray.

But these were unusual times that called for unusual measures if we were to struggle through—and by and large the people understood and supported us. It is something that you would not do in a perfect world, but we were hardly in a perfect world at the bottom of Confederation's ladder on almost every meaningful measure.

Meanwhile, undaunted, we proceeded to build new hospitals and clinics in Labrador, Roddickton, Port aux Basques, and Clarenville, and made major improvements to hospitals in Grand Falls, Gander, and St. John's, as well as various senior citizen homes around the province.

We established the first ever Status of Women Advisory Council, the first ever Arts Council, the first ever Environment Department (and attendant environmental assessment legislation), and the first progressive legislation enabling the establishment of ecological and wilderness reserves, a book publishers assistance program, a sustaining grant for the symphony orchestra, and provided funding for specific arts groups. We began setting aside moneys for a pension fund; at this time all pension payments came out of each year's budget. We eliminated gender pay discrimination and introduced a policy where 1% of the capital cost of all new public buildings was to be spent on Newfoundland art.

We expanded the schools' capital budget, reorganized the whole high school program with the introduction of grade twelve, and reorganized the trade school system into a professional community college system. The introduction of specific institutes, like the first bona fide school for the deaf, cajoled the federal government to help us support a new campus for the Institute of Fisheries and Marine Navigation (to become known as the Marine Institute), perhaps a one-of-a-kind post-secondary institution without equal in the world. We also built the first and only Fine Arts degree program at Sir Wilfred Grenfell College in Corner Brook.

On the resource side, while the eye was on the big prizes of fish, water, and oil, we did deal with the here and now simultaneously. New legislation was passed dealing with the forestry, streamlining and causing more reforestation and sylva culture, introducing the first Aquaculture Act, the development of a Labrador Resource and Transportation plan, updating mining legislation, introducing a prospectors assistance program (one of the discoverers of the giant Labrador nickel mine at Voisey's Bay availed of this program), overseeing the opening of the province's first gold mine, and having a Department of Rural Development with programs for leadership and small businesses.

We also expanded the Newfoundland and Labrador Development Corporation, which provided technological, administrative, as well as financial assistance to businesses. The corporation oversaw the Newfoundland Savings Bond Program (cancelled by a successive administration), which in one year collected over $20 million, and also administered a stock savings program with the private sector (which was also cancelled by a successive administration). Additionally, a loan guarantee program, especially for small and medium fish companies, was put in place along with other financial assistance programs for fishermen.

To fully appreciate the corporation's work, the former president, Ira Bridger, whom I appointed, has this to say:

> In 1967 the province established the Newfoundland and Labrador Industrial Development Corporation (NIDC) to provide long-term financing to industrial and resource-based projects, both through commercial investments or other financial arrangements. However, its role was a piecemeal approach, generally focused on large-scale projects. In any event, it was not a fully staffed organization engaged in promoting or providing financial services but rather an administrative mechanism that facilitated projects being advanced within a line department. Financial support for high-profile

projects could also be undertaken through other Crown corporations.

Assistance to enterprises engaged in fish harvesting and processing was provided largely through the Fisheries Loan Board. [It is interesting to note that as early as 1943, the then Commission of Government began offering loans to fishing companies willing to invest in fish processing plants.] The agriculture sector was assisted through the Farm Development Loan Board.

Some progress towards providing a broader range of financial support for small- and medium-sized enterprises was made in the early 1970s. This arose primarily from the federal government's creation of the Department of Regional Economic Expansion (DREE), which offered federal government support for various programs in regional economic development. Provinces could propose projects, which would be supported financially under General Development Agreements (GDAs) between the federal and provincial governments.

One of the initiatives arising from subsequent GDA proposals from Newfoundland was the creation of the Newfoundland and Labrador Development Corporation (NLDC) in 1972. Under a 10-year GDA, a revolving capital fund of $20 million for term-lending financial support to local business was established and to be managed by NLDC. Ninety per cent of the fund was provided by the federal government and 10% provided by the province. Operating costs for NLDC were shared 50–50. NLDC operated at arm's length from the provincial government and was managed by an independent Board of Directors (with equal federal and provincial nominees).

For the next decade NLDC provided debt funding to a variety of rural-based enterprises but lending activities were restricted to the primary processing or manufacturing sectors.

In 1982, DREE was transferred to the Department of Trade and Commerce, and with the creation of the Department of Regional Industrial Expansion (DRIE), the federal government decided to wind down many of the earlier initiatives undertaken by its predecessor (i.e., DREE). The GDA model was disbanded. The province was subsequently given notice that the federal government's participation in NLDC would end. The province decided to continue to underwrite both the capital and operating requirements for NLDC and to maintain its role as a mechanism for providing support to small- and medium-sized businesses while reassessing its future role in light of a review of a broader range of socio-economic development options.

In 1985, Premier Brian Peckford appointed a Royal Commission on Employment and Unemployment, which called for an integrated strategy for social and economic development and employment creation. The Summary Report "Building On Our Strengths" was presented in 1986.

A new president was appointed at NLDC in 1986 and the provincial budget for 1987 provided renewed support for the Corporation to expand and advance a wide range of innovative programs for small- and medium-sized businesses, which complimented the recommendations arising from the Royal Commission on Employment and Unemployment.

NLDC was given a broader mandate to invest in enterprise in all sectors of the economy. A number of new specifically designed and targeted programs were introduced, such as a Venture Capital Program (focusing primarily on technology commercialization) and a Youth Entrepreneur Program (focusing on entrepreneurs under the age of 25).[1]

A major innovation for promoting self-reliance was the issuance of Newfoundland Development Savings Bonds to provide capital funding for NLDC. The bond issue was primarily used to promote local enterprise and entrepreneurship. Bond sales were restricted to residents of the province, but some argued that there were more cost-effective ways to raise money that did not take into account the tremendous intangible advantage of providing a direct link to investment in one's own community. As a result, the bond issue received tremendous positive support from local residents, was over-subscribed, and raised over $20 million.

In addition to the revitalization of NLDC, the Peckford administration introduced a Newfoundland Stock Savings Plan and Venture Capital Tax Credit Program, which provided provincial income tax credits to encourage residents to invest in the provincial economy.

In 1987, NLDC created a subsidiary operation, the Enterprise Network Inc., which created, promoted, and initiated the development of a province-wide

---

1   Though NLDC was later disbanded by the Wells administration, and initiatives such as the Youth Entrepreneur Program were lost, it is interesting to note that the concepts developed at NLDC were re-introduced some years later within the Youth Ventures and Seed Capital programs promoted by the Newfoundland and Labrador Association of Community Business Development Corporations. In 2010, the province, through the Department of Innovation, Trade and Rural Development, also "reintroduced" a Young Entrepreneurs and Innovators Program.

Enterprise Network, a multimedia applications and support system for communications-and-IT-enabled socio-economic development in rural and remote communities, which also assisted in transferring the skills associated with the emerging information economy to business and economic development. This was an innovative, leading edge initiative that drew national and international attention.

As a Crown corporation, NLDC was able to form partnerships with community organizations and the federal government to plan and build the Enterprise Network service. In 1988 the Atlantic Canada Opportunities Agency supported the planning and initial pilot development of the Enterprise Network, and in 1991 a special Cooperation Agreement was signed by the federal and provincial governments to support the activities of the Enterprise Network.

Unfortunately, support for this initiative was later abandoned by the Wells administration. Nevertheless, the pioneering development work undertaken in Newfoundland and Labrador was followed closely by others and emulated in many other international jurisdictions.

There were other actions involving significant investments, including ongoing support for the Bay D'Espoir aquaculture program; support for our first gold mine at Hope Brook; tens of millions of dollars of federal-provincial money for technology upgrades to the two paper mills; support for the Sprung Greenhouse project; over $100 million in loan guarantees almost exclusively for the fish processing industry; tens of millions of dollars to a Rural Development Authority, which provided loans and grants for small rural-based businesses in forestry, farming, crafts; and leadership support through the establishment of Rural Development associations throughout the province.

Perhaps three major projects speak most dramatically to both "those immediate on-the-ground issues" and why through them we could see even more clearly why we had to push the big-three agenda, come what may.

COME BY CHANCE OIL REFINERY

THIS TROUBLED PROJECT CAME as a result of Joey Smallwood's "industrialize or perish" philosophy. When I came to power it was mothballed, and I had said during the campaign that I would see if something could be done to get the project going again. At the time it was the largest bankruptcy in Canada's history. I was able to get Petro-Canada, then a federal government–owned company, to pay for the mothballing costs. But this was for a finite time. I was trying to find someone who would take the place over and make it work. An almost impossible task! I am sure at the time there were very few who thought it was really possible, let alone probable. At least that was the information coming back to me. Additionally, the task was not made easier in the fact that most of the studies that had been done to assess the possibility of reopening the refinery all showed that it would take well over $100 million to rehabilitate the place. This has troubled me to this day, since it seems obvious that this was an inflated figure deliberately used to dissuade those who might have an interest in seeing Come By Chance reopen. The politics of refining oil in the Atlantic provinces during this time was very intense, showing as it does the lengths to which existing operators were prepared to go to protect their present position in the marketplace.

There had been some Middle Eastern interest with local Newfoundland business involvement, but this turned out to be a false attempt: while they professed private investment, with no public funds, subsequent meetings with them revealed a requirement for substantial public funds. But when all seemed lost on this venture and equipment was on site to begin dismantling (the mothballing time was at an end), there came an inquiry from a group in Boston who had read a news report in the *Boston Globe* about the refinery. This was Cumberland Farms, a company owned by the Haseotas family (of Greek extraction) who began with one farm and a cow and calf worth $84 in Cumberland, Rhode Island, in 1939.

The company had become successful in the convenience store business throughout New England and along the coastal states of the U.S. They had recently acquired additional convenience stores with Gulf gas stations, and hence were interested in a constant gas supply for their newly acquired assets. And thus was born a relationship between the provincial government and Cumberland Farms. Interestingly, and of great importance, was that although the company had no refinery experience or expertise, they were skeptical of the studies that showed that it would take well over $100 million to rehabilitate the refinery and were willing to hire independent experts in the field from Texas to examine the refinery and provide the company with estimates of how much it would cost to successfully restart the refinery.

Additionally, there was the cost of getting the large dock in shape and making it operational, an integral part of the whole operation. I remember well my conversations on this; the company and I agreed to do our own independent assessments and then compare our numbers. We went about doing our assessment in an unorthodox way.

We had recently appointed Tom Whelan as deputy minister of the Department of Public Works, an engineer and Newfoundlander who had spent many years working for the federal Department of Public Works supervising the construction of docks/wharves all over the province. Tom was a no-nonsense type of guy—ask him a question and you would get a straight answer—and not your typical federal bureaucrat. So I called Tom up and told him I had a special project I wanted him to do for me. I explained that we were in talks with a prospective buyer for the refinery and that both the company and I had agreed to do our own independent assessments on how much it would cost to make the refinery dock operational. He was interested. I told him that we did not have much time, that I was looking for a ballpark figure, that he could get whatever help he needed, and that I wanted an answer in a few weeks. Several weeks later, Cumberland had their figure and Whelan had submitted his figure. Surprisingly, both assessments said the wharf could be made operational for between $3 million and $5 million, a far cry from the $20 million that the other studies had determined.

Cumberland proceeded with the rehabilitation using, where possible, Newfoundland contractors, and almost all of the operational employees were from the province. And no government money or other government concessions were asked for or provided. Is there another project of its size in the history of Newfoundland's industrial development up to that time (1986) that has come on stream without some sort of government assistance (and in this case after the project had gone bankrupt)?

The refinery has been going ever since, producing 115,000 barrels of refined product a day and employing 550 people, having pumped over $1 billion over the years in capital upgrades. It was also awarded a Top 25 Employer distinction in Atlantic Canada.

The one negative aspect of all this was that in the final talks with the federal government, we were forced to advise Cumberland that the federal government would only agree to the sale if no product was marketed in the rest of Canada. This was a tough pill to swallow. In other words, the refinery's product could be sold in Newfoundland (a small market) or internationally, but nowhere else in Canada. I remember the evening Bill Marshall and I called Jim Haseotas (then president of Cumberland Farms) in Boston to inform him that we were unsuccessful in getting this condition waived and to see whether he would still proceed.

As we all know, Cumberland Farms went ahead with the project. But it always stuck in my craw that we had a buyer who did not want any money from any government and who was prepared to restart the refinery, and here was the federal government putting trade restrictions on the sale of the product from one province to another! In January, 2001, this restriction was finally lifted, fifteen years after the refinery reopened. One wonders if something like this could ever happen in any other part of the country.

Snatched from imminent destruction, the largest bankruptcy in

Canadian history up to that time, responsible for bringing down one of Japan's largest trading companies (Ataka), projected to have cost over $100 million to restart when it came in less than $30 million, and being in continuous operation ever since, qualifies the reopening of the refinery at Come By Chance as one of the unheralded economic success stories in the history of Newfoundland and Labrador.

CORNER BROOK PULP AND PAPER MILL

THE CORNER BROOK PAPER mill has a storied history—one of those enterprises of the 1920s much heralded by the prime minister of the time, Sir Richard Squires, as "putting the hum on the Humber (River)," a symbol of the exaggerated optimism and of the many riches that lay waiting to be developed in the hinterland of the island, which would make Newfoundland an exceedingly prosperous place. It became an economic mainstay of Corner Brook for over sixty years, notwithstanding the many concessions of trees and water necessary to get it going.

In 1984, Bowater Corporation, which had taken over the operation in 1938, announced that it was closing down and that it was no longer a viable operation, alleging that wood costs and transportation costs were too high. This came as a shock and a big blow to the economy of the west coast of the island. Of course, the province was on the front line to show the leadership needed to ensure that this tragic announcement would not happen and to allow some other company to take over the operation.

The early days after the announcement were difficult ones, since Bowater owners just seemed like they wanted to leave and that was that. They seemed disinterested in working with us to ensure an orderly transition where we would together seek other operators. Of course, the forests were provincial and the significant (110 MW) power plant in Deer Lake was also provincial. But I was not interested in looking at a provincial takeover for two reasons: I had a natural aversion to such actions (government trying to run a paper mill was not my way of developing the province, all the more given the abysmal record of government with a recent linerboard mill in Stephenville); and secondly, it was not at all clear, given the legislation under which the original deal was done, whether the province would be successful in any such effort. This did not stop me from using such an idea when I was frustrated with Bowater's early unco-operative approach when I exclaimed to them: "I guess what the Lord giveth, the Lord could take away."

However, co-operation improved and it was agreed that a divestiture committee would be struck to assemble all the needed information and to actively market the operation in the international marketplace. This was a massive undertaking and help would be needed. It was agreed that we would hire Woods Gordon, a well-known Canadian firm with expertise in this area. The late Len Delecat of the firm, a true gem of a man, competent and hard-working, was to head up the effort. All this hard work over many months culminated in us receiving several bids, with the final determination that Kruger Inc. of Montreal showed the most promise. Bowater was not entirely happy with this selection (I was told at the time that Kruger had snatched some markets from Bowater in the southern United States) but in the end complied with the decision.

Final negotiations then began with Kruger, the unions, and other interested groups. This process was a little more drawn out than the parties expected, with lawyers from both sides becoming so eager to impress their clients, that getting a final agreement seemed secondary. This came to a head one evening in the Cabinet room when both Kruger and the government agreed to have their respective lawyers leave the room, at which time Mr. Kruger and myself with a couple of advisers refocused the talks and highlighted key issues. Two big issues were that the government was looking for a commitment from the company of over $100 million over a number of years in capital upgrading of the mill, and they were also looking to employ a larger number of non-union contractors in the woods operations. At the end of the day, after tense talks with the unions and other parties, agreement was reached whereby these two big issues were incorporated into the agreement. Mr. Kruger was a wily negotiator and tried, right up to our press conference announcing the deal at the Sir Richard Squires Building (the government building in Corner Brook), to improve the deal for the company. Once signed, however, Kruger was committed to the agreement and has proven to be a very responsible employer in the province. At the time, the $100 million was seen as a substantial figure, and of course it was, but since 1984 the company has invested five times that amount and notwithstanding the significant downturn in the paper industry, the mill is still open and employs 600 in woods operations and 700 at the mill and the Deer Lake power plant.

THE FISHERY RESTRUCTURING AGREEMENT

THE OFFSHORE FISHERY HAS played a major role in the economic life of the province for decades. This was an offshore trawler-driven fishery and sustained several communities on the Burin Peninsula and other towns on the south coast. Each had fish plants where the trawlers landed the fish, and the plants employed hundreds of fish plant workers. When I was growing up in Marystown (before they had their own plant), communities farther along the peninsula were prospering from the offshore fishery: Grand Bank, Fortune, and Burin; in Fortune Bay, Harbour Breton, and Gaultois; and farther west along the south coast, Burgeo and Ramea.

The high interest rates of the early 1980s hit the offshore fishing companies hard. These companies—Fishery Products Ltd., Lake Group, John Penny, National Sea, and the Nickerson Group—who had in recent years expanded through bank financing, now found that they were unable to meet their bank obligations and turned to government for help. Protracted negotiation ensued, and through it all an agreement was reached among all the parties: the federal government, the provincial government, the fish companies, and the bank. It was called the Fishery Restructuring Agreement, signed in September, 1983. Through the agreement a new company was established, Fishery Products International, which absorbed the assets of the troubled companies, received an infusion of cash (over

$100 million), and reflected a new ownership structure: the federal government 60%, the province 25%, the bank 12%, and 3% allocated for employee participation. Sadly, as will be mentioned later, this highly successful company was sold to private interests without the attendant accommodations (so much a part of the original agreement) necessary at least for some additional time to reflect the historically rural and sociological dimensions of this industry.

CONSTITUTIONAL CHANGE

IF THIS WASN'T ENOUGH, in the early 1980s the Constitution issue became a subject of endless meetings and arguments between the provinces and the federal government.

Various attempts had been made earlier to "bring the constitution home" (patriation) to Canada. In other words, that future constitutional amendment to the British North America Act (the major written part of the Constitution) was to be done in Canada, severing that last constitutional provision which saw our country having to seek ratification for such a change through London. Premiers, intergovernmental affairs specialists, constitutional lawyers, territorial leaders, and aboriginal organizations spent countless days absorbed in discussion.

One of the big stumbling blocks in the past was agreeing on an Amending Formula that would guide additional constitutional reform in the future. And this would prove to be difficult this time as well. But Prime Minister Trudeau had additional ideas: with this patriation he wanted to add a Charter of Rights and Freedoms.

While many of us were not opposed to such an idea, it was one that would have a significant impact on the nature of the country over time and needed to be thoroughly discussed and debated. This was not something that the prime minister was particularly interested in doing; rather, he wanted to forge ahead with great haste. He saw this as a golden opportunity to get some of his most cherished ideas to bear constitutional entrenchment.

The other factor that drove the process was that the recent May,

1980, sovereignty association referendum in Quebec, although lost, was assisted in being rejected by the prime minister's timely, though vague, commitment to a "renewed federalism."

But it was the Charter of Rights and Freedoms that many of the provinces were concerned about, especially how such a charter over time would affect the division of powers, property rights, the ongoing powers of Parliament and legislatures versus the judiciary. There were already many federal incursions into provincial areas of responsibility, and many premiers and their advisers were skeptical as to whether such charter changes could further erode provincial powers duly detailed in the British North America Act of 1867. Hence, the provinces began to insist on questioning whether certain existing provincial powers could be changed without reference to the province, and in having other issues added to the equation that had been bones of contention between the provinces and the federal government for some time, such as strengthening the provinces' jurisdiction over natural resources and shared cost programs.

In June, 1980, the premiers met with the prime minister concerning possible constitutional reform, at which time agreement was reached on twelve items to be considered for such reform: this agenda would be referred to a Continuing Committee of ministers on the Constitution who would further consider the twelve matters referred to them. In August, constitutional matters dominated a Premier's Conference in Winnipeg and how the provinces would respond to various federal positions on the twelve issues agreed to in June. The pace was accelerating, and a major First Ministers Conference on the Constitution was held from September 7 to September 13, but no agreement was possible. There were many disagreements and a suspicion by some of the provinces (rumours were rampant) that the federal government was not dealing in good faith. The prime minister made it clear that our (Newfoundland's) items of greater fisheries and offshore jurisdiction, for example, were non-starters, to which we vehemently disagreed. So, in this kind of federal intransigence compromise was impossible.

The fears and suspicions of the provinces were given credence (some of us continue to believe that this September conference was just a set-up) when, on October 2—only a few weeks after our meeting—instead of looking for compromise, the prime minister announced that it was his government's intention to unilaterally patriate and amend the constitution with a Charter of Rights binding on the provinces. He proceeded to introduce a resolution in the House of Commons to this effect.

The provinces convened a meeting in Toronto on October 14, where five provinces (British Columbia, Alberta, Manitoba, Quebec, and Newfoundland) announced they would fight the federal resolution in the courts. And this we did with the Manitoba, Newfoundland, and Quebec courts hearing the matter. Later the provinces of Nova Scotia, PEI, and Saskatchewan were to join the opposition. Ontario and New Brunswick remained as supporters of the federal position.

The press described the provinces who opposed the federal action the Gang of Eight, not a particularly positive initial description but one that would stick, given the press's penchant of favouring the federal position and erroneously seeing the eight opposing provinces as obstructionists rather than concerned leaders about how our country was to evolve.

The actions of the eight were not simply to challenge the proposal in Canada but also in London, where Newfoundland made a submission to the Select Committee on Foreign Relations of the House of Commons, calling on that body to reject the Canadian government's unilateral bill.

On March 31 (an ironic time given that Newfoundland's entry into Canada occurred at the stroke of midnight March 31, 1949), the Newfoundland Court of Appeal in a unanimous decision ruled the federal resolution to be illegal and that the federal government could not unilaterally change Newfoundland's Terms of Union with Canada. Then on April 8 the parties in the House of Commons reached an agreement to delay any vote on the constitutional measure until the Supreme Court of Canada rendered its decision on the constitutionality of the measure. Finally, on September 28, the Supreme Court of Canada ruled the federal measure to be unconstitutional: "We have reached the conclusion that the agreement of the provinces of Canada, no views being expressed as to its quantification, is constitutionally required for the passing of the 'Proposed Resolution for a Joint Address to Her Majesty the Queen respecting the Constitution of Canada' and that the passing of this Resolution without such agreement would be unconstitutional in the conventional sense."

To this day the federal government characterizes this major defeat this way:

> In view of the opposition to this proposal, doubts expressed about the legality of the procedure and opinions given by the courts of appeal of Quebec, Manitoba and Newfoundland, the issue went to the Supreme Court of Canada. On 28 September 1981, the Supreme Court reached a majority conclusion that the federal initiative was legal; however, it expressed reservations about its legitimacy on the ground that it would run counter to the conventions and the spirit of the federal system. ("The Constitution of Canada: A Brief History of Amending Procedure Discussions")

And so this attempt by the federal government to fundamentally and unilaterally alter the Constitution of Canada went down to crushing defeat. Following this, Prime Minister Trudeau needed the provinces' support to carry out his constitutional project. Is there another democracy where a prime minister has so brazenly tried to impose his personal vision unto the people? And to think, two provinces saw no problem with such an effort!

And so all parties were back to the drawing board for Constitution making, with thankfully a more reasonable federal government.

The momentous days were from November 3-5, 1981. On November 5, the Constitution of 1981 was born! Through the evening of November 4, meeting in the Château Laurier Hotel, the four premiers of PEI, Nova Scotia, Saskatchewan, and Newfoundland, with senior designates from Premier Lougheed of Alberta and Premier Bennett of British Columbia, worked on a proposal presented by Newfoundland. By 12:30 a.m., this proposal, with some changes, was agreed to and retyped. It was agreed that I would present this amended Newfoundland proposal to the Gang of Eight's scheduled breakfast meeting that morning. Seven of the eight provinces agreed with the proposal without further amendment. Quebec opposed it. It was agreed by the seven that I would present this proposal to the full conference later that morning. Upon invitation from the prime minister, who was aware that there was a new provincial proposal, I presented the proposal and after a number of hours of discussion and additional amendments, the Patriation Agreement was born.

This series of events got very mangled later by various commentators, journalists, "scholars," and authors, and for thirty years the real story of how the deal came together was submerged. Full elaboration on this sad state of affairs is explained in Appendix I.

The immediate, large issues of the day here enumerated only strengthened our resolve that as important as they were, they could not lead (alone or in combination) to the goal that we sought: real, fundamental change leading to a proud and self-reliant place—a "have" province.

CHAPTER 7: THE BIG PICTURE — THE GAME CHANGERS

CHANGE ISSUE #1 — THE FISHERY

"The Newfoundland and Labrador cod, the so-called northern stock, are pretty fish with amber leopard spots on an olive green back, a white belly, and the long white streamlining stripe between the belly and the spotted back."
—Mark Kurlansky

"The history of Newfoundland, especially its earliest annals, is essentially a history of the cod fishery."
—D.W. Prowse

EACH TIME I THINK of fish I think of growing up in Marystown and how the cod fishermen cursed the crabs that would get tangled in their nets (a far cry from the lucrative crab fishery of decades later). I think of the older, retired inshore fishermen yarning in Thoms's store in La Scie and of my visit to the Horse Islands in the spring as sealing gave way to cod fishing. I think of the Canning family of Englee, a highliner fishing family who did not have time to complain as they toiled each spring and summer morning at 4:00 a.m., steering their trap skiff around the harbour headlands. I think of being in the trap skiff with the fishermen as we left Sandy Hook, southern Labrador, at 3:30 a.m. to head to the fishing grounds. I think of the Wentzels of Tub Harbour, the Rossiters of Snug Harbour, the Bradleys of Indian Harbour, of George and Mabel on Square Islands, and my friend in Croque to whom I loaned thirty-five dollars for food so he would not be dependent on the merchant, along with the hundreds of other fishermen around the island and off the coast of Labrador. When I think of fish I think of my grandfather Peckford with his fishing rooms at the Battery in St. John's, and others in Bay Bulls on the Southern Shore.

It was a hard life, but a good one and a special one. Yet we were just not making it.

Two of Newfoundland's biggest long-term resource mistakes concerned fish and water power.

I remember Gordon Winter, who was lieutenant-governor during my first three years as premier. He was one of the signatories to the Terms of Union with Canada in 1949. He, of course, had been reading the debates I was having concerning fish, water power, and the new offshore oil and gas potential.

Mr. Winter was not one to speak brashly or quickly. He gave everything a lot of thought. One day he and I were alone in his office at Government House reviewing some matter of mutual interest when he changed the subject and began asking me questions about my position on the fishery. A very interesting discussion ensued as we both debated the merits of federal versus provincial control of the fishery. Of course, I was quick to point out that it was not a matter of either/or, but a shared issue, truly in the spirit of the Confederation and the British North America Act of 1867 where certain matters were exclusively federal or provincial jurisdiction. But in other areas there was a dual responsibility between the federal and provincial governments. I could see that Mr. Winter had been mulling over this whole matter for quite some time and was uncharacteristically exercised about it. At the end of the discussion, which must have lasted a couple of hours, he looked directly at me and uttered, "Yes, I agree now. I think we made a big mistake in the Terms of Union concerning the fishery. We should still have some real say in the fishery."

It is an irony not lost on those of us who are interested in Newfoundland resource history, and the fishery in particular, of that which had helped mould our culture and make us who we are, that throughout our long history (1497 to 2012, spanning 515 years) we were virtually in control of our fishery for only thirty—yes, thirty—years.

From 1497 to 1587 Newfoundland was visited by several nations who fished its surrounding waters and took the fish back to their countries. The English did the same, with, however, an increasing number of English fishermen squatting on land in the various coves and inlets on the eastern part of the island, but always controlled by the English merchants and fishing admirals. After Sir Humphrey Gilbert claimed Newfoundland for England in 1583, the same mode of operation continued, with settlement legally prohibited, but with some English staying. The fishery was totally controlled by England and other countries.

The Treaty of Utrecht of 1713 gave the French certain fishing rights, and although they were unable to legally settle, the French in Article 13 were allowed "to catch fish, and dry them on land, in that part only, and in no other besides that, of the said island of Newfoundland, which stretches from the place called Cape Bonavista to the northern point of the said island, and from thence running down by the western side, reaches as far as the place called Pointe Riche" (Noel, 11).

So from 1713 onward both England and France were fishing legally the waters off the east coast of Newfoundland, with the French, as S.J.R. Noel says in his book *Politics in Newfoundland*: "France had nevertheless retained for her subjects important rights of easement upon a thousand miles, or roughly one-third, of its [Newfoundland's] coast" (11).

And the great democratic movements that brought Representative Government to the island in 1832, and full Responsible Government (self-governing dominion) in 1855, still saw this treaty in full force. And although changes were made in 1783 through the Treaty of Versailles that excluded the French fishing rights to two bays on the east coast, such rights were extended on the west coast of the island, which really gave the French more coastline than under the agreement it replaced.

Noel makes the important point:

Since the colony of Newfoundland was entirely dependent upon the fishery, responsible government was inevitably weakened if the colony could not regulate its most vital natural resource. In such important matters as Fisheries conservation the French could ignore colonial legislation with impunity. Also, Newfoundlanders bitterly resented the fact that the government-subsidized French fishery, by selling its produce at an artificially low price in southern Europe, tended to depress the value of Newfoundland's stable export in its largest market. (12)

In one of the truly great moments in Newfoundland history, further changes in French fishing rights were made (1857 convention between England and France), ostensibly to relieve the present tensions between Newfoundlanders and French fishing interests, only to see the French gain a more secure foothold through such arrangements. This caused an uproar in the country and led to a special resolution in the legislature condemning

[a]ny attempt to alienate any portion of our fisheries or our soil to any foreign power, without the consent of the local legislature. As our fishery and territorial rights constitute the basis of our commerce and of our social and political existence, as they are our birthright and the legal inheritance of our children, we cannot under any circumstances assent to the terms of the convention. (Noel, 13)

As a result of this resolution, the prime minister and the Leader of the Opposition went to London and persuaded the British colonial secretary, Henry Labouchere, to withdraw the convention and later in a communication to the governor of Newfoundland conceded:

> The rights enjoyed by the community in Newfoundland are not to be ceded or exchanged without their consent, and that the constitutional mode of submitting matters for that consent is by laying them before the colonial legislature; and that the consent of the community of Newfoundland is regarded by Her Majesty's government as the essential preliminary to any modification of their territorial and maritime rights. (Noel, 14)

Of course, the previous French fishing rights of the Treaty of Versailles prevailed, and hence Newfoundland continued to try and succeed as a society, even though the reason for its existence, its fishery, was not truly under its control.

Finally, a half-century later in 1904, with international events elsewhere in play involving England and France, an agreement between the two countries was reached, which saw the fishing rights of France in Newfoundland exchanged for previous English territorial rights in West Africa.

I will let Noel have the last word on the end of a sad tale that lasted centuries, on the one hand, and the optimism that the new agreement engendered:

> With the signing of the convention the prolonged struggle of the Newfoundland colonists to control the island's territory and resources came to an end. Newfoundland was at last master of its own house, politically as well as constitutionally, the equal of the other self-governing dominions of Canada, Australia, and New Zealand. St. John's was *en fête* for several days and Newfoundlanders everywhere looked forward with Prime Minister Sir Robert Bond: "to the time when even the memory of the French presence will fade like a fevered dream before the brightness of a new day."

So from 1904 to 1934 Newfoundland had control over its fishery. Sadly, 1904 was just seeing the results of the great railway fiasco, and a year later the beginning of the Grand Falls mill giveaway, to be followed, early in the 1920s, with the Corner Brook mill sellout.

There had emerged in the last few decades of the nineteenth century the view that the island was laden with resources and that a railway would tap this great potential, unleashing a great prosperity across the country. The vast timber resources would be seen for their great wealth and further prosperity could be assured. The problem with this notion, as I pointed out in my earlier book, *The Past in the Present*, was that if this were the case, why in heaven's name did we have to give so much away to get the Grand Falls and Corner Brook mills and the railway? It either made economic sense or it didn't. Hence, in the midst of this great industrial push, little was done on the real resource on which the country depended. The Amulree Commission's Report, which led to the suspension of self-government, tellingly points out: "We have already emphasized the fact that the fishery is the mainstay of the country—policies pursued by successive governments in recent years have tended to obscure this essential and all-important consideration."

And prophetically, given the later Smallwood government debacle of the Upper Churchill Falls contract and other concessions to Brinco, the Commission stated, "Unless this process [of major concessions to outside interests] is checked, similar results may be expected to follow in Labrador, which promises to become a favourite resort for concession-hunters."

And so the thirty short years of fisheries control saw us squander the first opportunity in our history to be masters of the very reason for our presence in this part of the world. Whiteway, Morris, and Squires had spun their toxic political rhetoric upon the country.

A report that I had commissioned after I became premier and that was conducted by Nordco, entitled, "It were well to live mainly off fish," makes a valid point on page 25 when it states, "The conspicuous lack of development of Newfoundland's fishing industry, during these early decades of the 20th century, left her in a disadvantageous position to compete in the world markets against rapidly developing fishing industries of nations like Iceland and Norway."

One would think that with the opportunity of Confederation with Canada in 1949 being the option that Newfoundlanders chose (at least according to what we know), our negotiators would have realized that Newfoundland needed another opportunity on doing it right on the fishery.

But it was not to be.

And now looking back on it, how could it be, really? I mean, what is thirty years, especially when you spend most of your time on other things like giving away forest rights and mineral rights? And look at the Newfoundland representatives who negotiated the deal: Albert Walsh, who had been a supporter of Squires, did well off the Commission of Government and became the first lieutenant-governor after Confederation; Philip Gruchy, manager of the Grand Falls mill, hardly an expert in the fishery; John B. McEvoy, a St. John's–born lawyer, trained in Halifax, worked as a legislative librarian in Halifax and later as a lawyer in St. John's—not your rural fisherman type; and Gordon A. Winter, St. John's-born and of the urban merchant class, unconnected to the fishery.

And then there was Joseph R. Smallwood, a Squires admirer and author of the 1931 book *The New Newfoundland* with its opening statement: "After more than three centuries' existence as a remote and obscure cod fishing country Newfoundland in the past decade or so has entered upon a new march that is destined to place her, within the next dozen years, in the front rank of the great small nations of the world. That new march is toward modern large-scale industrialism."

And so Confederation saw, for the first time by our own hand, the transfer of all meaningful say in the fishery to the bureaucrats on the Rideau Canal in Ottawa. And things did not get better. Smallwood, true to his philosophy of the 1930s, proceeded to fulfill his obsession with industrialization. A long series of enterprises was started and failed, and all the while the federal government was improving the social condition of the people through family allowances and old-age pensions but doing little of substance with the fishery. As a matter of fact, significant increases in northern cod catch by foreigners were beginning to occur; Nordco points out in their report that it rose from 40,635 tonnes in 1953 to a whopping 659,000 tonnes in 1968. In contrast, in 1968 the total inshore and offshore catch by Newfoundland was 121,000 tonnes.

There were many studies, but little real progress was made of addressing the fundamentals of the industry. The Nordco report (page 48) highlights this issue: "Within five years of the 1967 Royal Commission, the 'fisheries–rationalization' policy was in shambles."

And David Alexander in his book *The Decay of Trade* expresses a similar view:

> What seems utterly absurd is that Newfoundland's restoration as a major producer of fishery products has not been accomplished during the breathing space provided through union with Canada. Integrating with a larger country should have made recovery much easier by lowering overhead costs, providing scale economies with new social and economic services, and making available low cost development capital. (12)

With the election of Frank Moores as premier in 1972, a more interested and assertive provincial administration regarding the fishery was finally in place. A 1973 planning exercise ensued, which involved a push to ensure that the foreign catch of northern cod be caught by Canadians (and most particularly by those closest to the resource—Newfoundlanders), and importantly that there "be greater Federal-Provincial consultation in the determination of Canada's position at ICNAF meetings." (Nordco report, 49)

Finally, the province was beginning to assert that it had a role in the formulation of fishery policy off our coast. This position expanded throughout the 1970s as the province further developed this aspect of its policy, becoming even more certain with the five-volume "Setting a Course" report, which said among other things: "In view of the major impact which the Fisheries sector will have (as the stocks recovered as a result of the 200-mile limit and better resource management) on the local economy in the years ahead, it is desirable that the province should have a major input into Fisheries policy at every level."

The Nordco report noted another important point: "In 'Setting a Course,' the province has re-affirmed its intention to consider the social and economic needs of fishing regions in discussing plans for the fishery. This policy objective was in sharp contrast to the 'resettlement mentality' which had informed Fisheries policy some two decades earlier and as late as 1967 in the Royal Commission of that year."

The province strengthened its position on this issue in its white paper of 1978: "The Government of Newfoundland and Labrador holds the view that the limited participatory role by the provinces in the decision making process by the federal government relating to marine resources management must be replaced by one in which Newfoundland and the other provinces play a meaningful role in the decisions respecting resource management and all Fisheries-related matters."

The coming of the 200-mile limit, with attendant (temporary) larger fish volumes, and the federal government policy, which recognized the Newfoundland inshore effort, focused attention on how best to now manage the resurgent northern cod resource. Of course this is what led the Moores government, and later my administration, to call for greater involvement of the province in fishery policy matters. Unfortunately, the federal government had no intention of involving the province, and hence the province proceeded to try and persuade the federal government otherwise.

Three major documents stand out:

1. The August 18, 1980, "Towards the First Century Together: The Position of the Government of Newfoundland Regarding Constitutional Change."

2. The Nordco report "It Were Well to Live Mainly Off Fish," commissioned by my administration and published in February, 1981.

3. The five-year plan entitled "Managing All Our Resources," promised in my first Throne Speech and published in October, 1980.

I have already referenced the Nordco report. The other documents are ones produced internally by my administration and clearly articulate the province's position on the fishery and the desire to have greater say in it.

In the five-year plan concerning the rising projections for northern cod we noted:

> Before this catch can be harvested, the future management regime for the northern cod stock must be resolved by bilateral discussions between the Government of Newfoundland and the Government of Canada. The significance of this stock to Newfoundland and Labrador is overwhelming. It is the sole basis of our cod fishery from Cape Chidley to Cape St. Mary's.

It went on to say:

> A more structured federal-provincial decision making process based upon written principles and procedures has to be developed, all decisions must relate to written management objectives, and public hearings procedures must be developed so that proposed government actions may be reviewed.
>
> The application of these measures would be acceptable on an interim basis; the long-term solution must be entrenchment of provincial management

rights in the constitution. To achieve this, there
must be realignment of present jurisdictional
responsibilities.

This was clearly defined a few months earlier in the already
mentioned Constitutional Position document.

This was all hugely important for me at that time and for those
close to this policy in the government. We were only too aware of our
history, both distant and recent, of remote control fishery management
and its disastrous results.

Driving our position was also the knowledge that the federal
government had changed its position at the Law of the Sea talks from
one supporting our position of instituting national control to the end
of the continental shelf to just 200 miles, and then insisting that they
could, with their bargaining power, ensure that Canadian standards of
management and conservation would apply beyond 200 miles to the
continental margin, a position that was not sustained after the treaty. A
gigantic mistake to so trust the federal government! We had had other
earlier promises by Great Britain of having our own government restored
after its suspension in the 1930s, only to see this, a broken commitment.

Everyone seemed to ignore the geographic fact that the continental
shelf off Newfoundland extended beyond 200 miles in the areas known
as the nose and tail of the Grand Banks and Flemish Cap, where fish
spawning was prolific and necessary to manage for the integrity of
the fish resource inside the 200-miles area. Pierre Trudeau, in what
he thought would be a clever put-down of me and the province rather
than a display of fisheries ignorance, expressed his view at a publicly
televised conference about the fish having international and national
dimensions, that fish swim, only to be reminded by me that fish swim,
all right, in our context from offshore Newfoundland to inshore
Newfoundland waters. I am unsure whether the national press fully
grasped the significance of my statement, given their later infatuation
with Brian Tobin's silly Spanish public relations efforts concerning the
minor turbot species flap, long after the cod had disappeared and on
which he did precious little when he was an MP.

There is a fourth document: my letter of December 16, 1980, to Prime Minister Pierre Trudeau, which, perhaps more than anything else demonstrates the gigantic hill we were trying to climb given the blatant lack of concern of Newfoundland interests by the federal government. The letter highlights three issues concerning federal action dealing with the fishery:

1. The announced decision to establish an additional fishery region for the Gulf of St. Lawrence, headquartered in Moncton, New Brunswick, without any consultation with the province.

2. The intent of the federal government to introduce a new licensing policy that would see for the first time a specific quota for the inshore fishery, contrary to advice the province had provided.

3. And, if anything else could be more galling to a Newfoundlander, the trading of some of our northern cod stock to foreign nations for trade concessions of dubious value.

My letter ends with this:

> From the foregoing, you will see that from our perspective there has not been sufficient or proper consultation with the Government of Newfoundland on these matters. It is my belief that the kind of consultation which is necessary for coordinated action will only be possible when responsibility for these decisions is jointly held. This belief was at the centre of our proposals for concurrent jurisdiction during the constitutional discussions and I am convinced that present evidence demonstrates the necessity of achieving constitutional change.
>
> In conclusion, I would re-emphasize my grave concern over the three specific initiatives to which I have referred and urge that the process of

implementation of these initiatives be suspended until such time as more extensive consultations can take place, and we have the benefit of the findings of the Royal Commission presently examining the Newfoundland fishery. Moreover, I would urge you that any proposals for such fundamental change in the fishery be subjected to a process of public hearings before decisions are finally taken and that any such decision, when taken, be reasoned in light of the evidence presented.

Seven years later little had changed, even though we had our Conservative brethren as the government in Ottawa. On October 8, 1987, I was forced to write the following to John Crosbie, our Newfoundland representative in the Cabinet, concerning Canada's actions with France and the fishery:

The Government of Canada has offered non-surplus 2J3KL [northern cod] to France. The Government of Canada offers this non-surplus fish without any commitment from France to stop overfishing in 3PS [another fishing zone off Newfoundland]. How can you argue that you are safeguarding Newfoundland and Labrador's interests when you agree to give France non-surplus cod, when our inshore fishery has failed four years in a row, when most of our fish plants are only open for three or four months of the year, when we have the highest unemployment in Canada? Giving away more of our fish only ensures that UIC [EI] dependence will persist and our chances of longer-term employment for our people will diminish.

Parenthetically, we were also sent a bill by the Canadian embassy in Paris when our delegation had eaten there when we were "allowed" to be observers at some of the meetings with the Europeans. Lucien Bouchard was then the Canadian ambassador. Needless to say, we didn't pay it but informed Ottawa of the insult. Our own Joe Clark was the minister of External Affairs at the time.

Yet, notwithstanding all of this, we almost succeeded in our constitutional quest on the fishery. Most of the provinces were on board and it looked like we could see a breakthrough. However, the federal government remained stubborn on the issue, and with the prime minster's unilateral efforts at patriation, such issues as the fishery became secondary as the provinces fought to ensure that the prime minister's folly at unilateralism would fail, which thankfully the Supreme Court confirmed.

Through all of this, three of the major fish companies operating in the province ran into financial difficulty, and after delicate talks with the federal government it was agreed that a new entity would be formed, Fishery Products International, taking the assets from the three failing companies and merging them into this new entity, plus around $110 million. This company became a success and traded on the Toronto Stock Exchange. The management of the company, headlined by the highly competent Victor Young, ran an efficient operation, and had established a productive relationship with the communities where it operated. A special piece of legislation was passed in the legislature giving effect to all this and with provisions protecting Newfoundland's interests. Sadly, success in the fishery seems to infect us with some sort of suicidal virus, as interests from outside and inside the province vied for control of the company, and with a passive, if not willing provincial government, the provisions to protect the province's interests were dissolved and these interests succeeded in taking over the company. And while it is true now that many of the assets are now owned by Newfoundland interests, the *grand entente* between the government and local business interests, given the unique nature of the inshore fishery, has been lost and that is to the detriment of rural Newfoundland.

To add insult to injury, it was not long before the fears we expressed in 1980 and the warnings of many fishermen became a reality with the collapse of the ground fishery and its closure, heralding an end to rural Newfoundland as we knew it.

Our fight to gain some say or control was not universal in Newfoundland, which, of course, did not help our case with Ottawa, with the provincial Liberals being ambiguous at best. The Fishermen's Union, in its conflicted position of representing offshore trawlermen, inshore fishermen, and fish plant workers, and having their own contacts in the federal bureaucracy, were not co-operative.

Of course, just about everyone agrees now that the province should be more involved in fisheries management. Only one problem—there isn't any northern cod.

Dr. Leslie Harris, in his report (*Northern Cod Review Panel*, March, 1990) on the northern cod disappearance, highlighted a number of issues that the province had been advocating for years and decades regarding foreign fishing, extending national jurisdiction, joint management, and the principal of adjacency.

5. That Canada should seek international agreement to permit its management of all fish stocks indigenous to the Canadian continental shelf and that extend beyond the 200-mile economic zone; and, that failing achievement of this objective, Canada should take unilateral action to acquire management rights in accordance with provisions of the Law of the Sea Convention.

6. That the Government of Canada should re-examine its policies regarding the authorization of foreign fisheries within the Canadian economic management zone with the clear intention of eliminating any catch or bycatch of cod.

7. That Canada officially adopt a policy analogous to the Hague Preferences that would take into account in respect of stock allocations both the principle of contiguity and the "vital needs" of particular communities particularly depending upon fishing and industries allied thereto.

And he further elaborated that "the Government of Canada and the Government of Newfoundland and Labrador should jointly establish a Board or Commission in the context of which information can be shared, management objectives clarified and coordinated, policy directions set, and strategies developed."

Mr. Leslie Dean, former deputy minister and assistant deputy minister of Fisheries for the province, in a well-argued presentation ("Transition and Change: The Fishery in Newfoundland and Labrador Society") before the Royal Commission on Renewing and Strengthening Our Place in Canada, in March, 2003, said, "A solid collaborative policy approach is critical to the rebuilding of the Newfoundland and Labrador fishery on a viable and sustainable foundation" (10).

The Commission itself in its final report (June, 2003) highlighted its concern for the fishery by using the title "The Last Chance for the Fishery," and in most of its recommendations echoed what I (and the government I had led) had been saying twenty-five years earlier: joint management and unilateral action by the Government of Canada concerning the crucial fishing areas outside the 200-mile limit.

In 2005, I wrote a letter on the subject.

> My thesis has not changed: the fishery of Newfoundland and Labrador could have sustained much of rural Newfoundland. It was mismanaged; we should never have transferred the powers over the fishery to the federal government in 1949, and Smallwood's push to industrialize and ignore the fishery further exacerbated the eroding influence over the fishery. This transfer of power, the decades-long mismanagement, including the inaction of the federal government on foreign fishing and also our own inaction led by Smallwood, sealed our fate. We thought we couldn't fight the hand that **supposedly** fed us. The later formation of the union—at first a good thing but later mired in

internal conflicts between the south coast dragger
fleet, fish plant workers, and inshore fishers—diluted
its effectiveness for the all-important inshore fishery,
which was critical for a viable rural Newfoundland.

So in the last fifty years of the 20th century it
was first the transfer of powers (and that is the most
important factor), then our being led to downplay it
in the 1950s and 1960s, the conflicted structure of
the fishery both from a corporate and union point
of view, and then EI and all the rest that came later.

During the Patriation process of the early 1980s,
I had all the provinces on-side to consider changes
to fishery powers, but the Feds said no.

Looking back now, it is sad to think that Newfoundland as a
society could not come together on such a vital issue as this. What, I
wonder, does it say about us?

And so the first of our three major actions failed—perhaps the
one that of the three had the best chance over time to maintain a
viable rural way of life in coastal Newfoundland and Labrador.

We were dejected, yet there were many people who continued to
support our agenda, and my visits to rural Newfoundland invigorated
my spirit, like a visit to my new friend in Pilley's Island.

I was told that Wesley Pittman of Pilley's Island was a hardcase.
When, in 1972, I was into my first campaign in Green Bay District,
the boys from Pilley's who were introducing me around told me I
would have to make a courtesy call on Skipper Wes. I called him a
hardcase because he had a bit of a name. That's what the boys said, and
the boys knew, and given that I needed them (much more than they
realized), I wasn't going to argue. It seems he owned a few schooners
years back and fished them off Labrador like many fishermen from
Newfoundland did in those times. Apparently he lost a couple of
them—storms, he said—but the boys, well, they said there was this
dirty rumour making the rounds for years that they were insurance
jobs. To my knowledge, they never, ever confronted Skipper Wes

with this. Perhaps it was just good juicy gossip over a beer or shots of moonshine or just plain jealousy. Gossip in small communities was a wonderful thing; it kept people busy during the long winter nights, and the last thing you wanted was asking someone who would know some contrary information concerning it. Doing that might explode all that yarning—it was like a disease, and worse than most. I figured the boys wanted a subject for gossip and perhaps had some genuine envy because, notwithstanding Wes's sparse surroundings, he had, everyone said, "a bit of money." But Wes insisted to me, "I worked bloody hard for what I got and it ain't very much."

Anyway, before that day's campaigning was over I got to meet the man himself. He was a short, bald man with thick glasses halfway down his nose. He was wearing a plaid shirt, an old pair of trousers, and braces. He was about seventy-seven then, possessed of a lively mind and impish grin. He seemed a little reserved at first and I was soon to find out why. See, Skipper Wes was independent, all right, but he had a beer licence. In those days (the Liberal Smallwood era was just coming to a close), to get a beer licence you had to be "on the right side politically," and of course that meant Skipper Wes was a Liberal. Here he was talking it up with a young Tory candidate—and he knew I was aware of the situation.

Later, in my many visits to see him as his representative in the legislature, he maintained that he pulled one over on Smallwood and the Liberals because he really was a closet Tory the whole time. I sort of took that with a grain of salt and never pressed the matter again; I just enjoyed his many yarns, watching him savour his scotch, and seeing his genuine delight when I would turn up to see him.

It was on one of these visits that he up and told me that he was in the First World War, Royal Navy: "I got no records to show for it and the Canadian Legion knows it is true, but they are a no good lot 'cause they can't get my papers for me." This was a serious matter for him and he cursed at those around him who thought that it was just another one of his tall tales like his many exaggerated Labrador cod fishing yarns. I could see that of all the things we yarned about, this matter stuck in his craw. And I had found out that he was aware of the rumours of the insurance jobs but took that as a joke, that the boys didn't know any better. But his war papers, now that was another matter.

Well, I knew I had better try and do something about that! Of course, when I told him that I was going to check on it, he displayed his impish grin and exclaimed, "No young Tory could ever do something about such a complicated thing as that!" On reflection, there may just have been a bit of intrigue in this comment. He likely said it to urge me on.

So, together with my political assistant, we went to work on contacting the Admiralty in London. Between the jigs and the reels, many months later we were successful in getting, let's call it a certificate, verifying that Wesley Pittman of Pilley's Island, Newfoundland, was indeed in the Royal Navy and served overseas during the First World War.

On a sunny fall day I entered the porch of Wes's house and peered across the kitchen. There he was in the corner, sitting in his favourite old chair, pipe in hand, scotch bottle on the side table. He was partly leaning over trying to read from an old, dusty book, undeterred by his failing sight in the dimly lit room. He heard someone in the porch and growled a hello.

As I moved from the porch to the kitchen he growled again. Standing now in the middle of the kitchen, still unrecognized by Wes, I loudly announced: "Seaman Wesley J. Pittman, number 067541, His Majesty's Royal Navy, 1915–1917. Attention!"

At first confused, it slowly dawned on him that something special was happening. He rose to his feet, marched a few paces to stand in front of me, stood to attention, and saluted. He was now close enough to recognize me.

In as good an official military voice as I could muster, I declared, "Seaman Pittman, it gives me great pleasure to present to you your certificate of service in the Royal Navy!" I passed the certificate to him and, with a tear edging down his aged face, he exclaimed, "I never thought this would ever happen!"

My assistant, who had been waiting outside, entered and we took pictures of the event and had it displayed the next week in the local newspaper.

Skipper Wes died a few years later, a happy man, and was buried at Head's Harbour, the settlement of his youth, with the Canadian Legion proudly present.

CHANGE ISSUE #2 — CHURCHILL RIVER

"Labrador—'the land God gave to Cain'"
—Jacques Cartier

THE CHURCHILL RIVER OF Labrador consists of three major hydro-development sites: the so-called Upper Churchill, by far the largest at 5,280 megawatts, and two others on the lower part of the river, Gull Island and Muskrat Falls.

Every Newfoundlander and Labradorian knows of the Upper Churchill Falls development and most particularly of the Upper Churchill contract with Quebec. This was Smallwood's greatest failure of all. I remember being in Churchill Falls when this project was officially "opened," July 16, 1972, having been inaugurated five years earlier by Smallwood and Edmund de Rothschild. Premier Moores, Prime Minister Trudeau, and Premier Bourassa were all there. Funny how we all could be there (I was the newly minted first Conservative Member for the district of Green Bay) to celebrate the official sellout of Newfoundland water to Quebec!

This is one singular development that could have given the province historic and economic viability, to be a "have" province, if only we were getting our fair share of the revenues from current prices for electricity. This haunts all Newfoundlanders to this day and remains a bitter lesson in how not to develop a resource. People unfamiliar with the project are amazed and dumbfounded when they are informed of the details. In 1980, my administration published a booklet regarding Labrador Hydro Power entitled "The Energy Priority of Newfoundland and Labrador: Fairness and Equity in the Utilization of the Churchill Falls Hydro Resource." In it the Upper Churchill contract details are provided. Let me quote:

> Under the Power Contract, the price to be paid by
> Hydro Quebec for energy declines from a high of just
> under 3.0 mills per kwh in 1977 to a low of just over
> 2.5 mills per kwh in 2001, which price is maintained
> until 2016. The price is reduced thereafter to 2.0 mills
> pkh for the final twenty-five years.
>
> A total of sixty-five years in which the price that
> the power is sold for actually goes down over time,
> the equivalent of selling a barrel of oil for an average
> of $1.80 for 40 years, and then reducing the price to
> $1.20 per barrel for the final twenty-five years.

It is any wonder Newfoundlanders and Labradorians don't forget?

Several think tanks have concluded that Newfoundland's loss of economic rent on this project is somewhere between $500 million to $1 billion per year. In a 1978 briefing note from Newfoundland Hydro to Premier Moores, the economic rent loss to Newfoundland was estimated at $810 million for the year 1979. The Economic Council of Canada's report of 1980, entitled "From Dependency to Self-Reliance," although a timid and disappointing analysis in many ways, was forced to say in its Summary and Recommendations, "The contract with Hydro Quebec to develop Churchill Falls hydroelectric power has failed to return proportional revenues to Newfoundland."

This inequitable, unconscionable contract has been left to stand by successive federal governments with but mild attempts by some of them to help, such attempts being mainly a commitment by the prime minister to talk to the premier of Quebec. Sometimes it was insulting, as when I was approached at a constitutional meeting of first ministers by an envoy of Prime Minister Trudeau to indicate that if I was a little more compromising on the offshore, the PM would talk to Quebec about the hydro situation. The messenger could see by the look on my face that I was furious. I don't remember my exact response, but it would have been something along the lines of, "You must be joking—this is insulting: for a verbal promise through an envoy I am to relent on the last real chance for my province."

Later, Prime Minister Brian Mulroney at least put in writing that he had tried. In a letter to me dated February 16, 1988, Mr. Mulroney addressed our recent conversation on the matter:

> I have recently raised this issue with Mr. Bourassa, urging him to consider options for resolving the problems associated with the Upper Churchill contract and the development of hydro potential in Labrador and for a process that would encourage both parties to move forward on these issues. Mr. Bourassa has undertaken, without prejudice, to explore the matter further and I anticipate that he will be in a position to make his views known shortly. You should also know that the premier has rejected the idea of a federal intervener for the time being. I hope that my intervention will lead to a constructive dialogue on the issues at hand.

Other than this attempt, which, of course, went nowhere, there was little real sympathy by the federal government or for that matter by Canadians to assist in having the transmission of electrical energy handled on a national basis as the transmission of oil and gas was being treated. I travelled the country on the issue and most people were polite and that was about it. Hence, Quebec would remain holding Newfoundland hostage. I wonder if a similar situation would have been allowed to happen anywhere else in Canada. I remember that the well-known Newfoundland artist and designer of the Newfoundland Flag Christopher Pratt once suggested to me that there was one way to break this different treatment being used by Ottawa in the transmission of oil versus electricity, and that was to put the transmission lines in a pipeline!

After I became minister of Mines and Energy in 1976, I went to Quebec City to meet with the fairly new Parti Québécois Energy minister, Guy Joron. He was very friendly and expressed optimism that we could make progress on this file involving the Upper and Lower Churchill as a package. The meeting was in his office. Suddenly, who should enter but René Lévesque himself, jovial and of course smoking a cigarette. We all had a very upbeat conversation on the Labrador energy situation, and they would be following up with Hydro-Québec. Of course, Hydro-Québec saw that nothing materialized.

A very bizarre thing happened in 1978 when one evening I was made aware that Premier Moores was entertaining the premier of Quebec concerning energy. I was flabbergasted. I knew nothing of it. I immediately went to the premier's office to discover a flurry of activity. Vic Young was the premier's chief of staff at the time, and I was quickly ushered into his office and made aware that a framework agreement was pending with Quebec concerning the Upper and Lower Churchill River.

I demanded to see the premier, and after some shuffling about and my anger visibly rising, I was in the premier's office. He proceeded to give me a broad outline of what was going on and I listened with incredulity. There was to be a press conference that very evening to announce the arrangement. I asked a few questions and found the whole thing to be rushed, and just not enough elements there to make the deal worthwhile. I told the premier that I would not be able to support it and would have to make that known publicly. After being rushed from his office I was once more back in Vic Young's office with Vic (and I think a couple of Cabinet ministers), where I furiously, with tears in my eyes, denounced the deal and said this would not stand. I would resign and fight it. No amount of talk would appease me and I stood firm.

Lo and behold, the press conference was cancelled and the whole thing fizzled. Lévesque had to return to Quebec empty-handed!

Many years later, Janice Wells of St. John's, formerly of Corner Brook and a close friend of Frank Moores, wrote a book on the life of Frank. In it she recounted how Frank had told her how I had scuttled this wonderful deal he had worked out with René Lévesque. CBC interviewed her on the matter and later contacted me. I explained to the CBC that this was not at all the way the matter unfolded and that what was being offered was Quebec once again getting more of our power to use and sell, now from the Lower Churchill, with no change to the infamous Upper Churchill contract. If the deal was so good, why didn't Frank proceed with it, seeing he had the majority of ministers with him on the deal? Or, if the deal was so good, it should be able to take a few more days of scrutiny. It was a rush job and not in the best interests of the province. Funny, too, that for the many years after Frank left politics, I am unaware that he ever uttered a word that in any way corroborated Janice Wells's story. It seems like an attempt by an admirer to try and shed a positive light on her hero. Additionally, I had met Janice when she was writing the book (initiated by me when I heard she was writing such a book and I had not been contacted by her), and at no time during that "interview" did she mention this Churchill matter—odd, given her revelations in the book. I wrote Janice an email after that encounter on June 21, 2006:

> It was great seeing you again and having a few moments to talk about Mr. Moores.
>
> I was a little taken aback to learn that he considered me a socialist. I have some difficulty understanding how he could come to such a conclusion given my record. Did he ever share with you the reasons for such a view?
>
> You also mentioned some materials that his administration had prepared to distribute to the schools and which my administration cancelled. Apparently, he was upset with this decision. As I mentioned, I vaguely remember the materials and I cannot remember precisely why the distribution was cancelled. As I said to you I suspect the decision was made as a result of advice/recommendation from the Department of Education. I could perhaps find out for you if you wish.
>
> Any other matters just shoot an email.
>
> Regards,
> Brian Peckford

Ms. Wells never replied to this communication.

Without any breakthrough in talks with Quebec, the province embarked on legal action as well as being open to additional talks with Quebec. The legal action centred on the lease, a piece of Newfoundland legislation that provided a lease to Hamilton Falls Corporation, a forerunner of the Churchill Falls Labrador Corporation, the present owners and operators of the Upper Churchill Falls development. This lease transferred to Hamilton Falls Corporation the rights to the waters of the Upper Hamilton (Churchill) River. In Part 1, Section 2(e) the leasee had

> the right to transmit throughout the province any electric power generated as the result of the harnessing of the whole or any part of the Upper Hamilton and to export from the province such power; provided that upon the request of the Government consumers of electricity in the province shall be given priority where it is feasible and economic to do so ...

Newfoundland had earlier requested 800 megawatts from the development. With no adequate response on the request, Newfoundland exercised its legal rights under the lease to the courts. However, this was to be a long and arduous process with little chance of immediate to mid-term resolution.

Therefore, once I assumed the premiership in 1979, I assembled a number of legal experts to see what other options might be available. This legal team included Cabot Martin, Noel Clarke, Tom Kendell, Keith Mercer, and Edward Hearne. Our actual presentation to the courts (Newfoundland Court of Appeal and the Supreme Court of Canada) was handled by Leonard Martin with assistance from Edward Hearne, Noel Clarke, and David Osborne. We also consulted with legal experts around the world, including Dr. Geoffrey Marston of Cambridge University and Dr. William C. Gilmore of the University of Edinburgh. Through the work of that legal team, a number of options were presented to government; the one that the team thought had the best chance of success was a new piece of legislation entitled the Water Reversion Act. The government accepted this recommendation and action ensued in the courts. In other words, we decided after passage of the Act in the legislature that we would refer it directly to the courts to test its validity, rather than try to implement it with all the uncertainty this would engender.

The Newfoundland Court of Appeal agreed that the province was within its legislative competence to pass the Act.

However, the Supreme Court of Canada ruled on May 3, 1984:

> In conclusion, having found that the pith and substance of the Reversion Act is to interfere with the rights of Hydro-Québec outside the territorial jurisdiction of Newfoundland, it is my opinion that the Act, taken as a whole, is *ultra vires* of the Legislature of Newfoundland. Question 9 of the Reference must be answered accordingly. It therefore becomes unnecessary to answer the other eight questions.

Our hopes were dashed again.

And in 1988 the Supreme Court of Canada upheld the earlier decisions of the Newfoundland courts that our recall case was also invalid.

Of course, over time there are always those who question whether you have done all you can on a given public policy issue. And such was the case on my involvement with the Churchill Falls issues. In 2005, I appeared on a local CBC radio show and was questioned by Mr. Burf Ploughman, who implied that I had not done enough to get the Lower Churchill going and that there were buyers in New York State for the power. This led me to check my sources later and respond more fully to Mr. Ploughman.

Feb. 21, 2005
Mr. B.F. Ploughman
17 Pinebud Avenue
St. John's, NL

Dear Mr. Ploughman:

A few weeks ago you called the CBC radio afternoon show and indicated to the audience that when I was premier I failed to follow through on an opportunity to develop the Lower Churchill Falls. You quoted a press release that talked about the Power Authority of the State of New York and how they and other investors had the money to build the project and buy the power. I said to you and the audience at the time that I remembered the matter and that I had travelled to New York and that, notwithstanding the press release, no deal was able to be made. I then said that I did not remember any other details. You expressed amazement that I did not remember more details. Well, I did remember some, but I was not sure that I was completely correct. For example, I was pretty sure that a group of investors led by Franklin Roosevelt Jr. was involved and that there was a return visit to Newfoundland. I did not want to mention names and return visits unless I was completely sure that I was right.

I have had a chance to check the whole thing. There are no documents with the Government or Newfoundland Hydro on the matter, at least not now. This is so because there was no deal and no negotiations were held. I have talked to people who were in government with me at the time and to hydro people. All confirm that there was a meeting in New York and a visit to Newfoundland and that was it because of the impasse with Quebec. And on Friday, February 18, I have talked directly with Mr. Dyson, the then chairman of the Power Authority of the State of New York.

If you have read the recent articles in the

newspaper, *The Independent*, you know the rest. Essentially PASNY and the New York investors, especially PASNY (a big customer of Quebec power) thought that they would be able to get Lower Churchill power through Quebec. They soon realized that the Anglo-Saxon route was not economic at that time and that one of the remaining sources of power lay in Labrador. Mr. Dyson confirmed this in my conversation and volunteered that PASNY had actually met with Quebec to try and push the matter. All was for naught, however, as we know only too well when it comes to dealing with Quebec and Labrador power.

You may be interested to know that this was not my only effort to try and develop Lower Churchill. At the time of the PASNY interest, we had also talked to other eastern U.S. states and to Ontario. A federal-provincial Lower Churchill Development Corporation was formed. I sought out aluminum producers and met with Alcoa and several other producers over the years. I met with Quebec when I was Energy minister and tried to forge a deal, met with Premier Lévesque, Premier Bourassa, was involved in two court actions to get a better deal on the Upper Churchill, which could trigger development of the Lower Churchill and actually spent the people's money in studies relating to crossing the Strait of Belle Isle. You may remember a First Ministers Conference that was televised where I mentioned putting wires in a pipeline to carry Labrador Power through Quebec, a not too subtle reference to the ability of oil and gas pipelines to move across provincial borders. And there were endless efforts to try and get the federal government to allow for the wheeling of power through Quebec, as PASNY tried to do.

Given that you saw fit to very publicly present your views, you will not be surprised that I will do likewise. I will be sending this to the CBC afternoon radio open-line show in question and distributing it widely to all the press in the province and to many citizens of the province as well.

A. Brian Peckford

To indicate how set against Newfoundland Quebec really was, one has only to remember that the Parti Québécois had not recognized the Labrador/Quebec Privy Council decision of 1927 concerning the border between the two. We thought at the time that this was just political bluster by an Opposition party for local consumption. After the party became the government in 1976, reality sank in.

This was most clearly demonstrated to me when I attended a Mines Ministers Conference in Quebec City in the late 1970s. I arrived at the hotel the afternoon of the day of registration. There was to be a reception that evening hosted by the Quebec minister. I registered in the lobby of the hotel and was about to take the elevator to my room when I noticed a large map of Quebec hanging just behind the registration desk. There was no Labrador—it was all Quebec. I blew my top. I immediately complained to the people at the desk, went to my room, called to see where the minister was, and within a short period of time spoke to him. I indicated in no uncertain terms that this brazen display was unacceptable and that we would have to withdraw from the conference if this map remained on display and that I would hold a press conference announcing our withdrawal and why. The map was quickly removed.

The Churchill defeats were deeply bitter disappointments and it makes me now recall a staunch supporter.

I always liked small communities. I was raised in them, and as I got older I was always drawn back to them. In politics this can be good or bad. Good because you got to know more of your province, bad because there were fewer voters and time seemed always of the essence.

Nevertheless, I prevailed in one election campaign, much to the chagrin of the election planners, to visit the community of La Poile, an isolated community on the southwest coast of the island. I had prided myself that I had been to nearly all the inhabited places on the island, and La Poile was one that I had never visited, and hence I wanted to add it to my list as well as show my concern for those who lived there.

So with the required campaign staff press person or two and a megaphone at our fingertips, we set off in helicopter. Of course, the south and southwest coast is notorious for its fog, as the election planners kept reminding me. And so it was with great relief that, as we came to the coast from the north, we could glimpse that a glorious day lay over the community. The pilot landed the helicopter in one of the few places just large enough to do so, and we are off around the harbour/pathway to an appropriate location to deliver a speech on behalf of the party, our candidate, and myself, explaining why the people there should vote for us.

After tracking down a well-used pickup truck, I got into the back of the vehicle and with megaphone in hand began to wax eloquent to almost all of the inhabitants of the community.

In the course of my talk I happened to glance off to my left, and I noticed in the far end of a rocky field, just beyond the truck, an older gentleman sitting, likely out of earshot even for my well-performing megaphone. For a politician this is most aggravating, but I soldiered on, trying not to be put off by one of the elder citizens of the community, obviously a supporter of the opposing party.

After completing my speech and getting down from the truck to mingle among the people, I glanced to see if my wayward voter was still in his place in the field. Sure enough, he was still there keenly following the proceedings. I signalled to one of my campaign staff that he should, with the candidate, request that the people move just down over the hill to a pre-arranged lunch at the local school. I then whispered to him that I would be a little late for lunch, but given that it would take some time for everyone to get refreshments and a sandwich, I was sure to be there with lots of time to speak one-on-one and answer any questions.

As the people moved down toward the school, I jumped over the rail fence and made my way up the field to meet the challenge before me, sensitive that this might not be easy, a Tory premier meeting a senior citizen in a historically Liberal community.

It was one of those special days, warm and so clear that you could see for miles, and for a moment I savoured the peace and freshness that was all around me. I sat down next to my distant spectator.

"How are you today, Skipper?" I asked.

"Number one," he replied, with a slight twinkle in his eye.

"You never came down by the truck?" I inquired.

"No, boy, me legs are not what they used to be, can barely walk a few feet. And I don't like asking for help. But me ears are good. I heard most of what you had to say."

"Good for you," I said, trying to keep a brave face. "Well, perhaps then I can count on your vote come polling day. I am doing my best to get around to many of the smaller places and not just go to the big places where most of the votes are."

"No, 'tis a good thing you're doing, I'd say," he retorted, "a really good thing."

Mindful of my lunch obligation just down the hill and aware of the coy approach of my new acquaintance, I got up to leave and was about to bid a friendly goodbye when he raised his arm and with sudden conviction exclaimed, "No, don't go yet. Please, sit down. I won't be long."

His tone, more than the words, told me he had important things to say. I quickly sat down again.

"Do you know something?" he said in a quivering voice.

"What's that?" I said, half afraid to ask.

"Joey Smallwood said he had been in every community on the island. You're too young to remember. But I remember. I heard him say it on the radio. But dat's a lie. He was never in this place, because I have lived here for over seventy years and I should know."

Somewhat taken back, I responded, "Yes, Skipper, I have heard Joey say that many times. But I did not know if it was true or not," I responded eagerly.

His voice now raised, he exclaimed, "And another thing. You're the first prime minister or premier to ever set shoe leather in this place. Did you know that?"

Now fully surprised, I replied, "No sir, I did not know that."

"And I'm some proud you're here," he continued in a broken voice, "and I bet you don't know how many people vote Tory in this place, especially since Confederation with the Baby Bonus and old-age pensions. Let me tell you: two. And I was always one of them."

Somewhat shaken, I gently put my arm around the Skipper's shoulders and looked him straight in his watery eyes. "And you will never know how proud I am to meet you!" I uttered in my own quivering voice.

Well, we yarned a bit. Old buddies we were, or so it seemed— all in these few precious moments. I told him about my grandfather Peckford and his fishing exploits and about George Prole in Nippers Harbour, who was so much like him.

He told me of his life of fishing, the good times and the bad, and how he never trusted Smallwood and thought Confederation would make us lazy; all that free money wasn't good, he allowed.

Needless to say, in a few short moments I could have sworn I had known him all my life—a few tears from both of us, and then they were gone.

I rose to go, our hands clasped together. I made a solemn promise that I would return to see him. With that, we parted.

I galloped down the rock slope, over the fence, and barged breathlessly into the school and into the fray.

Two years later I accepted an invitation to speak to the annual Port aux Basques Progressive Conservative Association. La Poile is in this district, so I let it be known that I had a promise to keep, and that I had to go to La Poile on this trip. The schedule that had been so carefully prepared had to be scrapped, and I would spend an extra day in the area to accommodate all the other meetings that had been painstakingly arranged. We decided that on the day of the annual meeting we would leave early, helicopter to La Poile in the afternoon, and go on to Port aux Basques that evening for the dinner and dance and meeting.

By helicopter we went south from Deer Lake, crossing Grand Lake and moving down over the western edge of the Annieopsquotch

Mountains and Lloyd's River. The pilot told me that the weather reports were not good on the coast and that fog was likely to be rolling in. He knew my story and how badly I wanted to get to La Poile. So we continued. And then we saw in the distance the fog bank at the coast. We continued into the fog. But it was impossible.

We were now over the ocean and descended to about fifty feet so we could see water, and then travelled westward, intermittently seeing the water. We crawled along the coastal edge, land and water. Miraculously, we saw some lights and buildings ahead, and after several attempts we landed nimbly on the government wharf. What a flight!

People had gathered nearby after hearing the helicopter and knowing that, perhaps, given the fog, the wharf was the only safe place to land. We were in Rose Blanche, the first large community west of La Poile. We were able to hire a car and get transported to Port aux Basques to join the festivities already in progress.

When I got up to speak later that evening, I decided I would dispense with my original thoughts and instead I would tell the story of my attempt earlier that day to get to La Poile and why.

And I told it all in great detail. Slowly, and with every detail, the audience got a sense of the importance of the story and its emotive effect. As I finished to a hushed crowd, a person stood up near the back of the hall.

"Brian, I know the person you're talking about. He was my uncle. He spoke of you a lot and he always said you would return to see him. He passed away last week."

CHANGE ISSUE #3—OFFSHORE OIL AND GAS: THE LAST CHANCE

"I must go down to the sea again."
—John Masefield

WHEN I APPROACHED PREMIER Frank Moores and said I would like to have the vacant Mines and Energy portfolio, I knew that it was the place to be.

I was blessed with really good people who had been hired earlier by the government, especially Cabot Martin, Steve Millan, John Fitzgerald, and Lorne Spracklin. These people were invaluable in those early years: Cabot with his passion for the new opportunity and his devotion to Newfoundland; Steve, the steady, methodical Trinidadian; John, to remember what the rest of us forgot; and Lorne, the numbers man. It is extremely doubtful that we would have been successful later without the passion, persistence, and dedication of these four public servants.

The Petroleum Directorate was established and the important document "The Heritage of the Sea," our case on offshore minerals rights, was prepared and distributed to every household in the province, and the strong support of Premier Moores and the Cabinet validated our endeavours. This led logically to negotiations with all the oil companies who had an interest in the offshore to accept our regulations. I remember well all the trips to Calgary meeting with oil company executives. I particularly remember a meeting in New York when most of the companies came on side and were instrumental in getting Petro-Canada, then owned by the federal government, to accept our regulations.

Of course, the federal government was aghast at the audacity of Newfoundland to claim ownership of the mineral rights offshore and, I suspect, thought that we would soon abandon what they considered a silly and frivolous position. So the period from 1976 to 1979 was one of getting the Cabinet to agree to our many proposals for staff, legislation, and regulations, and to have a mandate to negotiate with the companies. The Newfoundland Regulations were gazetted in November, 1978, and the Petroleum Directorate was formally established after I became premier in 1979. In this atmosphere of competing jurisdictions and two sets of regulations, the oil companies withdrew in 1977–78 and no drilling occurred. Thankfully, they returned in 1978. Of course, the companies were not pleased with "having to serve two masters," and there were voices around the country who saw the province—and me in particular—as being provocative, if not belligerent, and the province acting like a banana republic.

I became premier in March, 1979 (on St. Patrick's Day), and the first discovery of oil at Hibernia occurred a few months later. However, it was not known at that time whether it was a significant discovery and whether it would be commercial. It was not until 1985 that it was declared a significant discovery. However, it was known that a significant flow of oil was encountered on that first discovery and that there seemed to be a large pay zone. So hopes were rising that this would turn out to be something worthwhile.

The first glimmer of hope in our quest came with the election of Joe Clark as prime minister in June, 1979. I had campaigned for Joe in his successful leadership bid of 1976, and he was well aware of the province's desire to gain control, like the other provinces, of its oil and gas resources. After many discussions and meetings, I received a letter from Prime Minister Clark on September 12, 1979, in which he said:

> I am happy to confirm the acceptance of the four principles which are set out as an annex to this letter. The four principles essentially confirmed Newfoundland's right to ownership of the oil and gas resources of our coast. The first principle reads: "The Province of Newfoundland should own the mineral resources of the continental margin off its coast insofar as Canada is entitled to exercise sovereign rights over these resources in accordance with international law. Such ownership should be to the extent possible the same nature as if those resources were located within the boundaries of the province. The legislative jurisdiction of the ownership should be the same as for those resources within the boundaries of the province."

This was a tremendous achievement—or so we thought at the time.

But it was not to be. The Clark government lost a non-confidence motion on the budget in March, 1980, an election ensued, and the government was defeated. The subsequent Trudeau government would not honour the letter, and our early hopes for a full agreement along the lines of the Clark commitment were dashed. It is a bitter irony, not lost on many of us, that the government fell as a result of a budget measure by then minister of Finance, a Newfoundlander, John Crosbie.

The echoes of times past rang in our ears: the fight for Representative and Responsible Government in the 1830s and 1850s; the promise of the fishery and the French fishing interests; the promise of the alleged immense wealth and prosperity that would flow from the centre part of the province with the paper mills of Grand Falls and Corner Brook; the major concessions of the building of the railway; the broken promise of a restored independent country; of Confederation with no real provincial fishery power; the Churchill Falls power contract; and Smallwood's industrialization at almost any cost.

Perhaps the least known, but of potential great importance, was of the great trade agreement negotiated by Prime Minister Robert Bond and the U.S. Secretary of State, James Blaine, originally agreed to by Britain but vetoed by them soon thereafter as a result of "Canadian" opposition to the treaty.

Through this treaty Newfoundland would have been allowed to export mineral products—and most importantly fish products—to the United States duty-free. Sadly, we remained a producer of raw fish shipped to the United States, with all the processing jobs in the state of Massachusetts. It would be ninety-four years later, long after Ontario had its own free-trade agreement with the United States (the Auto Pact), before we would see tariffs being reduced on fish exports, thanks to Brian Mulroney's courageous insistence on signing a free-trade agreement with the United States.

And so we were back to square one and having to deal with a government whose view of the country was one of a more powerful central government with its desire to ensure that jurisdiction of offshore minerals remained firmly in federal hands and that any sharing of management responsibilities and/or revenues would be decided solely by the federal government.

Meanwhile, I was having trouble with my Energy minister and former leadership rival, Leo Barry. He made it clear that in the pursuit of a deal on the offshore, he wanted a lot of freedom/flexibility, contrary to the practices then in place as it related to policy, especially large policy issues like the offshore.

There was in place at that time a series of Cabinet committees on policy: the Resource Policy Committee, the Social Policy Committee, and the Planning and Priorities Committee. In the normal course of events, any Cabinet paper that involved resource or social matters was referred to the respective committees before moving up the chain for full Cabinet consideration.

The Planning and Priorities Committee, chaired by the premier, was the senior Cabinet committee and dealt almost exclusively with new policy initiatives, including of course the offshore file. This was not the way that Mr. Barry wanted to proceed, and all the other members of the committee, including me, had trouble with the process that he wanted to have implemented. The committee made it clear to Minister Barry that there was a process and that he must follow that and get direction from the committee as negotiations moved forward; in many cases full Cabinet would have to be involved. It was obvious that the minister was on a collision course, either by accident or design, and so one morning after a day where the Planning and Priorities Committee had made its position very clear to the minister, he visited me in my office to submit his resignation, with me about to ask for it. This was not the only issue I had with the minister at the time. In recent weeks and months, the minister had been travelling outside the province on various matters involving the department, but without informing me of these travels. A recent incident had occurred relating to travel to meet individuals and companies in Chicago. The minister was obviously not a team player, and it was this very characteristic that I was implementing in the Cabinet process. It was not long before he became a Member of the Opposition, the Liberal Party, and then its leader.

This turned out to be a very favourable happening since it brought to the fore one of Newfoundland's most able ministers ever, William

(Bill) Marshall. I was fortunate that Bill Marshall, Gerald Ottenheimer, and John Collins (all leadership supporters) became integral parts of my Cabinet: Ottenheimer, Justice; John Collins, Finance; and Marshall, responsible for offshore and Newfoundland Hydro Corporation. All three understood government, its strengths and weaknesses, the role of a minister of Cabinet and of the premier. They were key advisers and loyalists, and always respectful of one another. With Collins on the budget, Ottenheimer on the Constitution, and Marshall on the key energy issues of offshore oil and gas and water power, this trio arguably had no match in Canada.

Marshall approached his job with conviction and analytical prowess. Here was a Newfoundlander through and through, steeped in Newfoundland history and tradition, painfully aware of our past resource mistakes and cognizant of the power and influence of an overarching federal government. It wasn't long before Marc Lalonde and Jean Chrétien, two of Prime Minister Trudeau's Energy ministers, and the federal bureaucracy realized that they had more than met their match in this Newfoundlander.

But a difficult road lay ahead, not made easier by some (a minority) of our own people and the national media, which often failed to actually read or listen to what we were saying. This is most aptly demonstrated by a letter I was forced to write to Peter Newman, then editor of *Maclean's* magazine, our only national magazine, on September 22, 1980:

In the discussion of offshore resources by your reporters in the September 22 issue dealing with the Constitution, I wish to make the following points:

1. I'm not aware that Mr. Trudeau offered what he said would be oil revenues equivalent to Alberta's.

2. What the federal government has "offered" is that "offshore revenues" would be owned by the federal government and the Province would get "significant revenues," much less than we would receive if the Province owned its

offshore oil and gas in the same way as Alberta owns its oil and gas.

3. There is no provincial power as it relates to "control" of the rate and kind of development in the federal proposal. A substantial rural fishing society must have power in this vital area; otherwise its delicate social fabric could be destroyed.

4. Finally, the federal government has indicated that somehow, when and if (don't hold your breath) we in Newfoundland become a "have" province, we will be treated differently (different federal-provincial revenue sharing, less for the Province) than other "have" provinces are treated.

I submit to you, therefore, that the brief general paragraph on this matter in the article referred to does not do justice to Newfoundland's position.

One would think that such a pointed rebuttal of the comments in the article would have stimulated further correspondence with the province and the magazine, who, following good journalist standards, would have wanted to get at the facts, at the truth. However, only silence followed.

At this juncture, chronologically, we were advancing on all three: the Churchill Falls issue regarding the lease was before the courts; constitutional talks were moving and we would be seeking greater say over the fishery through this process; and despite the setback with the defeat of the Clark government, we were still trying to advance the offshore file.

We were encouraged in this regard by a statement made by the new prime minister, Pierre Trudeau, in St. John's on May 5, 1981, in which he said:

My colleagues and I have constantly maintained that your best interests lie not in total provincial control of the offshore but in rather a negotiated partnership between our two governments in joint management. We consistently maintain that ownership is not the important issue and that reaching a negotiated agreement on shared management is the vitally important issue: either it will be negotiation or it will be a court decision. I am offering the choice to negotiate. I would still prefer that, because I feel it would be a better deal for Newfoundland and for Canada.

This very public statement, coupled with a later public television interview in which the prime minister indicated the federal government was prepared to accept the idea of sharing offshore the same as if the resources were on land until a certain level of wealth was attained, led us to believe that a good chance at achieving a negotiated agreement outside constitutional considerations was possible.

This led to a first negotiating meeting on October 2, 1981, and a further meeting on November 12, 1981, both of which addressed the principles that were necessary from the province's point of view in order to advance toward detailed negotiations and a final agreement. The second meeting incorporated these principles into a thirty-one-page document entitled "A Framework for an Agreement." Some of the principles in this framework included:

1. The Agreement should be permanent and entrenched in the Constitution making a determination of ownership by the courts unnecessary;

2. Joint Management;

3. One set of regulations;

4. The province being able to capture significant economic benefits;

5. Location of offices related to the offshore in
Newfoundland;

6. A compensation fund for the fishery in case of
pollution from offshore; and

7. Revenues to be shared as if the resource was on land.

It was clear, in writing, then, right at the beginning of these talks, what the province was seeking, and most importantly it seemed to us these principles were very consistent with Mr. Trudeau's public pronouncements.

We were shocked, therefore, when at a December 14, 1981, meeting the federal response failed to meet these basic principles. Mr. Marshall wrote the federal minister, Marc Lalonde, on December 18 requesting a ministerial meeting, which was held on January 8, 1982.

The province once again repeated its position and a further officials meeting was to be held, and another ministerial meeting in early February. To further elaborate and make crystal clear the province's position and to attempt to see a negotiated settlement, the province produced yet another document entitled "A Proposal For Settlement," dated January 25, 1982.

On February 10, 1982, only sixteen days after our "Proposal for Settlement" was presented, I was forced to write (telex) the prime minister:

The Government of Newfoundland is presently in emergency meetings on the question of our offshore negotiations.

Your statements in the province on May 5, 1981, left no doubt that you were prepared to set aside permanently your government's claim to exclusive ownership. However, everything put forward since then by your government denies this position. The key issue is that it now appears you have not agreed to put aside permanently your exclusive claim to ownership. We are prepared to do so. Unless you agree to this, clearly and unmistakably, it is impossible to have a permanent joint-management, revenue-sharing arrangement since at any time in the future any party found by the court to own the resource can elect to exercise its rights of ownership and destroy the agreement. This is exactly what happened in Australia where the federal government renounced a ten-year-old joint management scheme after winning in court. No agreement is worth anything, therefore, unless both parties are willing to set aside their exclusive claims to ownership permanently.

Your own minister, Honourable Marc Lalonde, has made some statements which were inconsistent with your statements of May 5, 1981, and in his telegram of yesterday reiterated that position. Your government's position of refusing to join Newfoundland's motion for a postponement in the SIU case is further evidence of this.

In any case, the issue is clear. Without both parties agreeing to put aside permanently exclusive claims to ownership, no agreement is beyond attack in the future by one party or the other.

Therefore, the Government of Newfoundland requests that you confirm in writing your agreement with the following position:

The Government of Canada is willing to put aside its claim to exclusive ownership of the mineral resources off Newfoundland and Labrador, both during negotiations and permanently, if an agreement is successfully concluded.

With this written commitment from both sides, the Newfoundland government feels that fruitful negotiations on joint management and resource sharing can continue without any fear that the agreement, once reached, is subject to challenge and destruction in the future.

Given the gravity of the situation, I earnestly request

an unequivocal answer by tomorrow. I have released this communication to the people of Newfoundland today.

No answer was received from the prime minister to this request. Further frustrating our efforts at this moment was the other matter referred to in the telex—the SIU case. This case before the court would necessitate the jurisdiction of offshore being considered, up to then not before the courts. The federal government's refusal to agree with us, to have this court case deferred until negotiations were completed, blatantly demonstrated that the federal government was really not serious in dealing up front with us on the issue.

Obviously, we were left with no choice but to take serious action; hence, on February 18, 1982, we referred the case of jurisdiction to the province's highest court, the Court of Appeal.

We had to show just how serious we were on this, and we held out hope that such an action may put sufficient pressure on the federal government that they would return to the negotiating table. But the federal government went about its business of undermining our position with two federal government actions quickly following one another: first, on March 2, 1982, the federal government and the Government of Nova Scotia signed an offshore deal; then on March 5, 1982, the federal government requested that we agree to suspend our Court of Appeal reference and go directly to the Supreme Court of Canada for a decision. We immediately rejected this request. Our minister of Justice, Gerald Ottenheimer, responded to Jean Chrétien, then federal Attorney General for Canada.

> The Government of Newfoundland cannot accept your proposal that the question referred to the appeal division of the Supreme Court of Newfoundland be referred immediately to the Supreme Court of Canada. The effect of acceding to your request would be to pre-empt the appeal division of the Supreme Court of Newfoundland of the opportunity of giving its judgment on this matter.

> The Government of Newfoundland is of the firm conviction that the people of Newfoundland have the right to a decision by the highest court of the province on a matter so vital to the future of the province. Furthermore, the government is of the opinion that the Supreme Court of Canada should have the benefit of the judgment of the appeal division of the Supreme Court of Newfoundland before it renders its decision.

These were uncertain times, to say the least, and this tussle over offshore resources was intensifying. A lot had happened in three short years: the Constitution talks, the court references concerning the Churchill Falls contract, and the economic recession—all bearing down on a very financially fragile government.

We knew by now that two of our three big issues were in jeopardy: our aim to get greater fisheries through the constitutional talks had failed, and the court references relating to the infamous Churchill Falls contract were problematic.

However, our third issue, the offshore, was still in play. Given the federal government's recent blatant moves to pressure us, I had to do something to strengthen my hand and keep the momentum in the face of this formidable adversary.

I called an election on April 6, 1982, to ask for a new mandate to negotiate regarding the offshore. The people responded, giving me and the party a great victory and increasing our majority in the 52-seat legislature from 33 seats to 44 seats. Surely this mandate would affect the federal government's approach and bring them back to the negotiating table.

Well, no!

The federal response was swift. On May 19, 1982, they unilaterally referred the offshore issue to the Supreme Court of Canada. The same day I responded: "The Government of Newfoundland is shocked beyond comprehension by this arrogant and cowardly act." I went on to refer to the January 25 proposal that was never answered.

Given that the federal government refused to respond
to our January 25 proposal and the fact that it was
unclear what answer the court would give to the
SIU case earlier this year, this government embarked
upon two specific courses of action to protect the
vital interests of the people of Newfoundland and
Labrador: I) we referred the matter to the Supreme
Court of Newfoundland, 2) we called an election
on the issue to get the views of the people of the
province.

We now find that the Government of Canada is
blatantly ignoring these two actions. Never before
has a federal government ignored the legitimate
rights of the Supreme Court of a province to
adjudicate on a matter of such importance to the
province. Never before has a federal government so
arrogantly dismissed the expression of opinion of a
people of a province on an issue which so greatly
affects them.

We appealed to the legislature for a unanimous resolution
condemning the action of the federal government and to call on
them to return to the negotiating table based on the proposals put
forward by the province. The legislature passed the resolution
unanimously. Additionally, we cancelled a ceremony celebrating the
new Constitution and called for a "day of mourning." We also called
on our five Liberal MPs and our senators for their support, and also
the two federal party leaders, Mr. Clark and Mr. Broadbent.

A note of some significant merit at this time was the support of
Liberal Senator Eric Cook—no small decision for a man who had
been a Liberal all his life. Bill Marshall had this to say on the matter:

By far the sharpest criticism was levied by Senator
Eric Cook in his address to the Senate several days
after the federal reference when he resigned from

the Liberal caucus over it, and sat throughout his remaining days in the Senate as an Independent. He scorned Prime Minister Trudeau and Justice Minister Chrétien for acting with "great impropriety" and their show of "shocking discourtesy and complete lack of statesmanship." He pointed out that the move dealt "a severe blow to the public perception of the Supreme Court of Newfoundland," whilst observing if these two lawyers had had any real experience of practising before the courts, they would have had second thoughts before treating with contempt one of the Superior courts of the nation.

Not unusual, the national media had a hard time understanding Newfoundland's position, even though it was put in writing in the clearest terms; they seemed to favour the federal position, which was factually contradictory. Puzzling indeed!

This lack of understanding is perhaps best exemplified by the contents of the most watched national TV news show of the day, *The Journal*, with Barbara Frum. Ms. Frum interviewed Mr. Chrétien (no one from the Newfoundland side was present, of course) concerning the offshore matter. But the facts were not provided, forcing me to write Ms. Frum on May 21, 1982:

> You failed to mention in your questioning two points:
>
> You left unchallenged Mr. Chrétien's contention that Newfoundland went to court first. For the record, the federal government enlarged the SIU case before a federal court to include ownership of the offshore, forcing Newfoundland to refer the matter to the Supreme Court of Newfoundland.
>
> Secondly, no mention was made of our January 25 proposal that was presented to the federal government, to which no reply has yet been received. If a prompt resolution is what the federal

> government wants, negotiation using this proposal
> can be much quicker than court reference.

Meanwhile, the Nova Scotia agreement and the federal government's unilateral reference to the Supreme Court kept the pressure on us notwithstanding our great election victory.

There were many who thought we should accept a Nova Scotia-type deal. However, we refused to accept a deal that did not reflect real management and revenue sharing—and that was the Nova Scotia deal.

On July 2, 1982, I wrote the prime minister on the offshore following up on a discussion I had with him on June 30 at a First Ministers Conference on the economy at Sussex Drive.

I pointed out to him the major issues consisted of real management and revenue sharing. I went on to explain why the Nova Scotia deal was inadequate and sought a meeting with him to see if we could come up with a basis to start negotiations again. In the letter I said, "In order to determine if the basis of a settlement is possible, I propose that we meet privately, without publicity, to pursue this matter in the very near future."

The prime minister's answer was disappointing, trying to claim that I was softening my approach to the permanence issue, and deflecting the request for a meeting between us. I responded and still requested a meeting between us for July 10, 1982.

Without a definite meeting date with the prime minister, I nevertheless agreed with the prime minister's suggestion of having the Energy ministers meet and review the issue. This occurred over the next few months, culminating in a September 2, 1982, federal proposal, which failed to address our positions of management and revenue sharing. I then met with the prime minister to ascertain whether this was the federal government's final position.

On October 6, 1982, I reported to the people of the province in a province-wide address:

> It is with deep regret that I report to you that we did
> not resolve the basic differences that would make

possible an agreement that was fair and reasonable to Newfoundland. The federal government is determined and will not change its position that it alone must manage and control the offshore. The federal government will not sign an agreement that will give Newfoundland a real say in managing these resources. The federal government insists that Newfoundland would only have an advisory role.

Sadly, it had taken seven months for the federal government to respond to our January 25 proposal—a response that was almost a total rejection of our reasonable positions, and of even greater import the response was contrary to the prime minister's earlier public statements.

It was always a mystery to me how five provinces could manage their oil and gas resources, and Newfoundland, once a self-governing dominion of the Commonwealth who brought the oil and resources with them into Confederation, was then to be refused the same management rights. We then suspended all talks with the federal government on this issue.

Needless to say, the federal government put on a powerful PR campaign to sell its proposal in the province, touting erroneously that we would get 100% of the revenues but conveniently ignoring the equalization revenues we would lose at the same time.

These were tough and difficult moments both for the Cabinet and the caucus. You knew what some were no doubt thinking and whispering. Had we gone too far? Should we now get the best deal we can? Is the Nova Scotia deal that bad? It was natural that "battle weariness" would settle in. It was at this time that we took a poll to gauge the mood of the people on the issue. What resulted was something like this: "You have fought the good fight; it is time to settle, get the best deal you can, and sign." I don't know now how many people I shared this with at the time, but I am sure it was only a few. It would have been political dynamite to have shared such information widely.

Then, prominent voices began to take issue with our ongoing

offshore position. In October the Opposition Leader, Stephen Neary, rejected our position while remaining ambiguous on whether he supported our January 25 proposal or the federal proposal of September 2. Then there was prominent businessman Harry Steele, part-owner of the regional airline Eastern Provincial Airways, blaming the bad economic situation of the time on the impasse over offshore, even though Nova Scotia, which had signed a deal, saw its unemployment rate rise as much as Newfoundland's, and Canada's rose by even a larger amount. And then there was a new publication of the time called "This Week," which criticized the government for issuing pamphlets explaining the offshore proposals.

Late fall of 1982 saw the prime minister shuffle his Cabinet; lo and behold, we got a new federal Energy minister, Jean Chrétien. Very soon he began making positive verbal comments about the offshore, indicating that there was federal flexibility and that he thought a deal could be forged between the two governments, one that could be different than the Nova Scotia agreement. Of course, we were very skeptical given the recent history and, therefore, approached these new federal statements with great caution.

The pressure was enormous for the province to get a deal, and now here was the federal government again, making these so-called positive noises. It was decided, therefore, that Mr. Marshall and Mr. Chrétien would meet to explore whether there were grounds to begin serious bargaining. In a bizarre twist, Mr. Chrétien insisted from the start that these talks would not be a formal exchange of written positions; rather, the two ministers would talk and just keep notes. In an unpublished paper he had written giving his recollections on the talks leading up to the Atlantic Accord (and which he shared with me), Bill Marshall explains:

> The second overt sign of Trudeauite aversion to confirm in writing federal seriousness of intent in negotiations came from Jean Chrétien when talks resumed following him replacing Marc Lalonde in December of 1982. We had been lured into the

second round on the promise of a deal different than the one accepted by Nova Scotia. At the outset of the Chrétien talks, I was not only assured the promise would be fulfilled, but also led to believe our revenue and management aspirations could be fully accommodated.

However, after the ministers held a number of meetings, it was time for the negotiating teams to begin sitting down and put into writing a draft agreement based upon the principles the ministers discussed. This process had no sooner started when Cyril Abery, the chair of our negotiating committee, reported to Bill Marshall that the talks were going nowhere. Marshall wrote Chrétien on January 24, 1983:

> I write you concerning the present offshore talks. You and I have had five meetings before any matters were referred to our negotiating teams. Our meetings were meant to establish the principles and agree on parameters that would lead to fruitful, successful, detailed talks between our negotiating teams. From the start you insisted that it would be beneficial if you and I did not exchange written positions on different items, although detailed notes were taken by both sides. I agreed with you for the sake of getting the talks going. During these meetings I thought we had made meaningful progress, and I think you did too. The fact that both sides agreed to refer some of the matters to our negotiating teams proves this.
>
> However, since the two negotiating teams have been meeting, things have changed dramatically. I find positions being taken by your team widely diverge from the positions you took during our talks. That was the reason for my first meeting with you after the teams started meeting, which I thought would

resolve the differences between you and your team. The further meetings between our two teams showed that you were not successful in having your position adopted by them.

Therefore, I requested a second meeting with you, which we had Friday past. You still maintained that your team's position is really not your position or that of the Government of Canada. However, your team's position is the only written position we have. All your positions have been verbal although noted.

Mr. Marshall went on to express his puzzlement and to request in writing from the minister his "understandings" on the seventeen items critical to the talks, from management issues of a joint board, revenue issues, national self-sufficiency, to sliding scale royalties, etc. This letter came as a result of private meetings between the two negotiating teams being held in the Meridien Hotel in Montreal, considered a good place away from the glare that would more likely be present in Ottawa or St. John's. The two ministers met and then the teams sat down to map out a framework agreement based upon instructions from the ministers. However, the federal team had the same position that it had displayed during the previous talks with former Energy minister Lalonde. Here is Marshall's interesting and revealing commentary:

I called Jean Chrétien. He said he would contact his negotiating team and set the matter straight. When the meeting reconvened, it was the same story. It was obvious I was not amused when I called him the second time. He was apologetic and full of assurances there had been some slip-up and he would set things right. The teams reassembled once more, incredibly with the same result. It was so eerie and weird that this could be happening in talks of such import to both governments.

The best description of my feelings over being toyed with a third time is expressed in the adage: "fool me once, fool me twice, me poor fool if you fool me thrice."

I had remained in Montreal. Jean Chrétien had gone back to Ottawa after we had agreed the officials could begin putting together a draft on the basis of the principles agreed by us. I was furious. I called him in Ottawa and asked him to come down to Montreal immediately. He said he was tied up and could not come right away, but he would come that evening.

In the interval, I sat down and prepared a letter to him listing the seventeen principles of the framework of the agreement that he and I had agreed would be fleshed out in an initial draft by our respective officials. After the letter was typed, I put it in my pocket and waited in my hotel room for my visitor's arrival.

He arrived alone and we sat down to discuss the situation. I began by getting right to the point in expressing deep concern over Paul Tellier's (the prime minister's chief of staff) refusals to discuss the framework we had mapped out. I then frankly told Jean Chrétien, while he may have believed he could conclude an agreement along the lines of our agreed framework, it was becoming apparent that the Trudeau policy had not changed and he could not deliver on his assurances. I suggested that Mark Lalonde was still pulling the strings. He was then told in unmistakable terms that negotiations could not continue on that basis.

Chrétien responded in the same refrain; namely, there had been confusion and he would straighten it up. After he went on in this vein for a while, I put my hand in my pocket and pulled out the envelope containing the letter. As I was doing so, I suggested the best way to clear up the confusion for once and for all was to provide a written outline of the framework of our agreement for the negotiating teams. They would then have our joint instructions and would be able to get on with preparing a draft of the agreement for submission to us. Then I advised him that I had prepared that outline and suggested he read it with a view to giving it to the teams.

When I took the envelope out of my pocket with the seventeen principles intended to serve as joint drafting instructions to respective teams of officials, Mr. Chrétien's eyes became fixed on it. I remember him rising from his chair whilst exclaiming, "But Bill we agreed there would be no writing." I recall responding that the federal negotiators were not accepting what we had agreed, so we had to reduce it to writing.

I, too, then got up out of my chair, holding out the envelope to him. Facing me, he started walking backwards towards the door with his hands up in front of his body as if to ward off some deadly blow, whilst incanting "no letter" to which I replied "just a little one, Jean." Then I heard him mutter "no writing," while continuing to back-pedal with his eyes transfixed on the envelope I was holding out to him. I recall responding with something like "just these few words, Jean" as he reached the door, whereupon he exited, slammed the door right in front of my extended hand holding the proffered letter, and beat a hasty retreat lickety-split down the hotel corridor. He was gone, never to return.

A response to Marshall's letter was never received.

We had no choice but to sever any more talks on the issue. It was obvious Chrétien's words were his own and he could not get them to become federal policy. He continually misled Mr. Marshall and failed to deliver what he had promised. Either he thought, once back in negotiations, it would be difficult for us to leave and, therefore, he could convince us to sign a Nova Scotia deal, doing something that his rival Marc Lalonde was unable to do and making himself look good in the eyes of the prime minister, or naively believing he could convince the PM and Lalonde to accept the Newfoundland position. The former is the more plausible to me. But this did not stop Mr. Chrétien from telling a local newspaper that "the people he was dealing with were not dealing in good faith."

Here was a man who refused to put his position in writing, was undermined by his negotiating team, obviously being controlled by others in the federal government, and then had the gall to describe the other side as bad-faith negotiators when we had put our position in writing and where our minister and the negotiating team were saying the same things.

Even the mayor of St. John's, John Murphy, a known Liberal, got in the act. Having contacted Chrétien, he wrote me a letter indicating that what the federal government was offering was a good deal. I responded to the mayor by pointing out the facts were not as had been painted by Mr. Chrétien and that we thought it only fair that positions be put in writing, concluding with "however, in the matter of the offshore, I regrettably have to note that your comments, based as they are upon one-sided and incomplete information, hardly serve the interests of all the people of the province."

The period from January, 1983, onward, after we severed talks, was the most difficult period of all. As Marshall says:

> The period between the break off of the Chrétien round in January of 1983 and June of 1983 saw the bleakest of days. There was nothing to negotiate and no one with whom to negotiate. The pressures exerted on us locally to sign and get on with

development, fueled by local federal acolytes and the Board of Trade, spiralled. Jean Chrétien kept the heat on with statements of his willingness to resume negotiations. But there was nothing to negotiate and no one with whom to negotiate in good faith.

Then the shocking news came in February. Our court ruled that the offshore was federal—we had no ownership rights whatsoever. The Nova Scotia deal, our own rejection of further talks, and now the unfavourable court decision, tested our resolve—especially in light of a budget that year that saw us having to increase our sales tax to 12%, the highest in the land, increase our corporate and personal taxes, impose a new capital tax on banks and trust companies, increase tobacco and liquor taxes, and raise fees on many other government services.

In April we played our last card: no more offshore negotiations until there was a change of government in Ottawa. And then the slightest glimmer of hope! Brian Mulroney won the leadership of the federal Progressive Conservative Party. There was renewed vigour in the party and a growing sense that it could win the next general election. Extensive talks with the party concerning offshore had been ongoing for some time, such that it was only days after Mulroney's ascension to the leadership that I was able to announce that the new leader and party had communicated to us in writing that the party was prepared, when it became government, to finalize with us an offshore accord that met the province's management and revenue positions. My response at the time, June 14, 1983:

> The Mulroney letter is a significant breakthrough in Newfoundland's long and often discouraging struggle to receive fair and equitable treatment on this resource which we were proud to have brought into Confederation.
>
> This agreement provides both the provincial and federal governments with a positive constructive role in the management process. It provides for our

province being treated equally and equitably with
other oil and gas producing provinces on the matter
of revenue sharing.
I am firmly of the view that the offshore will be
an important building block for Canada in the years
to come.

It is often forgotten that this commitment came from Mulroney
after our own Newfoundland Court of Appeal had ruled against us
and before the Supreme Court of Canada had ruled. It would have
been a credible position for Mulroney to announce that he would
make a final decision after a Supreme Court of Canada ruling. But
true to the commitment of an earlier leader, Joe Clark, Mulroney
never flinched—he delivered.

Mulroney wasted little time, only two months, in getting himself a
seat in Parliament by taking the seat of Central Nova in Nova Scotia in
a by-election as a result of the resignation of the sitting Member Elmer
McKay (Peter McKay's father), which allowed Mulroney to run there.

The Conservatives began improving in the polls and the Liberals
were slipping. Trudeau seemed vulnerable and a Conservative victory
now seemed at least possible, if not probable.

In February, 1984, Trudeau, seeing the writing on the wall,
announced his intention to step down. We were delighted!

Dampening that optimism of Trudeau leaving, and the possible
electoral success of the Progressive Conservative Party, was our defeat
at the hands of the Supreme Court of Canada on March 8, 1984. No
sooner was Trudeau to leave—our obstinate opponent to a fair deal
for the province—than this stunning rebuke of our claims by the
highest court:

In summary, we conclude:

(1) Continental shelf rights are, in pith and substance, an
extraterritorial manifestation of external sovereignty.

(2) Canada has the right to explore and exploit in the continental shelf off Newfoundland because:

(a) Any continental shelf rights available at international law in 1949 would have been acquired by the Crown in right of the United Kingdom, not the Crown in right of Newfoundland;

(b) Even if Newfoundland could have held continental shelf rights prior to Union, they would have passed to Canada by virtue of the Terms of Union.

(c) In any event, international law did not recognize continental shelf rights by 1949; such rights were not indisputably recognized before the Geneva Convention of 1958. [p. 129]

(3) Canada has legislative jurisdiction in relation to the right to explore and exploit in the continental shelf off Newfoundland by virtue of the peace, order, and good government power in its residual capacity.

In short, in our opinion both parts of the question should be answered in favour of Canada.

Just when we were gaining some hope, this decision put a dagger to the heart. You are no sooner off the mat than you are knocked down again.

Mr. Trudeau's resignation led to a Liberal Convention on June 16, 1984, at which John Turner was elected leader and automatically prime minister. In July, Turner moved swiftly, calling an election for September. The Liberal fortunes started to rise in the polls, and a Progressive Conservative victory, probable only a weeks before, now seemed very uncertain.

For once, luck was on our side. A secret deal between Trudeau and Turner saw a flurry of appointments to the Senate and other government agencies and some questionable appointments by Turner himself, all reflecting badly on the Liberals. In the public television debates during the campaign, Mulroney exploited this Liberal largesse and cronyism, putting Turner on the defensive and delivering a major blow to the Liberal fortunes. Mulroney's now-famous line during the debate, "You had an option. You could have done better," referring to Turner and his position on the appointments, resonated with the voters.

On election night Mulroney won a landslide victory of 211 seats in the 282-seat House of Commons, the largest seat victory in Canada's history.

The period from the Mulroney victory on September, 1984, to February, 1985, marks perhaps the five most important months in the history of our place. Talks began again on the offshore. Our minister Marshall and the federal minister Carney were at the negotiating table, taking instructions from their respective first ministers and Cabinets.

Gone were the acrimony, intimidation, and paternalism of the federal government. Commitments made were commitments met. Bill Marshall has commented upon the negotiations with the new Energy minister, Pat Carney: "No longer were we being treated as dupes in a game whose ultimate end was to force acceptance of outright federal suzerainty over oil and gas off our shores. This time it was for real!"

As a relevant aside, which I know will be hard for readers to believe, I remember an incident when we were in a meeting with then Energy minister Jean Chrétien over the big principle of us insisting on the establishment of an Offshore Board (with equal federal and provincial representation, with an independent chairperson with the full compliment of employees) and that it be stationed in the province. Shockingly, the federal side mused about where the children of the employees would go to school.

Marshall goes on to say:

> In the Carney round of negotiations there was
> no divergence between the word of the Federal

Energy Minister to me and what her officials told
our officials that they were instructed to translate
into the formal agreement. In fact, she saw to it that
a trusted and highly competent lieutenant, Harry
Near, co-opted specifically for the purpose, sat in on
the meetings of the officials to assure that Federal
Policy was being so translated.

The Atlantic Accord was born!

Our last game changer, our last chance, did not go down to defeat
by the refusal of a federal government for constitutional change, as
in the fishery; it did not go down to judicial defeat as in Churchill
Falls—but from such crushing defeats rose an agreement unlike any
in our history.

To quote a few of the main elements of the Atlantic Accord:

"To recognize the right of Newfoundland to be the principal
beneficiary of the oil and gas resources."

"To provide that the Government of Newfoundland and
Labrador can establish and collect resource revenues as if
those resources were on land, within the Province."

"To recognize the equality of both Governments in the
management of the resource."

"The offices of the Board and its staff shall be located in
Newfoundland."

"The two Governments recognize that there should not be a
dollar for dollar loss of equalization payments as a result of
offshore revenues flowing to the Province."

"The Government of Canada and the Government of
Newfoundland and Labrador hereby establish an offshore

development fund [See Appendix II]. The Fund will consist of a $300 million grant, cost shared 75% federal and 25% provincial."

And so for the first time in our history, we had negotiated an agreement that gave to Newfoundland meaningful and effective levers to be a major player in one of our own resources—this time, oil and gas.

Sadly, it is forgotten now that Brian Mulroney could have easily taken a tougher stand, armed as he was with a recent Supreme Court of Canada decision clearly and categorically adjudicating in the federal government's favour. But he did not.

NEVER A SECOND OR a minute during our talks with the prime minister or Minister Carney was advantage taken or pressure applied as a result of that decision. Yet, here we were with de facto ownership, consistent with national responsibilities, with the levers of ownership and jurisdiction. February 11, 1985, was a great day—the signing of the Accord.

I remember sneaking away for an hour or so to be by myself, driving to Signal Hill. I passed by the house at the bottom of the hill that Joe Peckford had built, glanced down Temperance Street to where Joe had his own "rooms" now all filled in and where the Terry Fox Memorial now stands.

Once on top of Signal Hill, I glanced out at the North Atlantic and my life passed before me: my parents, my great teacher and confidant, Brose Paddock, the basketball team in Springdale, the men who plied the waters of Green Bay, Pistolet Bay, the French Shore, and the Labrador Coast with me, advised me, and assisted me in "growing up," who experienced with me the frustrations and tribulations of people who were without, or troubled, or just plain looking for help or guidance—of making do, struggling with few resources and not whining and complaining; the people of Green Bay who stood by me at all times, many sensing, I think, the big picture, the greater good, and what I was seeking.

And my late new friend in La Poile would be a proud Tory today. Oil did not flow right away, of course; not until 1997 did the first oil flow from the first development, Hibernia. But when it did, it began the real movement to a better time.

Professor Richard Cullen, presently a law professor at Hong Kong University, published a book in 1990 entitled *Federalism in Action: The Canadian and Australian Offshore Disputes*, based on his doctoral thesis that he completed at Osgoode Hall, York University. In it he said, "Through these two Accords (Newfoundland's and then later Nova Scotia's, which was based on Newfoundland's), these two Atlantic provinces have gained, in important ways, more than they would have gained had they each won in court" (p. 193).

Later he continues: "The provinces have achieved the setting up of an offshore policy-making and management board truly independent of federal control. And they have also gained the same access to revenues from the adjacent continental shelf that the award of provincial sovereign rights thereover would have afforded them" (p. 193).

The last word concerning the Accord must go to Lin Jackson, in his book *Surviving Confederation*, who said of it:

> But it is no piece of paper; it is a brand new Term of Union which confers upon Newfoundland an unprecedented constitutional status with respect to the use of resources off its shores. One need only glance at the history of this area to realize that no other single factor contributed so persistently and significantly to retarding Newfoundland's economic growth and its social well-being over the centuries than precisely the fact that total jurisdiction of the oceanic resources upon which the local people always have depended, lay out of reach in the hands of others. The Atlantic Accord is not "historic," a "watershed," "the most significant document since Confederation" simply because Premier Brian

Peckford said it was. It is so because for the first time in our 500-year history the people and Government of Newfoundland have at long last been afforded a direct role in determining the management, use, and benefit of the great traditional resource of the banks of Newfoundland. (114)

On November 3, 2008, I received an email from Shelly Banfield, producer of the St. John's CBC Radio Morning Show, which said in part:

Hi Mr. Peckford:

I don't know if you heard the news yet, but Newfoundland is officially off equalization.

One day the sun will shine and have not will be no more!

EPILOGUE

POINT ONE

THE HIBERNIA DEVELOPMENT WAS the first development under the Atlantic Accord; we bargained hard for a reasonable deal and I think we succeeded. So the Hibernia Statement of Principles, July 18, 1988, was another great day marking as it did a real, tangible result of the Accord. But given the time, there were many risks and oil prices were a far cry from where they are today. The federal government had to step in and assist. Once again Brian Mulroney came to the fore as well as Michael Wilson, Marcel Masse, and John Crosbie, his Cabinet members. A $1 billion contribution and a $1.6-billion guarantee were needed. Later the project hit further trouble with the withdrawal of Gulf Canada and its 25% of the project. The federal government stepped in again, taking 8.5% with the remainder of the 25% taken up by Murphy Oil, Mobil, and Chevron.

Of course, such support from the federal government did not miss the eye of those from away who saw this as some terrible mistake, while millions of federal dollars were going into all sorts of projects for car plants in the country's heartland and into an area that had enjoyed for years the great advantages of an Auto Pact with the United States, when at the same time we were forced to sell unprocessed fish to the United States because we had no access like the central Canadians had with their cars and car parts. The *Globe and Mail* led the charge with its editorial on December 29, 1992. Its headline: "A Happy Ending to Hibernia—and Soon."

In the first paragraph it described the project as "the makings of a grand tragedy," and on a "historic scale" talked about the oil being the most costly on earth.

I was no longer in government when this was written, but I responded the next day with a letter to the editor:

> Let me express my utter disgust with your editorial of December 29 concerning the Hibernia Project. I find it strange indeed that the marriage of the private and public sectors which built this country finds so little favour with your paper. In advancing new frontiers, it has been this partnership that has been so important. It is no different with the first major offshore oil project development in this country. Strategic investment by the public sectors has been a characteristic of this country for decades. It is noteworthy that the strongest economies in the world today are those that have mastered the simple idea of strategic co-operative arrangements between the public and private sectors.
>
> Newfoundland and Labrador is eager to work based on gifts that nature has provided. Co-operation by all sectors is essential to make it happen. Already, Ontario, Quebec, and western-Canadian companies have benefited from the Hibernia project. We do not begrudge the billions of dollars that provincial and federal governments have invested in Ontario and Quebec and in energy and agricultural sectors in the west. In order for all regions to grow and contribute, fairness demands the same support to ensure the natural resources of Newfoundland and Labrador are developed for the benefit of all of Canada.
>
> In closing, I would like for your paper to provide me with the data—economic and financial—that was used to reach the conclusions in your editorial.

Needless to say, I did not receive a response to the letter and I am unaware of whether the paper later ever made amends for its unfortunate analysis and predictions. I have contacted the paper, and in getting them to send me many of their later editorials, I cannot find where they have acknowledged their monumental blunders regarding the price of oil and the cost of Hibernia oil.

And they were not finished. They followed this up with editorials on January 6, 1993, and January 12, 1993. January 6 was headlined "If Hibernia Can't Swim—Let it Sink" and the January 12 one was headlined "Hibernia or Uneconomics 101."

What is most shocking, besides the colossal errors (mocked as they deliberately inflated Hibernia to produce 700 million barrels—it will now produce over 1 billion) and bad predictions (as if they somehow were blessed with the only perfect crystal ball, saying oil prices will not keep up with inflation) is the zeal with which they denigrated the project. It is as if deep in the heart of the paper there was this gigantic fear that this just might succeed and we can't have that, so let's kill it now.

Ironic, isn't it, that this paper resides in Ontario, now a "have not" province, and Newfoundland, largely because of Hibernia, is a "have" province? Specifically, in the year 2011–12, Ontario will receive $2.2 billion in equalization and Newfoundland will not receive any. In other words, because of this great tragedy, Hibernia, Newfoundland *is now assisting* Ontario. This "farce," as they called it.

And I have just read a CBC report of July 5, 2011, that the federal government in 2008 and 2009 bailed out the auto industry, largely in Ontario, to the tune of—wait for it—$12 billion.

POINT TWO

THE HIBERNIA STATEMENT OF Principles, which we negotiated and signed in 1988, stipulated that a gravity-based structure was to be the production technology used and that it was to be built in Newfoundland (the first in the Western Hemisphere) at the new Bull Arm site (constructed with $95 million from the Offshore

Development Fund we had negotiated in the Accord). Its design, as well as the design of the flare boom and subsea lines, was to be done in the province, and the main support frame assembled and outfitted at Bull Arm in the province.

We were beginning to realize our aim of having an industry, not just a project. There were three provincial royalties: one before the project was paid for, one after the project was paid for, and a super royalty if oil prices rose significantly. Not bad compared with every other major resource deal ever done in the history of the place.

On February 21, 1997, I was in St. John's as a member of the board of CBC. I was suddenly confronted by a host of people at the Hotel Newfoundland, all of whom were invited there to witness the exciting, historic tow out of the Hibernia platform. I was humiliated, since I had to inform the curious, questioning people that no, I was not there to witness the tow out, because I was not invited. I made little of it then, although it hurt for a while and, for the record, I say it now.

POINT THREE

IN 2010, EFFORTS GOT under way to have a conference/ gathering to highlight and celebrate the 25th anniversary of the Atlantic Accord. Memorial University was involved, as well as individuals who were involved in the provincial government during the days when the Accord was being negotiated, present representatives of the provincial government, and the Newfoundland Ocean Industries Association.

Unfortunately, the format outlined for such a gathering did not find favour with the provincial government representatives and NOIA. The idea was to have the architects—that is, the politicians and public servants who actually did the deal there—to talk about the events and issues leading up to this historic document. Unbelievably, this did not happen, because of the lack of support from the province and NOIA.

The event then went forward with just the university sponsoring it under a Memorial Presents series whose "rules" precluded having someone from outside the university to speak. I was told, "Memorial Presents is always a MUN presenter on an issue of provincial importance, along with a panellist or two who provide some counterbalancing perspectives. Having someone of your status or Bill's as a panellist just did not make sense." And having someone like us would conflict "with their independence." And it is not their place to have a "celebration."

Well, needless to say, when I heard this I flipped my top and wrote to Memorial University.

I am having difficulty finding the words to respond to your comments.

Forget the "celebration" word. That is "different," I suppose, because we wouldn't want the hallowed halls of academia to go berserk over one of the greatest achievements of this land, especially in light of the railway, the Hum on the Humber, and the Exploits River Central Newfoundland boondoggle, the mining concessions to John Doyle, and the bankruptcy of Come By Chance (a story for another time, and its resurrection, which, of course, could not have the authors describe at some future university-inspired event), not to mention Labrador Linerboard or the Upper Churchill—oh yes—the ground fishery!

Parenthetically, the first blob of money out of the $300 million development fund under the Accord was to Memorial University for the Geology Building. How could they take it and remain independent?

"Oh, stop being so narrow, Brian, and not understanding the history and importance of a free and independent institution of higher learning," I can hear in my ears. I expounded on that at great length in my speech at MUN during the proceedings when I was awarded my honorary degree. Right on side, I am.

So let's not get hung up on the word celebration. Agreed! Not at the university—never!

But to say that you cannot invite authors, signatories to the Accord (1985), because that would somehow break or undermine the "independence" of the university or your series is surely a stretch— no, not a stretch; it is truly puzzling to me. How can you say "it did not make sense" to have any of the signatories there? How does one go about framing such rules? Does not the university have authors of papers, poems, novels, fiction and non-fiction, music, and visual art participate in the discussion of their creations?

Now, I do not mean to just have Bill Marshall or me and one or all of the federal signatories; rather, having the signatories, or some of them, introduce the topic and then others like Cullen and Locke or whoever follow with a full and open discussion.

Okay, so given the restraints that you describe, let's say this: it would seem to me most reasonable to have Mr. Marshall (given there is no cost) talk broadly about the principles of the Accord and to put it in some 1985 context; then the others, academics from all perspectives to present. I think this would be far more effective and realistic for those who will see/ hear the proceedings. It would give an air of balance and realism. Can one imagine that here is one of the authors right in your midst, a former learned judge, citizen, and public figure extraordinaire, and he is somehow viewed as ineligible from participating in what he helped create, a creation which has seen this land for the first time in its history become financially viable, one of only four "have" provinces in the Canadian Confederation? This is special and unique!

This becomes most bizarre when one looks at the facts. Take Mr. Marshall, for example. Here is a man who distinguished himself as a lawyer, then as a member of the legislature, and most particularly as minister of Energy, and then having an exemplary period on the highest court in the province, the Court of Appeal. He is known far and wide as highly intelligent, learned, and fair, with integrity to burn. If anyone takes the time to read any of his decisions, his fairness, integrity, and sense of justice overwhelms. His formal politics ceased when he became a judge. Please explain to me how the university's policy of independence can deliberately exclude such a man who was a critical part of the Accord's creation and final agreement from being asked to participate in a discussion/gathering on the 25th anniversary of the Accord? Remember, it was the province through Mr. Marshall at the table who insisted on principles approved by me and Cabinet that saw this Accord move forward and then accepted by Ottawa. And let's not forget these principles had already been rejected by an earlier federal government.

It seems to me that the university cannot, on the one hand, espouse open and free expression and independence, if on the other hand it disallows some people who happened to be in politics twenty years ago and just happened to be the author of the subject of a public university–initiated discussion from being a part of that very discussion. I suspect if I was to pursue this through appropriate channels, a legitimate discrimination challenge could be launched.

To put it another way, the university is a public institution. It is to serve that public and provide information and analysis and a very wide, diverse perspective to that public. It prides itself on openness and free expression. It is contradictory to its mission to establish rules and policy for a public forum, which this 25th anniversary discussion espouses, in a manner which discriminates against certain people from being heard because of their political past (or is it something else of which I am unaware?) and who are very relevant to that discussion, especially given that these people were the authors of the subject being discussed and who no longer are formal participants in the political process and have not been for twenty years.

I am, of course, speaking here to the *university* and not to you as an individual, but obviously this episode has hit a very sensitive nerve.

Brian

If this is not one of the most amazing things you have ever heard, I don't know what could be.

The university wanted to talk about the pros and cons after the Agreement had been in operation for twenty-five years, fine. But on the 25th anniversary of that which made us a "have" province?

Here is the only university in the province (public and all) to highlight arguably one of the most important economic, resource, and financial agreements ever signed in the history of Newfoundland (and from which they benefited handsomely and continue to benefit), and to do so without inviting those who were the negotiators, signatories, and architects of the agreement.

ACKNOWLEDGEMENTS

IN A PROJECT OF this sort there are many people to thank. Two former members of the House of Assembly, Mr. Charlie Brett and Mr. Fred Stagg, as well as Mr. Ira Bridger, former president of the Newfoundland and Labrador Development Corporation, graciously agreed to provide written material that is used in this book. The Legislative Library in St. John's was exemplary in its assistance to me, both in person and by email communication. Andy Fowler, the manager, and Andrea Hyde were both enthusiastic in assisting me on various research topics. Andrea was just superb at finding many items. David Vardy, former clerk of the Executive Council, was of great assistance in tracking down information concerning the Atlantic Accord and the Bowater divesture. Ron Penney, former deputy minister of Justice, also assisted on this and provided valuable advice. Hal Stanley and Herb Clarke, two highly competent clerks of the Executive Council during my time as premier, were also very helpful. Leslie Dean, former assistant deputy minister of the provincial Department of Fisheries, assisted me on Fisheries matters; Sandy Roche, former deputy minister of Development, assisted on linerboard mill matters; Peter Withers, former deputy minister of Municipal Affairs, assisted on the municipal issues. Des Sullivan, former executive assistant to me and to Frank Moores, has been very helpful in remembering various important incidents and in general advice to me. Frank Ryan, my leadership campaign manager and in all my provincial elections as premier, was always there for valuable information and insight. My elder bother, Bruce, was also of assistance when I went looking for various pieces of information. Shirley Miller of Cape Breton Island was very helpful on family tree matters. Dr. John E. Fitzgerald provided information and advice relating to the Confederation period. Bill Marshall, as the book clearly indicates, was of immeasurable help and support. And, most particularly, my wife, Carol, who had to put up with the books and papers loosely scattered about for a couple years, not to mention the many mood swings of an aging former first minister. I must make special mention of the public servants and their support personnel who served on the Atlantic Accord and Hibernia Project negotiating teams. The province can be very proud of this group of competent, dedicated Newfoundlanders. The teams' names are listed in Appendix III.

Thanks also to Flanker Press and Garry Cranford for agreeing to edit and publish.

APPENDIX I: PATRIATION OF THE CONSTITUTION

A. INTRODUCTION

As mentioned in the main part of this book, the events of November 3–5, 1981, that led to the Patriation Agreement have become distorted and in many cases are inaccurate. In researching for this book, I was surprised at the extent of this misrepresentation. Of course, I should not have been so surprised since only days after the Agreement had been reached there were stories in the media that described events leading up to the Agreement that were at variance with what I had experienced at the conference. Disturbed by this, I called a local reporter, Randy Joyce, since deceased, the week of November 8 and taped an interview with him recalling the events of the previous week and how the Agreement came together. I kept the tape; its full contents have not been released. Unknown to me, my two deputy ministers (Cy Abery of Intergovernmental Affairs, since deceased, and Ron Penney, living in St. John's), who were involved with me at the patriation meetings, were reading the same press reports and had decided that it would be important, for the record, to get together and write down what happened. This document is dated November 12, 1981. It has never been released publicly, until now. Importantly, the two deputy ministers also kept three very important documents of the patriation meetings, also being released now for the first time. The first is a brief proposal that I prepared on the afternoon of November 4 (which was meant to be presented to some of the provinces that day but the

251

meeting never happened) in an attempt to seek common ground on the issues. The second document is the amended version of this proposal and enlarged by the Newfoundland delegation, which included Justice minister Gerald Ottenheimer, my two deputy ministers (mentioned above), and a special adviser, Cabot Martin. The third document is the Newfoundland amended proposal, which became the provincial proposal presented to full conference on November 5.

Here are the three most important misrepresentations.

> 1. *The Agreement resulted from notes on scraps*
> *of paper developed by Attorneys General Jean*
> *Chrétien of the federal government, Roy Romanow*
> *of Saskatchewan, and Roy McMurtry of Ontario*
> *who had assembled in a kitchen of the Château*
> *Laurier Hotel in Ottawa.*

The evidence points to the Agreement being developed at a suite in the Château Laurier Hotel from a written proposal presented by the Government of Newfoundland—first to British Columbia, Alberta, and Saskatchewan, and later that evening to an enlarged meeting including Nova Scotia and Prince Edward Island. Four premiers were present (Newfoundland, Saskatchewan, Nova Scotia, and Prince Edward Island), as well as a number of ministers and officials. Amendments were made to the Newfoundland proposal and late in the night/early the next morning, this amended proposal was retyped and became the provincial proposal. It was agreed that night that the premier of Newfoundland would present this amended proposal to the Gang of Eight provinces (all except Ontario and New Brunswick) at an already-scheduled breakfast meeting the next morning, and if agreed, to be presented to full conference later that morning. Seven provinces agreed to the proposal at breakfast, with no amendments, and agreed that the premier of Newfoundland should present it to full conference that morning. Quebec disagreed with the proposal. It was presented to full conference, as agreed, and after a number of amendments the Patriation Agreement was born.

> 2. *The Patriation Agreement was rushed through at the last minute without proper consideration.*

The evidence indicates that the Patriation Agreement was the culmination of seventeen months of formal deliberation by the eleven provincial governments of Canada. It began with an agenda of twelve items. It was sidelined when the federal government took a unilateral action to try to patriate the constitution with a charter of rights and freedoms without reference to the provinces. Several provinces challenged this federal action in the courts and the Supreme Court of Canada ruled this federal action unconstitutional. Further meetings were then held between the provincial governments and the federal government resulting in the Patriation Agreement.

> 3. *The provinces were selfish and did not cooperate in this project.*

The evidence suggests that the provinces were eager to forge a new agreement regarding patriation and a charter of rights and freedoms. There were obvious concerns regarding provincial jurisdiction and the charter and other matters, but the provinces presented four proposals: the April Accord proposal (1981), the proposal prepared by British Columbia (presented privately to the prime minister on November 3), a proposal by Saskatchewan to full conference on November 4, and finally the amended Newfoundland proposal (now a provincial proposal) of November 5, which led to the Agreement.

These inaccuracies show up in different forms in many publications and websites, including a book written soon after the Agreement was reached entitled *The National Deal: The Fight for a Canadian Constitution* by Robert Sheppard and Michael Valpy, and in the past year in a book written by Ron Graham entitled *The Last Act: Pierre Trudeau, the Gang of Eight and the Fight for Canada.* There were even fanciful theories circulating that Pierre Trudeau was the "behind the scenes puppeteer" manipulating all the proceedings, and another even more incredible suggestion that Jean Chrétien was the father of it all.

Chronologically, after I did my taped interview and filed the tape away, and the deputy ministers did their record of events and filed them away (including the proposal documents), the next significant event (at least from our viewpoint) was an article published in the *National Post* in 1999 entitled, "Night of the Long Knives: Who Dunnit?" by professors Barry Cooper and Ted Morton of the University of Calgary. Here, again, the now established misrepresentations of events were described for all to see. It even had Newfoundland being really "a messenger" in the patriation meetings and proceedings. And some unfortunate slights were directed at us. Obviously, my two deputy ministers and I were not amused when we read the article. Presented here are the responses sent to the professors by my deputy ministers. These are also being released publicly for the first time. Perhaps the most significant is Cy Abery's letter, which deals with the misrepresentations in the article.

My first comment on all of this was to be in this book, but I was pre-empted by events of last year when the University of Alberta, through their law faculty, Constitutional Affairs division, held a conference on the patriation issue, it being the thirtieth anniversary of the event, and invited me to attend. Not wanting to pre-empt my book's publication and the documents I was to release, I simply made a written summary of my taped interview of November, 1981, and hence highlighted my disagreement with the accepted version of events. That same weekend two books were released: one, already referenced, was Mr. Ron Graham's book (an article promoting it was carried in the *Globe and Mail*) and the other was the book *The Patriation Minutes* by Howard Leeson, former Saskatchewan deputy minister, and involved the night of November 4, 1981. His book goes some way to correct the record. This conference was followed by another one on the subject of patriation hosted by the University of Quebec at Montreal, at which time I made a more detailed written presentation. Both the summary of the taped interview and the Montreal presentation are provided here.

I am also releasing for the first time an exchange of letters between myself and Judge Binnie, then a member of the Supreme Court of Canada. This is important because it highlights most clearly the extent of the misunderstanding that existed as it relates to Newfoundland's constitutional position and, therefore, how easily things could get garbled on the patriation issue and hence gain such public credibility. What is very perplexing, however, is that on the day of the actual patriation event, Prime Minister Trudeau (well-known to be at variance with many of my views on other matters), in a public comment recognized the role Newfoundland played in the proceedings. Yet a different version took root and the prime minister's comments were ignored.

Then there is the book written by David G. Wood and published by Key Porter Books in 1985 entitled *The Lougheed Legacy* in which, on page 229, Mr. Lougheed is quoted as saying:

> At the end of the meeting, the Premier of Newfoundland stated he had a proposal, different from Trudeau's, which he wished to present. Since it was already late in the day he decided not to present it to the conference at that time but defer it until the following day . . . hence, Mr. Peter Meekison, the Alberta Deputy Minister of Federal and Intergovernmental Affairs, was sent to the Château Laurier Hotel to work with Newfoundland on Premier Peckford's proposal . . .

This book was followed in 1999 by another publication, *Constitutional Patriation: The Lougheed-Lévesque Correspondence*, with an introduction by Peter Meekison and published by the Institute of Intergovernmental Relations, Queen's University, and the Canada West Foundation. In the introduction Mr. Meekison says, "The fact that a draft compromise proposal emerged should not have come as any surprise to anyone given the various comments during the day, particularly after Premier Peckford had indicated his intention to put forward a proposal" (p. 9).

Also in this publication is Mr. Lougheed's letter to Mr. Lévesque dated March 8, 1981, which includes numerous references to the

Newfoundland proposal, including the one referenced above in the book *The Lougheed Legacy*. Let me quote another from that letter. This is point number 27 on page 26 where Lougheed is addressing Lévesque and now referencing the November 5 breakfast meeting: "When you arrived at the meeting you were given a copy of the Newfoundland proposal and you had an opportunity to discuss it before the Group of Eight adjourned."

Further research that I have conducted has uncovered the correspondence of Mr. Mel Smith, deputy minister of Constitutional Affairs for the province of British Columbia and a key player at the patriation meetings. Mr. Smith was involved with Trinity Western University in Langley, British Columbia, and has left his correspondence at the archives of that institution's library. I have found a letter/memo dated November 10, 1981, that Mr. Smith wrote to his minister summarizing the events of the patriation the week before. On page 5 of that memo, Mr. Smith says the following:

> Mr. Gardom instructed me to attend a working session of officials in Premier Blakeney's suite in the Château (Rm. 481) at 9:30 p.m. on Wednesday evening. I did so. At the beginning present were Messers. Cy Abery of Newfoundland, Peter Meekison of Alberta, Howard Leeson of Saskatchewan, and myself. *Our work centred around a three-page document entitled "Constitutional Proposals submitted by the Government of Newfoundland, at the First Ministers Conference, Ottawa, November 3–5, 1981." This was obviously the document to which Peckford had made reference near the conclusion of the Wednesday meeting.* [emphasis added]

B. INTERVIEW

The following is a summary of a taped interview I did (the whole interview is twenty-four pages) with the late Randy Joyce of the St. John's

Daily News, *conducted on November 8, 1981, at the premier's office, St. John's, Newfoundland.*

THE PATRIATION PROCESS AND FINAL AGREEMENT OF NOVEMBER 3–5, 1981

When the conference got started, the eight provinces' position was that of the Accord of earlier that year (April), to which they had agreed. The prime minister's position, and thus that of the federal government, was the Federal Resolution before the House of Commons. As the conference proceeded, the prime minister seemed to show flexibility on the Amending Formula and the provinces showed some flexibility on the introduction of a Charter of Rights and Freedoms.

On November 3, the eight provinces assembled and assisted British Columbia in a proposal that they were crafting. It included the Accord plus a small charter involving democratic rights and fundamental freedoms. That afternoon, there being no closed meeting with the prime minister, we let it be known that we wanted a meeting with him to present a proposal. Premier Davis was contacted and asked whether he would support such a proposal. He said he would study it and indicated that he was willing to act as an intermediary with the prime minister. We had already appointed Premiers Buchanan, Lougheed, and Bennett to represent us but agreed that Davis could be part of the delegation. The meeting was held with the prime minister, but he rejected the proposal.

At breakfast the next morning (Wednesday, November 4), the eight premiers there showed unanimous support for British Columbia to present the rejected proposal at the meeting of premiers and the prime minister later that morning. This was important to the premiers then, since if the conference failed later they wanted it on the record that they had made such a proposal and that it would show that the provinces were being flexible and really wanted the conference to succeed. This was agreed to at breakfast. At the last minute before the meeting was to begin, British Columbia reneged on presenting the proposal. Premier Bennett had contacted Premier Lougheed at the last minute and indicated he had changed his mind. We were all shocked, but what could we do? Premier Blakeney also had a proposal to present, and we had persuaded him to allow Premier Bennett to go first. Now that British Columbia was no longer going to present their proposal, when the meeting began Premier Blakeney proceeded to present his province's proposal. It was discussed at great length, covering all the key issues that were in play at the time. In the end, though, the prime minister would not accept it.

The meeting seemed to be heading for a stalemate, and it was then that I began writing down a few ideas on where I thought common ground was possible: namely the prime minister's seeming flexibility on examining various options for an Amending Formula and the provinces' seeming flexibility on considering a charter, although the elements of that were still in flux. I was hoping to present this to the premiers' Wednesday afternoon meeting that had been tentatively arranged. The meeting never happened, and hence this proposal never got tabled. I have a copy of that proposal. It was proposing the following:

A. Acceptance of the eight provinces accord.

B. Acceptance of a full Charter with two amendments:

1. Minority Language Education rights to be included, but those provinces who opted out would have to hold a binding referendum.

2. An amendment to Mobility rights to permit a province to pursue affirmative action programs for job creation as long as that Province's unemployment rate was below the national average.

At the end of that morning's session, the prime minister was more or less resigned to a failure (or was this a tactical move on his part?) and mused about just doing patriation and over the next two years having a double referendum: one on the Amending Formula and one on the charter.

Early that evening the Newfoundland delegation—minister of Justice,

Gerald Ottenheimer; deputy minister of Intergovernmental Affairs, Cyril Abery; deputy minister of Justice, Ronald Penney; and special adviser to the premier, Cabot Martin—worked on a proposal and consulted with me on it. A proposal (I have a copy) was prepared building on the early ideas in the proposal that was never presented, and with my approval Penney and Abery went to the Château Laurier (fourth floor) to discuss the document with officials from Alberta, Saskatchewan, and British Columbia. Soon Premier Buchanan of Nova Scotia, Premier MacLean of Prince Edward Island, and Premier Blakeney of Saskatchewan attended that gathering. Meanwhile, I had spoken on the phone early that evening to Premiers Bennett, MacLean, Blakeney, and Buchanan.

Mr. Abery called me at the Four Seasons Hotel mid-evening to report that he thought some progress was being made, that he was getting a generally favourable reaction to the proposal, and that I should be ready to come to the Château later if this positive reaction continued. Meanwhile, Minister Ottenheimer contacted Minister McMurtry of Ontario and informed him of what was happening. He seemed pleased and said he would ensure that Premier Davis was informed that evening. Around midnight, Mr. Abery called again, saying that good progress was being made and he thought I should join the group to further advance the proposal.

I hailed a cab at the Four Seasons and went to the Château Laurier to join the group. Three premiers (Blakeney, Buchanan, and MacLean) were there and some of their officials/ministers, and officials of British Columbia (Smith representing Premier Bennett), Alberta (Meekison, representing Premier Lougheed), and, of course, the Newfoundland deputy ministers. Minister Romanow of Saskatchewan joined much later. Ministers Howe and Morris were there from Nova Scotia and Minister Carver of Prince Edward Island, all three having been there most of the evening. A lot of discussion ensued.

I underscored that we were there to fashion a bargain, not organize a defeat. A lot of discussion centred on the charter, the notwithstanding clause, Minority Language Education rights, and the Mobility rights. At the end there was agreement on the elements not much different than what was in our proposal. The final proposal was prepared and typed by our delegation, after having been approved by those present, and was to be presented at breakfast of the eight provinces that morning, seven hours later. Minister Carver of PEI, under instructions from the group, contacted Minister Mercier of Manitoba to ensure that the province would have the information before breakfast the next morning. Premier Lyon had to return to his province to campaign, but Minister Mercier was in touch with him.

Contrary to a lot of commentary over the last thirty years, there were four premiers present that night, and representatives of two more were present, British Columbia and Alberta, and two other provinces not present were contacted that night, Manitoba and Ontario (who were not part of the eight-province group). So eight provinces knew about what was happening that night. Quebec was informed at breakfast that morning of November 5, and New Brunswick was informed just before the proposal was presented to the conference later that morning. At breakfast, six of the provinces (Quebec said it could not support the proposal and Premier Lévesque was unhappy about our proceeding that night and abruptly left the breakfast) supported Newfoundland in its desire to present the proposal at the conference that morning.

C. DOCUMENT OF MR. CY ABERY AND MR. RON PENNEY

November 12, 1981

Constitutional Conference
Sequence of Events
November 4–5, 1981

This document was prepared by Deputy Minister Cyril Abery, Intergovernmental Affairs Secretariat, and Deputy Minister Ron Penney, Department of Justice.

- By the afternoon of November 4, Premier Peckford was convinced that a consensus was still possible, based on

Patriation, the April Accord, and the Charter of Rights. There was no opportunity to present this at the time although he did have a Draft Compromise ready to table (attached).

- The afternoon meeting ended in disarray at about 6:00 p.m., but with agreement to meet the next morning at 9:00 a.m.

- Premier Peckford and Blakeney agreed that officials from Newfoundland, Saskatchewan, and Alberta should meet Wednesday night to see if a common position could be attained. This meeting was set for 9:30 p.m. in room 481 at the Château Laurier.

- The Newfoundland Delegation returned to the hotel (Four Seasons) and it was agreed that we should draft up a proposal to bring to the 9:30 meeting with Saskatchewan and Alberta.

- At about 7:30 p.m., Ron Penney and the undersigned went to Ron Penney's room and jointly prepared a proposal (attached). This was then reviewed with the premier, Mr. Ottenheimer, and Cabot Martin, and a couple of changes were made as noted on the original.

- The premier's view was that he intended to table this as a proposal the next morning but was willing to make changes to get other provinces onside, provided that the main elements remained and the overall scope was not changed.

- This was then typed up and Ron and I went over to the Château Laurier at 9:30 p.m., where we were met by Howard Leeson of Saskatchewan. Shortly thereafter Peter Meekison of Alberta and Mel Smith of British Columbia arrived.

- We distributed the proposal and indicated that the premier was going to present this to the conference the next morning although he was prepared to make some modifications (attached).

- Saskatchewan, Alberta, and British Columbia indicated that the draft was generally acceptable with some modifications. There was a view that a more detailed proposal should be made, but we argued strongly that it should be kept very straightforward and clear. This was finally agreed to by the other provinces.

- The changes suggested were as follows:

    a) That the federal government would never accept the delegation clause and that they should be deleted (Saskatchewan and Alberta). This was agreed.

    b) That the *non obstante* clause should cover fundamental freedoms as well as legal rights and equality rights. Alberta was very firm on this point, both because of their position and also because they believed it was necessary to have something to bargain with if necessary. This was agreed upon.

    c) That the clause on Minority Language Education rights should be made more positive by stating that the Provinces agreeing would agree up front with provision for other provinces to join later but not be forced to have a referendum (Alberta). This was also agreed.

    d) That the parties relating to aboriginal rights should be deleted because it was not clear what they meant and that the native groups were not satisfied with the clauses anyway (British Columbia stressed this matter). This was also agreed.

- These changes were then incorporated into the second draft, following discussion with the premier by telephone (attached).

- It was agreed that the premiers should be called together and that Nova Scotia and PEI should be included. Premiers Lougheed and Bennett were not available.

- A meeting was convened at about midnight between Premier Blakeney, Premier Peckford, Premier Buchanan, Premier MacLean, Peter Meekison representing Premier Lougheed, and Mel Smith representing Premier Bennett. Also involved were the undersigned, Howard Leeson, Harry Howe of Nova Scotia, and Edmund Morris of Nova Scotia. Roy Romanow of Saskatchewan also joined in towards the end.

- The second draft was agreed to by the six provinces. Mr. Ottenheimer had had discussions during the night with Roy McMurtry of Ontario and it was felt that it would probably be acceptable to Ontario. This view was shared by most of the provinces at the meeting.

- It was unclear whether Manitoba, New Brunswick, or Quebec would agree.

- It was agreed that the Group of Eight premiers would have a meeting at 7:45 a.m. to review this draft again.

- The meeting adjourned at about 1:30 a.m.

- The next morning the premier presented the paper to the prime minister. All provinces, except Quebec, agreed.

- The prime minister made several suggestions, three of which were accepted:

  a) A five (5) year sunset clause for any legislation enacted using the "notwithstanding" clause.

  b) The deletion of the second sentence in the proposal regarding Minority Language Education rights. This was after the Provinces would not agree to his suggestion that it not be proclaimed until all had agreed.

c) The inclusion of a First Ministers Conference regarding native rights.

- New Brunswick suggested that the change regarding Mobility rights be made positive by permitting affirmative action programs when a province's employment rate was below the national average (rather than unemployment rate above). This was agreed.

- The changes were incorporated in the text and the final version was signed by the nine provinces and the federal government in the room about 1:00 p.m. (5th Floor of the Conference Centre). The French version was subsequently signed in the main Conference Hall at about 2:00 p.m.

Cyril Abery
Deputy Minister
Intergovernmental Affairs Secretariat

Ron Penney
Deputy Minister
Department of Justice

D. DOCUMENTS AT THE PATRIATION CONFERENCE

FIRST PROPOSAL

Draft Compromise

The Newfoundland Delegation and I prepared this document, but it was never presented. The proposed meeting of some provinces was to be the afternoon of November 4, but it never happened.

Wednesday Afternoon
November 4, 1981

1. Acceptance of the eight provinces' Accord.

2. Acceptance of the full Charter with two amendments.

3. (A) Those provinces which agree with minority language education agree now. Any province which disagrees with this can opt out but must hold a referendum on the issue in that province. Referendum decision will bind that province.

4. (B) An amendment to Mobility rights to permit a province to pursue affirmative action programs for job creation for its citizens until that province's unemployment rate was no greater than the national average.

SECOND PROPOSAL

This is the actual document presented to the provinces the night of November 4. The date shows November 5 because this is what we had intended to present the next day, not thinking that we would get agreement the night of the 4th with some amendments.

Constitutional Proposal
Submitted by the Government of Newfoundland
At the First Ministers Conference
Ottawa, November 5, 1981

The Government of Newfoundland, in an effort to reach an acceptable consensus on the Constitutional issue which meets the concerns of the federal government and a substantial number of provinces, submits the following proposal:

1. Patriation

2. Amending Formula

- Acceptance of the April Accord Amending Formula with the deletion of Section 3, which provides for fiscal compensation to a province which opts out of a constitutional amendment.

- This change would mean that a Province opting out would have to bear the financial consequences of its act.

3. Charter of Rights and Freedoms

- The entrenchment of the full Charter of Rights and Freedoms now before Parliament with the following changes:

a) With respect to Mobility rights, the inclusion of the right of a province to undertake affirmative action programs for socially and economically disadvantaged individuals as long as a province's unemployment rate was above the national average.

b) *Non obstante* clause covering sections dealing with legal rights and equality rights. This would make it possible for Parliament or a Legislature to override these provisions of the Charter in certain specified circumstances.

c) With respect to Minority Language Educational rights a procedure would be adopted whereby the section would come into force in any province whose legislature adopted the proposal. If within two years a legislature had not adopted the section a binding referendum would be held in that province to determine the issue. The Newfoundland Government would introduce in the House of Assembly the necessary resolution to adopt these provisions of the Charter with respect to Newfoundland.

4. The provisions of the Act now before Parliament relating to equalization and regional disparities, the rights of the aboriginal peoples, non-renewable natural resources, forestry resources, and electrical energy would be included.

THIRD PROPOSAL

This is the amended version of the previous document agreed to the night of November 4. It was presented at breakfast on November 5 and then to a full meeting later in the morning of November 5, forming the basis of the final agreement.

November 5, 1981

In an effort to reach an acceptable consensus on the Constitutional issue which meets the concerns of the federal government and a substantial number of provinces, we submit the following proposal:

1. Patriation

2. Amending Formula

   - Acceptance of the April Accord Amending Formula with the deletion of Section 3, which provides for fiscal compensation to a province which opts out of a constitutional amendment.

   - The Delegation of Legislative Authority from the April Accord is deleted.

3. Charter of Rights and Freedoms

   - The entrenchment of the full Charter of Rights and Freedoms now before Parliament with the following changes:

(a) With respect to Mobility rights, the inclusion of the right of a province to undertake affirmative action programs for socially and economically disadvantaged individuals as long as a province's unemployment rate was above the national average.

(b) *Non obstante* clause covering sections dealing with fundamental freedoms, legal rights, and equality rights. This would make it possible for Parliament or a legislature to override these provisions of the Charter in certain specified circumstances.

(c) We have agreed that the provisions of Section 23 in respect of Minority Language Education rights will apply to our provinces. Any province not agreeing to be bound by this section continues to have the right to accept the application of the section to their province at any future time.

4. The provisions of the Act now before Parliament relating to equalization and regional disparities, and non-renewable natural resources, forestry resources, and electrical energy would be included.

FINAL AGREEMENT

November 5, 1981

In an effort to reach an acceptable consensus on the Constitutional issue which meets the concerns of the federal government and a substantial number of provincial governments, the undersigned governments have agreed to the following:

1. Patriation

2. Amending Formula

- Acceptance of the April Accord Amending Formula with the deletion of Section 3, which provides for fiscal compensation to a province which opts out of a constitutional amendment.

- The Delegation of Legislative Authority from the April Accord is deleted.

3. Charter of Rights and Freedoms

   - The entrenchment of the full Charter of Rights and Freedoms now before Parliament with the following changes:

   (a) With respect to Mobility rights, the inclusion of the right of a province to undertake affirmative action programs for socially and economically disadvantaged individuals as long as a province's employment rate was below the national average.

   (b) A "notwithstanding" clause covering sections dealing with fundamental freedoms, legal rights and equality rights. Each "notwithstanding" provision would require reenactment not less frequently than once every five years.

   (c) We have agreed that the provisions of Section 23 in respect of Minority Language Education rights will apply to our provinces.

4. The provisions of the Act now before Parliament relating to equalization and regional disparities, and non-renewable natural resources, forestry resources, and electrical energy would be included.

5. A constitutional conference, as provided for in Clause 36 of the Resolution, including in its agenda an item respecting constitutional matters that directly affect the Aboriginal peoples of Canada, including the identification and definition of the rights of those peoples to be included in the Constitution of Canada, shall be provided for in the Resolution. The Prime Minister of Canada shall invite representatives of the Aboriginal peoples of Canada to participate in the discussion of that item.

Dated at Ottawa this 5th day of November, 1981.

CANADA
(Signed)
Pierre Elliott Trudeau
Prime Minister of Canada

ONTARIO
(Signed)
William G. Davis, Premier

NOVA SCOTIA
(Signed)
John M. Buchanan, Premier

NEW BRUNSWICK
(Signed)
Richard B. Hatfield, Premier

MANITOBA
(Signed)
Sterling R. Lyon, Premier
*Subject to approval of Section 3(c)
by the Legislative Assembly of Manitoba*

BRITISH COLUMBIA
(Signed)
William R. Bennett, Premier

PRINCE EDWARD ISLAND
(Signed)
J. Angus MacLean, Premier

SASKATCHEWAN
(Signed)
Allan E. Blakeney, Premier

ALBERTA
(Signed)
Peter Lougheed, Premier

NEWFOUNDLAND
(Signed)
Brian A. Peckford, Premier

E. LETTERS CONCERNING THE PATRIATION OF THE CONSTITUTION

On April 15, 1999, Professors Ted Morton and Barry Cooper authored an article carried by the *National Post* entitled "Night of the Long Knives: Who Dunnit?"

The article espouses a version of events concerning the Patriation of the Constitution November 4 and 5, 1981, that has been allowed to gain credence and which is really at variance with what actually happened. As a result of that article, my former deputy ministers of Intergovernmental Affairs, Mr. Cyril Abery, and my former deputy minister of Justice, Mr. Ron Penney, responded directly to the professors with the following letters and for the first time provided copies of the original documents that Newfoundland prepared which had led to the Agreement.

Suite 2
47 Harvey Road
St. John's, Nfld A I C 2E9
April 21, 1999

Professors Ted Morton and Barry Cooper
Political Science Department
University of Calgary

Dear Sirs:

I am writing with reference to your April 15, 1999, article in the *National Post* entitled "Night of the Long Knives: Who Dunnit?"

More specifically I refer to your statements that:

"Since when does Newfoundland broker national unity deals? Other first-hand accounts suggest that Newfoundland's role was that of delivering the message, not creating it; that its real authors are Saskatchewan Premier Allan Blakeney and his attorney general Roy Romanow. The 'Peckford document' was decisively influenced by Romanow, McMurtry, and Chrétien, and behind them stood the master puppeteer himself."

My name is Cyril Abery and I was deputy minister of Intergovernmental Affairs for the Government of Newfoundland from 1972 through 1984. As such I was intimately involved in all constitutional discussions leading up to and including the events of November 4 and 5, 1981, in Ottawa.

I do not know your sources of "other first-hand accounts," but the events of the night of November 4 and morning of November 5, as you describe them, are both totally inaccurate and misleading. Mr. Romanow, whatever his role on the overall process, was not the "instrument" of Ontario and Ottawa for "influencing/dismantling the Gang of Eight," as you state. Indeed, he was not even involved in the events of the evening of November 4 until well AFTER the so-called "Peckford document" was completed.

To help you understand the events of the afternoon/ evening of Wednesday, November 4, 1981, I am enclosing copies of a number of documents, which, to the best of my knowledge, have never been made public (although Peter Meekison, former DM, Alberta IGA was given a copy sometime in 1982 when he visited St. John's and met with Ron Penney and me).

The first enclosure is a copy of a document entitled "Constitutional Conference, Sequence of Events, November 4 and 5, 1981." This was prepared and signed jointly by Mr. Ron Penney, then deputy minister of Justice for Newfoundland and me about a week after the Constitutional Conference in Ottawa when the events were still quite fresh in our minds. We did so because even at that early date there were misleading and inaccurate accounts surfacing.

You will note from the first document that it was Howard Leeson, not Roy Romanow, who represented Saskatchewan at the meeting in the Château Laurier on the evening of November 4, 1981, and that others attending at the start were Peter Meekison of Alberta and Mel Smith of British Columbia. It was only much later in the evening (about midnight) that representatives of Nova Scotia and PEI were involved. Manitoba and Quebec were not represented at all until breakfast the next morning. Ontario and New Brunswick were also not involved, having never been part of the Group of Eight.

The second document attached is a handwritten copy of the first draft, dated November 4, 1981. The handwriting is mine and was written in conjunction with Mr. Penney in his room at the Four Seasons. This was amended as noted and typed up at the Four Seasons. Document 3 (attached) is the type-written draft which we brought over to Room 481 at the Château Laurier at 9:30 p.m. for discussion with Messrs. Leeson, Meekison, and Smith.

It is important to note that the items included in this draft were not in any way considered by us (i.e. the Newfoundland delegation) to be original ideas—far from it. Rather, they were merely a summary of what Premier Peckford and ourselves believed were the main elements of a possible compromise based on all the previous discussions and negotiations that had taken place. However, Premier Peckford fully intended to table this document at the conference the next morning if subsequent meetings that night with the others did not lead to an agreed-upon text (which they did).

Document 4 (attached) is the second draft which was agreed upon by ourselves, Peter Meekison, Mel Smith, and Howard Leeson. The changes from the first draft and the reasons for the changes are noted in Document 1. It was this second draft which was presented to and agreed upon by Premiers Peckford, Blakeney, Buchanan, MacLean, Peter Meekison representing Premier Lougheed, and Mel Smith representing Premier Bennett at about 1:00 a.m. on November 5 in the Château Laurier and subsequently presented to the conference by Premier Peckford the next morning following the breakfast meeting.

You will note from Document 1 that Mr. Romanow joined the midnight meeting towards the very end, but was not involved in any of the discussions leading up to the revised draft. Whether he subsequently had discussions with Mr. McMurtry and/or Mr. Chrétien prior to the start of the conference the next morning and brought them onside is something I have no knowledge of but is no doubt a possibility.

Finally, attached is Document 5, which is a portion of the actual agreement which was signed at the conference table on the 5th floor of the Conference Centre at about 1:00 p.m. on November 5 by the prime minister and the premiers/representatives of the nine provinces. You will note that this is in English only. The French version was the one signed before the cameras in the main Conference Hall at 2:00 p.m. (As I recall, Trudeau said something like "Let's sign it now just in case someone changes their minds on the way downstairs!")

Quite frankly, I do not know what role Mr. Romanow, Mr. McMurtry, and Mr. Chrétien played in the overall scheme of things. Undoubtedly it was significant.

However, what I do know as a fact is that they were not involved in the Château Laurier meetings on the night of November 4, nor did they play any part (overt or covert) in our deliberations that night. Unless you subscribe to the theory that all the officials, ministers, and premiers from six provinces were manipulated without even knowing it, your statement that "'the Peckford document' was decisively influenced by Romanow, McMurtry, and Chrétien, and behind them stood the master puppeteer himself" is a complete and utter myth.

If you wish to verify the sequence of events as outlined above and in the attached documents, you might wish to contact Peter Meekison who still resides in Edmonton and whom you undoubtedly know. I believe that Mel Smith still resides in Victoria and Howard Leeson in Regina, but I have lost contact with them over the last few years. Ron Penney still resides in St. John's and is currently chief commissioner and solicitor for the City of St. John's.

I am confident that they are as amazed as I am at how expertly we were all manipulated that night in Ottawa, and how we still haven't cottoned on some eighteen years later!

I would also be pleased to elaborate further should you so wish. My telephone number is (709) 738-2944. However, you should note that I will be out of the country from April until early June. I look forward to hearing from you in due course.

Best regards.

Yours truly,
Cyril Abery

And here is Mr. Penney's letter to the professors:

10 Inglis Place
St. John's, NF
A1A 4B7

April 30, 1999

Professors Ted Morton and Barry Cooper
Political Science Department
University of Calgary

Dear Sirs:

Re: November 15, 1999, Article *National Post*

Cyril Abery has given me a copy of his letter of April 21, 1999, to you with respect to the above, which accurately reflects the involvement of the Newfoundland delegation in the events referred to.

Aside from the issues of fact and the negotiating record set out in Mr. Abery's letter, there are two other serious concerns that I have with the article.

The first is a failure to attempt to contact members of the Newfoundland negotiating team, such as Cyril Abery or the undersigned, to get the "first-hand account" rather than rely solely on "other first-hand accounts." I would have thought that the only way in which a version of events can be tested against other versions is to have all versions available.

The second is the tone, perhaps unintended, of your comment: "Since when does Newfoundland broker national unity deals?" I read this as an insinuation that the members of the Newfoundland delegation were either intellectually incapable of performing such a task, or that we do not have the necessary status within Confederation to undertake such a role, either of which is equally offensive.

The Newfoundland delegation played a key role in the entire Patriation debate, defending the interests of Newfoundland within the context of our federal system, and the role of the provinces in that system. I am proud of the part we played, but I am disappointed about the myths which have arisen about what actually happened and which continue to be supported in articles such as yours.

Yours truly,
Ronald G. Penney

Thankfully, the two professors responded to Mr. Penney's letter, one actually apologizing, sort of. Given that Alberta is often unfairly criticized by the national media, people from Alberta should not criticize other provinces, and not specifically Newfoundland, one should note.

University of Calgary
Faculty of Social Sciences

April 30, 1999

Dear Mr. Penney:

Thank you for your letter of 30 April. We appreciate receiving Mr. Abery's account and supporting documents. We propose to undertake further research and interviews to try to sort out apparent inconsistencies in the various accounts.

I also want to apologize for the line about Newfoundland brokering unity deals. It was a cheap shot; similar to the ones Alberta often gets in the national media. I don't like them when they are directed at Alberta, so henceforth I will be careful not to direct them at other provinces.

Sincerely,
Ted Morton

The other letter does not come right out and use the word "apologize."

University of Calgary
Faculty of Social Sciences
Department of Political Science

May 3, 1999

Mr. Ronald Penney
19 Inglis Place
St. John's, NFLD
A1A 4L7

Dear Mr. Penney:

Thank you for your faxed letter of 30 April regarding the piece Ted Morton and I wrote for the *National Post*.

You are, of course, quite correct to insist that we ought to have contacted all the participants in the original conference. We relied on published accounts, and Mr. Abery's notes and other materials he made available were not published.

Second, there was no intention to cast into doubt the intellectual resources of the officials of any of the delegations. There was (and I speak only for myself) an intention to call into question the honesty or perhaps the straightforwardness of the prime minister. In my opinion, he was the most Machiavellian of our prime ministers. Not too long ago Lloyd Axworthy remarked that he was surprised at the extent of evilness of the president of Yugoslavia. He clearly underestimated something. I would submit that the premiers and perhaps their staff underestimated something with respect to Pierre Trudeau. This is not a matter of intellect (though Trudeau is very smart) but of integrity. The question of the timing and significance of Trudeau's offer of a referendum, for example, has yet to be explained, at least to my satisfaction.

Perhaps at some future occasion it may be possible to gather together the participants and compare recollections and interpretations.

In any event, thank you again for writing.

Cordially,
Barry Cooper, FRSC
Professor

There are several things that are of interest to me about this letter. Of course, there really isn't an apology, although an acknowledgement that their research for the article was shoddy given that they failed to contact people who were actually in the room when the patriation deal was being created. Sadly, academia feeds off just some facts and a lot of myth and it makes for great conspiracy theories—lots of articles but poor scholarship. To continue to advance the proposition of behind-the-scenes manipulation by Trudeau in light of the evidence of those who actually were participants is really a stretch. And finally, the so-called "first-hand accounts" phrase has now been clarified as I mentioned earlier; there was only one account, that of Mr. Romanow, who arrived on the night of November 4, late and after the agreement had been completed.

I also responded to the article by writing directly to the *National Post*, who carried it in their April 27, 1999, edition.

Over the years, I have read the views of a number of commentators on the events surrounding the Patriation of our Constitution. All of them I have found were either wrong or in some cases incomplete. I kept notes at the time of this important occasion and in due course I will make them public. For now, I would like to make a few points concerning the article by Ted Morton and Barry Cooper ("Night of the Long Knives: Who Dunnit?" April 15).

1. The so-called Peckford Document was prepared by me through the night of November 4 and presented the next morning at the breakfast meeting and subsequently to the formal gathering.

2. The statement "other first-hand accounts" suggest that Newfoundland's role was that of delivering the message, not creating it, which is untrue. Many of the provincial delegations discussed through the evening and night various elements that they thought might be probable compromises.

3. The statement "'the Peckford Document' was decisively influenced by Romanow, McMurtry, and Chrétien" is untrue. During that evening and night, ideas being advanced by all the provincial delegations were discussed, and it was later, in reviewing the major elements, that the document was prepared.

4. The theme of trickery by Prime Minister Trudeau—the theme of the article—is not how I would characterize the events.

5. While I agree with Mr. Lougheed that there was no desire

or attempt by the Group of Seven to exclude Quebec, we should have tried harder to keep Quebec involved.

A. Brian Peckford

Of course when I say me, I really mean the Newfoundland Delegation, specifically Minister Gerald Ottenheimer, Deputy Ministers Cyril Abery and Ronald Penney, and adviser Cabot Martin. A document was prepared by us and presented on the evening of November 4, first to Alberta, Saskatchewan, and British Columbia, and then later that evening to PEI and Nova Scotia. The PEI attorney general contacted Manitoba. The document was finalized, with some adjustments, in the early morning (1:00–1:30 a.m.), presented to eight provinces at breakfast (New Brunswick and Ontario were not a part of the group), and then approved by the breakfast meeting to be presented by me to the full conference later that morning. It was and formed the basis of the Patriation Agreement.

F. FURTHER LETTERS CONCERNING THE CONSTITUTION

I was out of the country in February when an article appeared in the *Globe and Mail* headlined "Senior U.S., Canadian judges spar over judicial activism." In that article Judge Binnie made some incorrect remarks about my position during the constitutional meetings of 1980 and 1981. Luckily, a person saw the article and sent it to me. I wrote Judge Binnie the following letter on March 20, 2007:

The Honourable Mr. Justice William Ian Corneil Binnie
Judge
Supreme Court of Canada
301 Wellington Street
Ottawa, Ontario
K1A 0J1

Dear Mr. Binnie:

In an article ("Senior U.S., Canadian judges spar over judicial activism") in the *Globe and Mail* newspaper of Saturday, February 17, 2007, one paragraph says:

> Judge Binnie cited an attempt by former Newfoundland Premier Brian Peckford in the early 1980s to have his province's right to control fisheries written in the constitution. When former Prime Minister Pierre Trudeau asked how he could possibly balance fish against human rights, he quoted Mr. Peckford as saying, "That's your problem."

Now, of course I do not know if this is an accurate quote by the paper of what you said. However, I have not seen any comment to the paper from you denying this quote. I assume it to be correct, therefore, and know that if in fact this is wrong you will be sure to set matters straight.

I have no recollection of us ever meeting. Although you might have been amongst the bevy of counsel at the federal-provincial Patriation talks, I do not recall your presence.

I find it very disturbing that you would use such a quote from one party to an alleged happening without knowing the views of the other party referenced in the quote. It just might be that the second party may not agree, either having a totally different version of the conversation or indicating that such a conversation never occurred.

There were many things said in the heady days of the constitutional Patriation talks of the early 1980s, in many formal and informal meetings.

However, at no time do I remember such an exchange with the prime minister of the time. It was not uncharacteristic of the prime minster to "set up" such a question to try and make something that was contained in the question a fact.

For example, at one public forum carried by national TV, the prime minister had tried to link my constitutional position with Quebec's because I had voiced some support for an unrelated Quebec social program.

I do remember Mr. Trudeau saying that fish swim; hence, it is all about national and international matters and provincial involvement is out of the question. Whereupon I retorted, "yes, from offshore Newfoundland to inshore Newfoundland!" Sometimes legal niceties get in the way of real things.

And if I had to quote some of the things I remember that were said in these meetings in the cut and thrust of debate, which, I suspect, occurs among judges in the consideration of a decision, and to say that such comments represented a given position, then the chance of fruitful debate and reaching a consensus would be small indeed.

We all knew that it was not a question of a particular federal-provincial right versus "human rights." Rather, we understood that the prime minister and many other parties at the table were desirous of adding to the constitution in the Patriation process, some advocating a Charter of Rights and Freedoms and others, at the same time, requesting consideration of other matters to be changed or added to the Constitution. There were provinces that were desirous of changes/additions as it related to non-renewable resources, for example, resulting in the addition of Part VI, Section 92A. There were other issues like regional disparities and equalization (Part 3, Section 36) and aboriginal rights (Part 2, Section 35) that were added.

But even more to the point of the quote, that Newfoundland was entertaining some kind of strategy of bargaining various rights, let me quote from a Government of Newfoundland public document dated August 18, 1980, entitled "Towards the Twenty First Century—Together: The Position of the Government of Newfoundland Regarding Constitutional Change":

> The entrenchment of democratic rights and fundamental freedoms is a means of giving explicit constitutional recognition to the values which have served Canada well. Newfoundland, therefore, supports a Charter of Rights which will entrench the democratic and fundamental freedoms of Canadians. (p. 9)

No ifs ands or buts, no bargaining! This was 1980, long before the meetings and debates among the first ministers took place that led to the 1982 Constitution Act. So contrary to bargaining rights, the province was clear from an early date on the Charter, and the federal government had this document.

It is true that Prime Minister Trudeau was agitated with tiny Newfoundland vociferously arguing for a realignment of powers in Fisheries, a more balanced approach to the management of the resource between the two levels of government. I mean, it is one thing for a number of the provinces to be arguing for strengthening the Non-Renewable Resources provision, but Newfoundland on Fisheries and more balanced and joint decision making? That was quite another! How dare they? It sort of took him off his game plan and made him cranky. And, of course, add to that the fact that we were seeking some fairness in hydro transmission and had just discovered oil offshore that we were saying should be treated the same as if it was on land, and you have the makings of an exasperated prime minister whose real interests were Patriation and the Charter. He knew there would be trouble on his western flank, but on his eastern flank too?!

This leads me to the other equally disturbing part of the quote where you say I was trying "to have his province's right to control fisheries written into the Constitution." It is hard not to read this as you saying that the Province was looking to control the fishery. As you can tell from the above considerations, the Province was looking for more say over fisheries matters—a sharing of responsibilities, not control. The 1980 document already referred to provides a full description of the Province's position. It is detailed and too lengthy for this letter. However, some points must be quoted, all from page 18: "The Government of Newfoundland is not requesting exclusive provincial legislative jurisdiction relating to Fisheries. Rather, the proposal requests a sharing of the legislative jurisdiction."

Secondly, "the Government of Newfoundland recognizes the legitimate role of the federal government in many aspects of the fisheries and the degree of provincial involvement required would not undermine this legitimate federal involvement."

And thirdly, "the proposal made would not 'balkanize' the fisheries or lead to over-fishing because the federal government would retain full authority regarding the conservation of fish stocks."

I now realize the difficult job of historians, and one of the reasons I find it necessary to write this letter. While we all know that there is a time to advance one's own particular agenda, and that sometimes it may infringe upon how some view what is the "larger good," I can assure you that those involved in the Patriation process knew and understood the local, provincial, and national perspective and how such weighty matters are an evolving process and why, in the end, a deal was struck. In my particular case, even without any changes on fisheries, in the last hours the Newfoundland delegation that I led made two written proposals that assisted in the final successful outcome.

Honourable A. Brian Peckford
Qualicum Beach, BC

Judge Binnie replied on March 28 on Supreme Court of Canada stationary.

Dear Mr. Peckford:

Thank you for your letter referring to an article that appeared in the *Globe and Mail* on February 17, 2007. The background you provide is most interesting. As you may have gathered, the topic of my conference speech was not at all what the *Globe and Mail* emphasized. I enclose a copy of what I prepared in advance for the translators.

In 1980 and 1981, I was in Ottawa having been retained to so some work for the Department of Justice on (amongst other things) the Constitutional File. I, therefore, followed with some interest the public discussions. I do recall quite distinctly reading Trudeau's comment to the effect "How am I supposed to bargain fish against human rights?" reported in (if I recall) the *Globe and Mail*. I remember it because my wife snorted with amusement when she read it. It certainly sounded like an authentic "Trudeau-ism" and made sense only in the context of Newfoundland's desire to achieve greater control over the fisheries at the time. It was certainly how I think it was interpreted by many of the lawyers in the federal Department of Justice.

In the debate with Justice Scalia, I wasn't pretending to address any point of historical controversy. I was responding to Scalia's argument that "originalism" could be followed without "freezing rights," because if the people want to "update" a bill of rights they can always do so by constitutional amendment. As you know better than most, constitutional amendment is not a very feasible option in this country. The discussion on that point was brief and quite peripheral to our respective concerns.

Yours sincerely,
Ian Binnie

The Honourable Mr. Justice William Ian Corneil Binnie
Judge, Supreme Court of Canada
301 Wellington Street
Ottawa, Ontario
K1A 0J1

On April 25 I responded to his letter.

Dear Mr. Binnie:

Thank you for your letter dated March 28, 2007.

You mention my letter was undated. I sent the letter by three modes: regular mail, email, and fax. Both the email and fax record the date and hence why in my typing I excluded it.

You say that what was being talked about at the conference was much different than what the *Globe and Mail* covered. I hope you will tell them so. But, nevertheless, the story did quote you as saying "Judge Binnie cited an attempt by former Newfoundland premier Brian Peckford."

Thank you for clarifying that you know of no quote from me in response to what you say was a quote from Mr. Trudeau stating: "How am I supposed to bargain fish against human rights?" I take it, given that there is no mention in your response, that you now agree that Newfoundland was not seeking "control" over the fishery.

As described to you in my letter, the Newfoundland position (support of a Charter without conditions) was made quite clear in a public document (published in August) before the meetings in the fall of 1980. Hence, Mr. Trudeau's statement was a false representation of the situation, slick but inaccurate. It was quite likely a deliberate ploy to denigrate one of the Gang of Eight, which, of course, would gain great favour in many quarters of central Canada at the time. The juxtaposition of fish and human rights sounds so far-fetched to the average person; how outlandish and unreasonable.

The press would "lap it up." In this context, yes, the quote is likely a Trudeau-ism.

It is unfortunate, therefore, in light of the evidence, that, although not uttered, such a type of statement ("That's your problem") is seen by you and, at the time, by members of the federal Department of Justice as reflective of Newfoundland's response.

In my experience the *Globe and Mail* newspaper, as a source, is very unreliable, having on two specific occasions carried stories about me (one that had me at one time being president of the Provincial Teachers Association, and the other regarding a free trip I was supposed to have taken on a local airline), both of which were shown to be completely false. And, of course, this very exchange was sparked by a *Globe and Mail* article that you say "the topic of my conference speech was not at all what the *Globe and Mail* emphasized."

There are many other myths (in addition to the two you espouse) circulating about those last days and hours that led to the Constitutional agreement. For example, upon randomly going to a website on constitutional patriation, I note that it talks of only four provinces being involved during the last night. This is false. Seven of the provinces were directly involved that night, and all ten the next morning. And this site talks of providing information to students! The Canadian Encyclopedia website does not record proposals made by Newfoundland at all. Similarly, the book *National Deal* by Robert Sheppard and Michael Valpy talk of officials meeting on the final night. In fact, four premiers were present.

A. Brian Peckford

The comments of Judge Binnie at the conference referenced in the *Globe and Mail* article and his statement in his letter are startling, given that they come from a person who held such high office. Even though he states that the *Globe and Mail* did not carry what he emphasized, he does not deny saying what the paper says, and more galling even when confronted with the evidence of Newfoundland's position (a written document of August, 1980), one that he should have read, given that he was working with the federal government on the Constitutional File, and further, that he had no evidence that I said what he alleged in the paper—he makes no attempt to acknowledge he was wrong.

Cunningly, he moves from the position of "control" of the fishery in the remarks quoted in the paper to "greater control" in his letter, rather than forthrightly saying he was wrong on the point. Factually, this, too, is wrong; to be utterly accurate, it was going from nearly no control to some control. No small distinction! And it was not Newfoundland's response, "That's your problem" at the time, as he continues to suggest. It was a preconceived notion that most federal bureaucrats had about Newfoundland's position. It was their attitude of Newfoundland's position, but it was not Newfoundland's position.

APPENDIX II:
ATLANTIC ACCORD PROVISION (SECTION 42) — CANADA NEWFOUNDLAND OFFSHORE DEVELOPMENT FUND

List of Projects and Value

1. Centre for Earth Resource Research $27,085,000

2. Offshore Survival Centre $6,315,000

3. Skills Training Projects $4,500,000

4. Computer-Aided Engineering Design Centre $1,150,000

5. Career Development Awards Program $18,000,000

6. Centre for Offshore and Remote Medicine and Telemedicine
   $2,883,500

7. Centre for Cold Ocean Resources Engineering $7,500,000

8. Centre of Excellence in Marine Signal Processing
   $7,600,000

9. Research and Development Block Fund $7,649,965

10. Offshore Technology Transfer Opportunities Program
$5,000,000

11. Petroleum Training Program $22,600,000

12. Industrial Infrastructure Planned Program $733,546

13. Management Training Program Marystown Shipyard Ltd.
$1,000,000

14. Infrastructure Planning Marystown Shipyard $343,341

15. Enhancement of Fabrication Facility Marystown Shipyard
$40,000,000

16. Access Road to Cow Head Facility $573,228

17. Administrative Support Program $1,492,500

18. Marine Offshore Simulation Training Centre $12,429,810

19. Segmented Wavemaker Institute for Marine Dynamics
$3,500,000

20. Institute for Social and Economic Research $292,972

21. Community Information Centre Program Agreement $449,980

22. Public Legal Information Association of Newfoundland
$98,000

23. Hibernia Onshore Site Development and Engineering
$95,000,000

24. C-Core Modelling Centrifuge Facility $3,556,200

25. Hibernia Operational Training Program 1 $990,625

26. Hibernia Operational Training Program 2 $689,220

27. Vinland Industries Ltd. $1,793,095

28. Arnold's Cove Commercial/Industrial Park $588,617

29. Ultimateast Data Communications $1,444,326

30. Ocean Engineering Research Centre MUN $776,000

31. Marketing Assistance, Marine Institute Memorial University
$206,000

32. Bull Arm Marketing $750,000

33. Upgrading Turf Point Wharf $2,032,174

34. Instrumar Multi Phase Meter $1,047,020

35. Canadian Centre for Marine Communication Newfoundland
Geomatics Project $2,500,000

36. Cabot College Petroleum Products Training Capability
Enhancement Project $2,601,500

37. Centre for Cold Ocean Resources Engineering (Phase II)
$3,500,000

38. Dynamic Positing Project $550,400

39. Turf Wharf Phase II $466,895

40. Industry Development Block Fund $3,606,085

41. Enhancement of Growth of Marine Technology $2,600,000

42. Refurbishment of Marine Institute South Side facilities
$3,105,000

43. Refurbishment of the Skills Training Fund $1,000,000

APPENDIX III

Atlantic Accord Negotiating Team:

Cyril Abery (Chair)   David Vardy
Cabot Martin   John Fitzgerald
Ron Penney   Barbara Knight
David Norris

There were many support personnel including Jim Thistle of the
Department of Justice.

Hibernia Statement of Principles Team:

Peter Kennedy (Chair)   Clyde Granter
Gordon Gosse   Lorne Spracklin
Hal Stanley   Gilbert Gill
Cyril Abery   Ron Penney
Cabot Martin

Hibernia Statement of Principles Technical Team:

John Cummings
Ray Grouchy
David Oake

APPENDIX IV: PEOPLE OF NOTE

JOHN CROSBIE

The first time I met John was when I ran for the presidency of the Green Bay Liberal Association in 1968. John had attended the meeting of the district association to elect an executive, these officers to be delegates to the announced Leadership Convention of the party. Premier Smallwood was also in attendance (as I relate elsewhere in this book) and took a characteristic intrusive role in the outcome of the meeting. Strangely enough, John did not intervene as one would think he would to ensure that the premier remained objective rather than brazenly supporting my opponent in the election of the president. Anyway, because of my disillusionment with Smallwood and the dictatorial way the so-called new Liberal Party was being organized, contrary to all the public statements Smallwood had made about it being a democratic party, it was later that I joined Crosbie's leadership team upon an invitation from him to become involved.

This was a wonderful learning experience for me as I criss-crossed the central, northeast, and eastern part of the island (Baie Verte to Clarenville) from late June to October looking to attract people to the Crosbie campaign, get them organized and attend nomination meetings to get Crosbie delegates elected to the Leadership Convention. Crosbie at that time, and which is no doubt a shock to many now, was a very poor public speaker. Even in a one-on-one situation he was aloof, and that habit of closing his eyes while he spoke or someone was speaking to him drove us campaign people crazy as we would hear people complain about this weird behavioural phenomenon after the meetings that John attended. Everyone knew he was a lawyer, must be smart, was a minister in the Smallwood government, and came from one of the most well-known merchant families in the province, but to see this type of behaviour in one looking for support seemed most unusual and downright odd.

I remember one sojourn with him in Twillingate/New World Island where we had arranged for him to attend a meeting in order to assist us in gathering some supporters in a very Smallwood-leaning district. That was a mistake. There was simply no way we could compete here with the madly loyal Smallwood supporters, whose anti-merchant bias was on full display and who, even when confronted with some solid arguments for Crosbie, would often cite his inability to give a stirring speech. I remember our car ride back to Gander that night with John insisting on driving at lightning speed over miles of dirt road. I thought at any moment we would end up in a ditch or worse—crash into a utility pole or an oncoming vehicle.

Concerning my later unfortunate incident with John where he insisted that he had forgotten our earlier arrangement with the campaign, I tried to put it behind me. Of course, I worked for him as a sort of executive assistant to the Liberal Reform Group (after our agreement to continue to be paid was honoured) from November, 1968, until the next June. It was here that I really got my first glimpse of John up close. He was, and remained, as most people know, a hard worker, many times involved in the minutia that should be left to others. And he was stubborn. He came to most decisions, then, on his own, and then gathered people around to agree with him and to assist in implementation. So, while I kept in touch throughout that time with many of the wounded Crosbie supporters, there was little research that I was asked to do. This was a shame, since here I had an office on New Gower Street, a secretary, and time to assist more fully in seeking out information and researching various issues that were coming before the legislature.

My next encounter, of course, was serving with him in Frank Moores's caucus after the March, 1972, election. And from 1974 to 1976 I served in Frank Moores's Cabinet and saw John in action on that level. Once again John distinguished himself for his hard work but also for his obstinacy: when he took a position it was impossible to move him away from it no matter what substantive or political reasons given. This was always evident, but I remember most particularly on the Labrador Linerboard issue, where he was the lead minister, and the Brinco water rights issue. Interestingly, in his book *No Holds Barred*, John characteristically deals with these issues as if he alone was involved, when in fact Cabinet ministers, the premier, and the full Cabinet were party and involved with these important issues.

John left the provincial Cabinet in 1976 and ran in a by-election in October, won and became a Member of the Progressive Conservative Opposition led by Joe Clark. During his time as Joe Clark's minister of Finance and Newfoundland's representative (1979) in the federal Cabinet, nothing stands out, except for Mr. Clark's commitment letter regarding offshore (a pyrrhic victory given the short seven-month life of the government) and the fisheries matters which remained unresolved. So the great hopes that we had for Newfoundland's prospects with our "fish and chips" ministers in Ottawa came tumbling down with the defeat of the government in Parliament as a result of the budget of our very own John Crosbie. I guess it is here that one sees demonstrated the hamartia as described earlier—his obstinacy, and I guess at the same time Joe Clark's as well in his lack of leadership in not facing down his Finance minister.

Perhaps the two most interesting (at the time frustrating beyond belief) incidents concerned two significant events: first, my leadership run, and second, the first meeting as premier and he as federal minister.

My leadership team was very organized and we were lining up prominent people who would support us. Frankly, we did not have that many. Ours was mainly a grassroots campaign. But John Crosbie, given that I had been involved with his leadership campaign against Smallwood, knowing that he was not enamoured with most of the other candidates, and the fact that many of the people who had supported Crosbie were supporting me, we figured this would not be a difficult thing—only the timing. Well, it proved to be a very difficult thing. By the time Crosbie did throw his support my way— after a personal visit from my campaign manager, Frank Ryan, who had also been involved with Crosbie—it really was too late to have an impact. We had all the hard work done. One of the major turning points was when three very prominent PCs came out supporting me: Bill Marshall, Gerry Ottenheimer, and Dr. John Collins. These three individuals were known as honest, bright, and very devoted Conservatives. They were to play pivotal roles in my administrations. We were confident that with a good speech at the convention, we would be in there competing for top spot. This is another sad story in my relationship with John. Why he was holding out, I honestly do not know. No doubt there was a tinge of jealousy since it was no secret that John really wanted the premiership, not the position of federal minister for Newfoundland. And here was a rural fellow, who had been one of a number of campaign managers on his own leadership campaign, now challenging for the very job for which he yearned.

With the leadership concluded and after taking over the reins as premier, the federal election of May, 1979, produced a minority government but with the federal Conservatives in the majority, Joe Clark as prime minister, for whom I had campaigned in his successful leadership bid, and John Crosbie as minister of Finance. It was customary (and in this particular circumstance assumed to be a very pleasant affair) for the premier and the federal minister to get together at an early moment to review the outstanding bilateral issues existing between the two orders of government. The date was set and we were to meet in St. John's. There was a hitch. I was informed by my press secretary, Frank Petten, that John (Mr. Crosbie) would meet me at a suite in Hotel Newfoundland. How unusual! Another fit of pique, the stubborn streak? Of course, I let it be known in no uncertain terms that there would be only one setting for the meeting: the premier's office at the Confederation Building. And, of course, John relented and the meeting proceeded, as all meetings with like participants have proceeded before and since.

John published a book in 1997 entitled *No Holds Barred*. I never read it then. At the time I was tied up in some project that took up my time. I remember, however, a number of people contacting me, asking if I had read the book, since, they said, he was hostile to me. I sort of passed this off as John's bluster and that was that. Well, of course, for this book, given that I was to discuss John, I was forced to get his book and read it. What a shocker. Stupidly, I had not read it, and therefore had not responded to the many false statements, half-truths, and selected comments ascribed to me. It really is an egocentric tirade: how good he was and how bad most other people were. In retrospect, that was John. I emailed Alvin Hewlett, my former chief of staff and former Member of Green Bay, the following:

> Believe it or not, I did not read Crosbie's book when it came out in 1997. I think I was travelling doing the salmon inquiry for the Government of British Columbia. Anyway, I have just read it, a requirement if I am to talk about Crosbie in my book. Wow—what a nasty, or should I say, visceral attack on me and through me the province and the citizens in those sections where my name is mentioned. What perhaps is most disconcerting is that many statements are factually incorrect, others partial truths, and other phrases a deliberate attempt at cherry-picking. And hardly any of it with supporting documentation. All and all, a disappointing, ego-driven tirade. I am surprised that Geoffrey Stevens would allow his name to be associated with something so second-rate.

I honestly did not realize that John could be so blinded, one-sided, and bitter once he began to write about politics and people.

It's a bit ironic to title a book *No Holds Barred* when it is so obviously selected holds which are open and others which are not. John's sudden loss of memory or omission of his breech of trust to me, his late coming to my leadership, his absence at a crucial meeting on the offshore with then Finance minister Michael Wilson, the just-referenced meeting in my office, are some of the holds that are barred. Yet he remembers I was elected secretary of the Green Bay Liberal Association. By the way, it really was vice-president! When one chooses such a title for a book, it's open season I'm afraid.

And, of course, no one could make a political decision on their own if associated with John, since he knew all. For example, in his book in referencing the Green Bay Riding Association meeting where I was elected vice-president, John goes on to say, "Like thousands of other Liberals he followed me into the Conservative party" (p. 78). There's the arrogance for you—and untrue. I had joined the PC Party before John and at the time phoned and told him so. Similarly, in speaking of his federal leadership plans, he says: "I had made a point of getting Newfoundland premier Brian Peckford on my side . . ." meaning, I suppose, there was work to be done to get my support (p. 209). There was never any doubt about my support even if I was privately reluctant—he was from Newfoundland and being loyal to the province and potentially having a Newfoundlander prime minister far overshadowed other concerns at the time. And John knew that.

The book is full of personal attacks. On page 239 he references "the ruthlessness of Brian Peckford," but shows an absence of evidence to substantiate such an appellation. The greatest sin, you see, was to oppose John Crosbie on anything. He took that personally because in his mind he was always right, so how could anyone have a credible opposing view (not unlike Mr. Trudeau)? Unlike both Moores and Mulroney, where it was possible to hold an opposing view on one thing but work co-operatively on other things, Crosbie could not engage in such activity. This, then, often led to hyperbole, such as when he labels me on page 354 as "selfish and ungrateful." Funny how Ottawa so quickly federalizes people. Ironically, John had fallen into the Smallwoodian mindset of Ottawa's manna from heaven theme; we were given things from Ottawa, never entitled to them. And don't dare criticize on an issue if you had achieved something for the province on another unrelated issue.

On page 55 he goes so far as to say he "wanted to wreak vengeance on them [Peckford and Wells] and their miserable governments for their appalling attitudes." This is pretty strong stuff, since it is not much of a mental stretch to conclude that he was also insulting the people of the province. It's reminiscent of his outbursts later in Marystown and St. John's over the fishery; Marystown concerning his support of some mainland corporate interests and the other when he was announcing the northern cod moratorium as minister of Fisheries.

On page 355 he states that I wanted to bar non-Newfoundlanders from fishing for northern cod. Wrong! The policy was Newfoundlanders first, because of the principles of adjacency and historic use, principles well recognized around the world; if after this was achieved there were still fish available, then other Canadians. He criticizes me for trying to get the best deals possible for the reopening of the Come By Chance refinery and the Lower Churchill. I plead guilty!

Need I say more?

FRANK MOORES

Frank was different. Crosbie and Moores came from wealthy families, both drank a lot—Moores, his Scotch, Crosbie, the dark rum—attended private schools in Upper Canada, and were used to getting their own way. After that the similarities ceased. Frank was easygoing where Crosbie was serious; Frank liked a frolicking good time, Crosbie a no-show for such things; Frank his many women, Crosbie devoted to Jane; and Frank an aversion to hard work, Crosbie attracted to it.

It would be a huge mistake, however, to imply that Frank lacked brains. He was quick, had an excellent memory, and could master a lot of material quickly when he put his mind to it. It was getting his mind to it, and holding it—that was the problem.

I remember when I first worked in the premier's office, having been appointed special assistant in 1973. I think I also acted as parliamentary assistant. Anyway, the office was in disarray. Charlie Brett (the then Member for Trinity South and good friend) was doing his best to arrange things. It was a mighty task. Just getting responses out to letters written to the premier seemed like a mighty task. And it wasn't being done in a timely manner. On one of my first days I was in the premier's private office (I think just me) talking to the premier. I insisted on a one-on-one because I wanted to tell him just how bad the organization of the office was and get his okay to bring some sense to the place. I used as an example his desk before me, cluttered in piles with letters—some opened, some not opened—and that this needed to be cleaned up.

"Well, Pecky, just look at you; trying to change the world. My son, if you can do it, no problem. You got my blessing."

It was this nonchalance that would frustrate one as you tried to do something that would help him and all of us. He often just didn't seem to care that much. And then there were times when he would get this burst of energy for the job, and for a few days he was on top of everything. And great to be around.

His womanizing was legion. While serving as his parliamentary assistant I had occasion to be ordered by him, while seated in the legislature, to proceed to the legislature gallery and escort a woman, unknown to me, to his office on the eighth floor. I did and returned to the legislature. In a few minutes, the premier left his chair and informed me that he would be away for a little while and proceeded to his office via the private elevator. Within the hour he was back, looking refreshed, showered, with a clean shirt and tie, and gave us all the impression he was very much interested in the ongoing debate. On campaign stops around the province he was known, at overnight stays, to have access to women of the community. And I remember I was to accompany him and his press secretary to Ottawa for a conference via Montreal. The conference was on a Tuesday, but we three were going to Montreal on Friday for the weekend, or so we were informed.

And he could be generous. I remember when I finally persuaded him to come to my district to be the guest speaker (he had never been there before) at the PC District Association annual meeting, dinner and dance. Of course, he almost didn't make it, showing up late by helicopter on a misty evening just before dark (and well fortified with alcohol).

A few days before, when I had reminded him of the event, he said to me, "Well, what are the problems in your district?"

I responded, "Premier, there are many: road problems, forestry issues, health care, and so on. If you just mention that you are aware of the road, forestry, fishing, and heath care issues, and that you will be tackling them with me, that will be fine."

"No, no," Frank said, "What can we do right now? What do you want?"

Taken aback, I stumbled and uttered that a very dedicated group had been working with me and the Department of Health on a new long-term care facility for Springdale and that they had a lot of the groundwork already completed.

"Well, that's it," he said, "I will announce it."

After his arrival and just before we headed to the event, Frank said to me, "What is it that I am going to announce?"

I was flabbergasted. He had already forgotten! I explained to him about the nursing home facility and all the work that had been done, the involvement of the people of the town, the Department of Health, and all related organizations. I also mentioned there were many other issues that over the years we would have to tackle, like forestry, the fishery, and the local ferry service.

Off we went to the event and Frank suddenly became very animated, shook hands, mixed with the people, and everyone was in a good mood and happy to meet the premier. Dinner followed; no problems. Then the meeting was handled quickly and I introduced Frank.

He got up and began his speech—how glad he was to be here, wonderful town, great people, and so on. And he knows there are issues with roads, ferries, forestry, and the fishery, and that he and Brian are going to tackle them together. He also knows that the people of the town have been working hard to get a nursing home here in Springdale for the area.

"Well," he said, "I am announcing that this new facility has been approved by government."

The audience was in shock! No one thought that this would happen so quickly. There was still some work to do and the Department of Health was very careful in not getting the people's hopes too high that it would happen that soon. Hey, but here it was, announced by the premier. And that was that.

Of course, I had to do a lot of shuffling in government to see that this commitment was realized; the Department of Health had to get approval from Cabinet, but this was the premier and he had committed government to it and that was final. Frank liked doing things like that and he did them often during his time as premier.

Another time when I was Municipal Affairs minister, he asked me to accompany him to his district. There was a fair amount of negativity coming from his district that he really had not visited, and this visit was to try to counter this local problem. Well, we ended up meeting with all the municipal councils on the north shore of the Bay of Islands. What a whirlwind series of events. At each meeting Frank would quickly commit to almost whatever the councils asked for. I was there interrupting and trying to smooth things out and keep some kind of lid on the dollar value and number of commitments that were being made.

Unfortunately, Frank could scheme and things were not always as they seemed. One of his favourites was to have his driver bring the premier's car over early in the morning and park it in the premier's parking spot. Everyone thought the premier was in early to work when he was still home, recuperating, often from a previous night's intense activity. Additionally, he seemed to enjoy small numbers (I think he was more comfortable), and small Cabinet cliques and other business cliques developed early on in his premiership. There were always lots of rumours and backstabbing going on. This manifested itself in many unsavoury ways: one being the Public Works scandal involving a local electrical contractor and a later suspicious fire at one Cabinet minister's apartment, as well as illegal fishing and hunting escapades. One of my first acts as premier was to rid ourselves of the fishing camps the government had in Labrador, which were often misused for partying and not legitimate government entertaining of dignitaries.

Let me record three particular instances on this theme.

I was only minister of Municipal Affairs and Housing a short while when early one morning I heard footsteps coming down the long hallway to my office. It was early and this had been the first time I heard someone else coming in that early. So I was suspicious. I got up from my desk, moved out into the hallway, and looked around. Two men were coming toward me. Who should this be but the premier, Frank Moores, and one Craig Dobbin (now deceased), a local influential businessman. Was I surprised! I called out good morning and as they got nearer I invited them into my office, more than certain it was me they were here to see.

There was this prime piece of land that Newfoundland and Labrador Housing Corporation had that interested Mr. Dobbin; the premier indicated that I should talk to the corporation about having it released and "handled in such a way" that Mr. Dobbin would get it. Well, I was taken aback by the subject and perhaps as much by the brazen approach the two were prepared to make to get the land. I indicated that this did not seem like it should be considered and that therefore doing such a thing was really something I was not prepared to do. Arm twisting ensued, but I stood firm, perhaps more so as the implication of what was being proposed sank in. It became clear to the two as I read their faces that they realized they had made a tactical error, thinking that I would bend under such a visit. So almost as quickly as they appeared they left with Frank, mumbling, "Well, Pecky, get on to the Housing Corporation today. I'm sure you can do something here to help." I bid them a good morning. I did nothing about it. And Frank never raised it again.

Frank realized that I would not compromise on matters that were obviously unethical and bordering on the illegal. So other issues were kept from me that fell into this category as I continued in his Cabinet.

The sale of the Stephenville linerboard mill is a good example of this. This mill, poorly conceived by Smallwood, and unfortunately pursued and executed by Moores/Crosbie, was finally closed (after more than $300 million of taxpayers' money) and then put up for sale. Given that it was owned by the government, a public process was instituted to see if there were any buyers manufacturing other paper products to run it, using wood from the island, not from Labrador, one of the fatal flaws of Linerboard's demise. I found out (how, I do not remember; perhaps from another minister or a public servant), after the process had been under way for some time and the selection of a buyer was imminent, that there was likely "not so nice behind-the-scenes arrangements" going on that very day. This was late morning and I checked to see where the premier was and found out he was meeting in his dining room with several ministers. I barged into the meeting. I immediately inquired if the meeting was about the sale of the mill and was told that it was being discussed. I indicated that from information I was given, Abitibi-Price had submitted the best bid and that this seemed like a simple decision. Well, the premier and a number of the ministers began some advocacy of another bid by Consolidated-Bathurst, a company then owned by the prominent "behind-the-scenes mover and shaker" Montreal businessman Paul Desmarais. As a matter of fact, while I was arguing the point, Frank placed a call to Desmarais and a conversation ensued, only part of which I could hear. It seemed as if Frank was negotiating over the phone with Desmarais. After this phone conversation I made it clear that the mill must go to the company that submitted the best bid as determined by the public servants who were analyzing it and that I would be taking such a stand at the Cabinet table and that rigging one bid to make it seem the best bid after the fact would not work. I think I then walked out of the dining room. Later at a Cabinet meeting, a recommendation came forward for the mill to be sold to the best bidder, Abitibi-Price.

Perhaps an even more galling (in the sense that this was under my ministerial responsibility) event was the issue of a hydro deal with Quebec on the existing Upper Churchill development and the development of the much discussed Lower Churchill project. Frank had patched together a framework agreement with Premier Lévesque without my knowledge, and I found out about it the evening of the signing. The announcement was to be the next day. I remember hurrying to the premier's office and inquiring as to what was happening. I was ushered into the premier's office and informed of the arrangement. This was an unbelievable circumstance. For my purposes here, it reinforces the point already made about Frank's modus operandi, his willingness to completely co-opt ministers, and the gall in thinking that everyone would just go along with what he had secretly negotiated, regardless of its merits and negative repercussions, economically or politically.

Disappointingly, Frank seemed not to get it. After doing such things and knowing I knew, he would continue in like manner. In

1978, rumours began circulating about his pending resignation. I was in his office one day during this period and he informed me that he was going to resign very shortly and he thought he should tell me. Of course, I thanked him for the courtesy. He asked whether I intended to seek the leadership. I responded that this would be a big step and did not know if I would or not; I would have to talk it over with family and friends. He quickly responded that he thought I should, that I could be assured he would not take sides in the pending leadership competition. He was adamant about this and thought such a position would be good for the party—to have a wide-open race with the retiring leader remaining on the sidelines. Well, of course I took this with a grain of salt given my previous experiences with him, but his statements were so emphatic that I half-believed him. How foolish! He had no sooner resigned when he was secretly organizing for Bill Doody, one of his ministerial confidants and leading candidate to replace him.

These kinds of experiences greatly colour my views on the man, although most would say that he was the only one at the time who could unseat Smallwood. And I believe this is true. The early days of his administration saw major change in the way government operated, and most of this was to the good, including a Public Tender Act strongly influenced by Bill Marshall, a minister in Moores's early Cabinet and later to be of tremendous assistance to me as minister of Energy.

On Frank's passing, I issued the following:

Frank Moores, Premier of the Province of Newfoundland and Labrador 1972–1979. I first met Frank Moores in the provincial election campaign of 1972. What was most striking as this point was his passion for organization of the PC Party of Newfoundland and his desire to change the way politics was conducted in the province.

I served as executive assistant and parliamentary assistant to Premier Moores from 1972 to 1974. I served in Mr. Moores's Cabinet from 1974 to 1979 in the portfolios of

Municipal Affairs and Housing, Mines and Energy, and Rural and Northern Development.

Mr. Moores delegated responsibility. This was a major sea change in the conduct of government, contrasting sharply with previous administrations in the province. While much attention over the years has been paid to his time in Ottawa as a consultant, little attention has been paid to the fundamental changes that were accomplished under his administrations.

Simply put, it was under Frank Moores's leadership that governance in the provincial government entered the twentieth century. The Public Tender Act brought accountability and transparency to the conduct of business between the private sector and government. Now companies and the public were assured that if one bid on government work that price and ability would be the criteria by which proposals were judged, and not political connections and influence.

Secondly, the strengthening of the public service, the Public Service Commission, and the organization of government were further important reforms that occurred in Mr. Moores's administrations.

Thirdly, and arguably Mr. Moores's greatest legacy, was his approach to resource development in the province. Rather than participating in the depopulation of rural Newfoundland, he actively fostered a reinvigorated rural Newfoundland through the Department of Rural Development, a bolstered Department of Fisheries, active enlightened fishery policy (which often contrasted with the federal approach and contributed to the province having influence in overall fishery policy for the first time since Confederation), and progressive forestry policy.

It was under Mr. Moores's administrations and leadership that the genesis for all future offshore oil and gas policy was formed and articulated. Mr. Moores was one of the first leaders who spoke for real provincial influence and self-reliance and who fought the federal dependency idea that had become prevalent in the first three decades of Confederation.

A. Brian Peckford

JOEY SMALLWOOD

Of course, from the time I was seven or eight years old I had heard the name "Joey Smallwood." He was a fixture in Newfoundland politics when I was growing up. He was the premier. He was the boss man. I saw him in action as a teenager at a rally in Lewisporte where he invoked admiringly the names of Sir William Whiteway and Sir Richard Squires. Of course, it was much later that I discovered the shady deals of Squires, but he was supposed to have put the hum on the Humber and Smallwood liked that. The next time I saw him was when I was prancing up Elizabeth Avenue with everyone else at the opening of the new campus of Memorial University. An additional university experience was when he showed up with full Cabinet on stage as he announced grants and salaries for students attending university. I remember it as a sort of surreal experience. I had had experience as a temporary social worker by this time and this lavish display of new money seemed so out of place given the many social problems I had experienced, not least of which was the meagre assistance that was provided to widows, children, and disabled people. Later in the House of Assembly when Smallwood sat in Opposition as head of a Liberal Reform Group, I remember debating with him late one evening about the Upper Churchill contract. It was clear that Smallwood was about the business of trying to justify, for the record, the many dubious deals in which he was involved, and of course this included the infamous contract. In true form, Smallwood went on for a long time. Finally, at one point I rose to rebut him, lamenting the lack of an escalator clause on the price being charged by Newfoundland in the contract, exclaiming that the Greeks in classical times were aware of inflation.

Two further encounters have already been related: his phone call to me during the heady days of 1971–72 and his appearance at the formation of the Green Bay Liberal Association.

One further encounter when I was premier is perhaps the most revealing.

The only living father of confederation, Joseph R. Smallwood, was still active in the early eighties attempting to complete his *Book of Newfoundland*. His company had a building off Portugal Cove Road in St. John's and several people were hired to assist Smallwood in completing the work. I wasn't impressed with the work to date on the project, but it was something Smallwood wanted to do, so several "old friends" (no doubt who had benefited from Smallwood's largess in times past) had helped finance some of it and people were hired to assist.

It was during this period that I received a frantic call (was there any other kind?) from Joey imploring me to meet with him as soon as possible because he had this fantastic opportunity for Newfoundland to describe to me—that it was something beyond the wildest dreams of the most optimistic of our citizens. Aware of Smallwood's weakness for hyperbole, I took this sudden new opportunity with the more than usual grain of salt and told him that over the next couple of days I'm sure we could meet to more fully discuss this exciting development. Well, this could not wait for a few days; it was doubtful, he insisted, if this could wait a few hours. So not unlike others before me, I succumbed to this typically brazen Smallwoodian approach. I invited him for dinner that evening at the premier's dining room at the Confederation Building. It was a night to remember! How many people have spent twelve continuous hours with the man?

The province's own flag debate was raging at the time. I had introduced a bill in the legislature which would see to it that the province had its own flag. Up to then we were using the Union Jack and I was intent on changing that. A select committee of the legislature had held public hearings, designs for the new flag were invited from the public, and the committee had reported and recommended a design created by the well-known artist Christopher Pratt.

"You can't do that!" Smallwood said as he settled in to the dining room table.

"Do what?" I said.

"You can't go ahead with that silly flag. Don't you realize you will be dead politically?"

"Well, times have changed," I responded. "I think the province is ready for it."

"This is crazy; haven't you heard the open-line shows? The Canadian Legion is against it, the Catholics will never support it. Stop it before it is too late," he shouted.

"Well, I can't stop it now, and furthermore, I don't want to stop it," I replied firmly. "We must have our own symbols; it's important for our own identity, of who we are, and what we can become. The Old Country is not this place. And all the provinces have their own flag and we must establish ourselves in every way possible."

This did not go down very well. I could hear Smallwood grumbling under his breath. The evening was off to a rocky start.

Undeterred, Smallwood continued to explain his many encounters with the veterans and the strong opposition of the Catholics to the Confederation battles in the late 1940s. They would bring the government down and I should not be picking fights with them. I should be getting on with more important issues and leave this alone.

I did not remember the next day what we had had for dinner that night; the discussion consumed everything. There was no pause.

"And I have the issue and the opportunity, right now," exclaimed Joey.

"You have?" I answered sheepishly.

"Yes I do. We are ready to open the Come By Chance refinery. Shaheen has the money arranged, I guarantee it," he proudly announced.

And so began a frenzy of discussion about the Great Refinery and

Mr. Shaheen and how only he and Mr. Shaheen could get the thing going again.

The Come By Chance refinery was the brainchild of Smallwood and Shaheen during the late sixties and early seventies and opened with great fanfare in the early seventies (I was there), with the ship the *Queen Elizabeth II* docked in Placentia Bay for the gala affair. Unfortunately, the whole enterprise failed in short order and it became at the time the largest bankruptcy in Canadian history. It was partly because of the financing required of the government that saw John Crosbie and Clyde Wells break with Smallwood and form their own Liberal Reform Group and attack the deal from the Opposition benches. After the closedown of the refinery, the Newfoundland Conservative government was able to negotiate with the Liberal government in Ottawa for Petro-Canada, then a federal Crown Corporation, to keep the assets in good standing for a period of time so that the provincial government could look for new owners. After the set period of time, the refinery could be dismantled and sold for scrap.

Given this blot on Smallwood's record, he was eager to wipe this colossal failure away. And he and Shaheen were busy trying to do just that.

Our heated discussion at the dinner table was adjourned when Smallwood invited me to his Portugal Cove Road office/residence, so that we could continue the discussion and he could show me some of the work he was doing on *The Book of Newfoundland*.

So off we go to Portugal Cove Road, less than a mile from our dinner surroundings at the Confederation Building.

After we were suitably comfortable and our wine (later cognac) was poured, I thought I would take the offensive and try and bring the matter of the refinery to a head.

"Why did you have Shaheen and his people follow me during the PC Leadership Convention and then have a suite for him right next to mine at the hotel?" I asked abruptly.

"You wouldn't talk to a great industrialist, a great friend of Newfoundland, the man who wanted to invest hundreds of millions of dollars in Newfoundland. You said that day in the hotel when

Shaheen wanted to get a meeting with you that you wouldn't talk to him," exclaimed Smallwood.

"That's right. He is not reliable or dependable," I rejoindered.

Smallwood blew up! "He had the money then and he has the money now. And now you have got to do something about it. You can't afford to see millions and millions offered and not act on it. Shaheen is in Paris right now. I spoke to him today. I spoke to him yesterday. I speak to him almost every day. He has met with banks and he has a deal for hundreds of millions of dollars to get the refinery started again. He can get the crude from the Middle East and in the North Sea and he can even get some from Nigeria. You know all about the oil. We can build one of the great petrochemical complexes of the world, right here in Newfoundland, right in Placentia Bay."

I retorted as strongly as I could, "But Mr. Smallwood, you know Shaheen, he is likely just putting you on; it does not mean very much. He is just using you to get to me and the government—get a half-baked promise from the government for some vague assistance and then lever the banks and vise versa. Don't you see that?"

"You're crazy, you're mad," Smallwood shouted. "You can't let Newfoundland down. This great entrepreneur who has the money; he knows all the bankers and how to get the money. He told me today that he had the money, he told me so today . . ."

"Okay," I said, "you believe he has the money. I do not believe he has the money. But I will take your word for now. And I will check it out tomorrow. If we can get written confirmation from the banks that he has all the money in place, I will meet with him. How's that?"

Smallwood shouted loudly. "That's fantastic! You will do this first thing tomorrow morning?"

"Yes, I will," I answered.

"I didn't say he had all the money," Smallwood interjected, "but he has hundreds of millions committed. Do you understand?"

"No, no," I quickly said, sensing Smallwood was moving away from his earlier bombast. "From the way you have been describing it, anyone listening would have to conclude that Shaheen had all the money he needed."

313

"All I am saying is that he has a lot of money arranged and I'm sure he will get more if needed," Smallwood responded.

It was now well-nigh midnight, and given that Smallwood had what he wanted, I was itching to get moving. No such luck.

More wine and cognac followed and we proceeded to talk on a variety of issues. Smallwood was interested in the simmering dispute regarding offshore oil and gas and how he had moved earlier to ensure it belonged to Newfoundland when he had a plaque posted on the seabed. Of course, I reminded him that his friends in Ottawa were not recognizing this at all. It was viewed as a symbolic act without any validity constitutionally. He had little response to this but to say that Trudeau was a great friend and that he would look after Newfoundland. This last statement was like a red flag to a bull to me.

Raising my voice, I exclaimed, "That is where you and I disagree most . . . someone to look after us. That's crazy—that is all we have known—that's what I want to change. The oil is off our coast, we brought it into Confederation, and we deserve the same kind of deal as Alberta has on its oil."

With a flourish he brushed my comments aside with his oft-stated refrain of the glories of Confederation.

In the midst of all this he was not unmindful of the opportunity and put a plug in for his son Bill (who represented for twenty-three years the constituency I now held), whom he described as brilliant and that the government could really use him. Astonished at this, I remained silent and moved on quickly to leave. It was now after 2:00 a.m.

"But, but, you have not seen the work on my books!" he said.

I listened to a long recounting of how he got started on the project and some of the people who would be in these next volumes. When I got a chance an hour later, I reminded him that I was told some months earlier by one of the workers on his book project that my grandfather Peckford was to be included since he had the first motorized boat in the inshore fishery. He was a little taken back by this revelation, but he quickly regained his composure and weakly indicated, not convincingly, that he had known about this. He tried to move on, but I persisted.

"I bet you didn't know that Joe Peckford campaigned for Squires?"

With a start, he exclaimed, "For Squires, your grandfather?"

"Yes, that's what I have been told."

With a glint in his eye, and almost a smile, he said, "Well, there's hope for you yet."

"Like you, I suppose," I rejoindered, "only you were a socialist."

Newly aroused, and with a gulp of cognac, he shouted, "It's one thing to go from a socialist to a Liberal; it is quite something else to go from a Liberal to a dirty Tory!"

It being close to 4:00 a.m., I let the matter drop.

A second attempt to leave was thwarted as he rushed to the tape machine and began playing many of his speeches. A new bottle of cognac appeared and Smallwood was now in his glee. I watched him as he listened to his voice—completely engrossed—shouting above the speech to utter, "Now, isn't that good. What do you think of that—brilliant, no?"

Two hours of this and I could take no more. I rose and Smallwood finally shut off the tape machine.

"I am leaving," I said.

"And what about Shaheen—you promised."

"As I said last night, I will get on to it today and get back to you as quickly as possible."

"Right, right, great, we'll have ourselves a refinery again," he said joyously.

Was I glad to get into the fresh morning air! The ceaseless bombardment of all things Smallwood had been suffocating. Yet, as I took in the freshness, I suddenly felt a tinge of sadness and disappointment. I was sad because I knew in my bones that this new Shaheen thing was a sham—Smallwood chasing another dream—and then again I questioned myself that perhaps I was being too judgmental and I really needed to hold my assessment until later in the day. I was disappointed for another reason. I had always wanted to have a long discussion with Smallwood about our history, political theory, the great ideas and minds of history, and to engage him in poetry and the poets. Through the night I had tried, on a number of occasions, to turn the conversation in these directions, but except for a brief comment on Squires and Churchill the ground seemed barren indeed. Did he really not know? Was he just too consumed that night with Shaheen and himself, showing off his office and taped speeches, that nothing else mattered? I was almost afraid to believe that a myth had been destroyed, that what I had heard about the depth and breadth of his knowledge was a bombastic creation. And although I had come to detest many of the things he had done and tactics that he used, I still harboured the idea that there was some real substance to the man on the grander scale. It hurt somewhere inside to realize that perhaps this was false. I quickly shut it from further thought.

Within a few minutes I was in my office. It was too late/early to go home. I jumped in the office shower to freshen up, read some of the mail on my desk, and waited for 9:00 a.m. to come.

At 9:00 sharp, I phoned the Department of Finance. After making sure they knew who was calling, I said, "Now, boys, don't think I'm crazy, but I want you to contact our agents in Paris and the banks. I'm told Shaheen has the money raised to take back the refinery and reopen it. I want to find out if this is true."

There was a silence, and then the obvious response with a touch of incredulity, "Who told you that?"

"It was Smallwood," I said, breaking down a little, since it was not my intention to reveal the source. "He has been after me to see Shaheen because he contends that the money is raised for the refinery. I promised him I would check it out and get back to him."

Regaining some composure and authority I continued. "In any case get on to it right away. I want to get to the bottom of the matter as quickly as possible."

I proceeded to give them the information, scanty though it was, that Smallwood had provided me. Calls were made; checks and double-checks were done.

With a heavy hand, the next day I picked up the phone and placed a call. In as even a voice as I could muster I said, "Mr. Smallwood, there is no money in place anywhere in Europe. Shaheen had visited some of them, but no money has been pledged. It's all a sham. I'm sorry, but—"

"No, no. I was just talking to Shaheen, everything is in place—hundreds of millions—you have it all wrong. We can get the whole thing moving. It will be a godsend. We will be heroes—just you wait and see. I mean you could not have ch—"

Gently, I placed the phone back in its place and went back to work.

DON JAMIESON

I had first encountered Don Jamieson when I was a student at Memorial University. A number of education students were agitating for improvements to the salaries of teachers in the province. We had submitted a brief to the premier's office and through that action became known to the media. Don, at the time, had the very popular supper news program on the private NTV television network. A couple of the students including yours truly were asked to appear on the program to explain our position. This was an exciting moment for us students and we were able to explain our position to a provincial audience.

It was many years later as a Member of Premier Frank Moores's government that I again met Mr. Jamieson, as I most often called him. Of course, I was aware of the many interactions of the Moores government with the federal government through Mr. Jamieson's office given that he was Newfoundland's representative in the federal Cabinet. Moores and Jamieson had a good relationship and both liked their scotch, which didn't hurt the relationship, and a lot of healthy horse trading ensued. There was Mr. Jamieson's riding to be considered in any federal money and then there were the priorities of the province. I remember, for example, the horse trading involving monies for the beginning of the road in Burgeo in Mr. Jamieson's riding and the provincial insistence on some monies at the same time for the Great Northern Peninsula Highway. This is not to say that Mr. Jamieson was not concerned about the whole province (because he was), but naturally he had a responsibility to his riding as well, especially as it relates to the Burgeo area, which was a very isolated part of the province and deserved to have a road connection. This was an era of significant federal spending, and given that the federal government was providing up to 90% of the money, Mr. Jamieson carried a lot of weight in the federal-provincial development agreements of the time. Moores understood this and tried to accommodate Mr. Jamieson. This included ensuring that transportation was provided to Mr. Jamieson to get to his residence in Swift Current, more than 100 miles from St. John's; this included both providing a helicopter or a car and driver for him. Such goodwill helped facilitate many an agreement and keep relations positive.

I was minister of Mines and Energy when the Aluminum Company of Canada (ALCAN) announced the closure of the fluorspar mine in St. Lawrence, in Mr. Jamieson's district. Although plagued over the years with tragic safety and environmental problems, it was still a major economic driver during this time. Hence, its closure was a major issue involving the federal and provincial governments. The meetings among the three parties—the two governments and the company—culminated in a planned final big meeting in Ottawa with the intent of settling all the outstanding issues involved in the closure. I had been briefed by my mines safety people that there were a number of significant safety issues that were still outstanding in the company's closure plan. Talks with the company and the department had not resolved these issues satisfactorily. I don't know whether the company thought that at such a high level meeting I would not raise these issues or what was their motivation, but there was a definite understanding from the conversations at the beginning of the meeting that the premier, the company, and Mr. Jamieson thought that a final signing off on the closure plan was what we were all there to see happen. I was forced unfortunately to throw cold water on this expectation and argue that all the safety issues that the department had raised had not been resolved, sometimes arguing with my own government and insisting that there was still work to be done, that a final resolution was impossible at this meeting. After lengthy discussion, I was able to have a final decision cancelled and that a meeting between the company, myself, and safety officials from the department take place in Montreal in a few days to hammer out the remaining issues. It being late afternoon, the formal part of the meeting concluded and a more liquid evening continued well into the night.

A couple days later a meeting was held in Montreal. There was a lot of tough talk at the table between the parties, and a private meeting, involving me and two executives from the company, where excessive pressure was applied to have the issues resolved without further concession from the company. I actually walked out of this meeting and returned to the bargaining table. I think it became clear to the company that their last best shot was at the Ottawa meeting and that pressure tactics of whatever manner would not work with me. A decided co-operative approach soon appeared from the company at the bargaining table and a full and final resolution was achieved.

My next encounter, of course, was on the campaign in 1979. Mr. Jamieson had been persuaded by senior people from the Newfoundland and Labrador Liberal Party that he could win a general election that I had just called. He returned to the province triumphant, arriving at St. John's airport with one of the largest motorcades even seen in the province. During the campaign I met him only once, at the TV leaders' debate, where I thought he did a good job.

With the election over, Mr. Jamieson became Leader of the Opposition. There was not a better Opposition Leader in the history of the province. He was not your traditional confrontational leader of the Opposition; his very nature was non-confrontational and he looked for a way to co-operate with government.

I was eager to get the co-operation of the Opposition on a number of measures, especially the introduction of a committee system for the consideration of the estimates of the budget. This would give the members a real opportunity to become more involved in the legislative budget process. I invited Mr. Jamieson to my office to discuss the new House session. Aware that he was a scotch drinker, I had my office inquire of the kind of scotch he enjoyed. It was a special scotch. We could not get it in the province, so I promptly ordered some from Ottawa. On the appointed Friday afternoon, he visited and we conducted our business in short order after which I offered him the scotch. He was impressed!

Mr. Jamieson proved to be a very responsible Opposition Leader and we were able to make changes to the legislature that improved its efficiency and involved the members more in its deliberations.

As I have said, Mr. Jamieson was not made for the cut and thrust of a provincial legislature, nor for a federal one, for that matter. He was more in the diplomatic mode. It was appropriate, then, that the prime minister appointed him Canadian High Commissioner to the United Kingdom.

PIERRE ELLIOTT TRUDEAU

I think the first time I heard of Pierre Trudeau was in the early sixties when I was at Memorial University in St. John's. It was the federal Liberal leadership happening and this former Justice minister was one of the candidates. He was musing about a just society and he projected an image of a young, vibrant upstart, supposedly in tune with the young generation. I was never that taken by him although many of the people I knew became almost instant supporters. It all seemed a bit contrived to me and without much substance.

Later a number of incidents explain my continuing suspicion of the man.

Early on in my time as premier a vacancy in the office of the lieutenant-governor occurred and a new appointment was imminent. One morning while driving to work, I heard on the radio that Dr. Anthony Paddon had been appointed. This was highly unusual. While it was the federal prerogative to appoint, there was/is a custom or convention that the prime minister would consult or advise in advance the premier of the province of the person to be appointed.

I think there are two reasons for such a custom. First, common courtesy would demand such co-operation—one government to the other within the Confederation. Of course, the province would have all the day-to-day interaction with the lieutenant governor, financially support the governor and his operation, and have all orders in council or decisions of the Cabinet signed off by him. Secondly, it is a very practical reason in that the premier and provincial government would not be blindsided by the inevitable questions from the press and the public. Of course by this time some of the big disagreements between the two governments were apparent, making it difficult not to see this as a deliberate snub of my administration.

On another occasion the Honourable Don Jamieson, federal minister of External Affairs, later to be my opponent in my first provincial election as premier, invited me to Ottawa to attend an evening dinner for Elliot Richardson, the then American Secretary of Commerce. Mr. Jamieson thought that I would enjoy such an evening. And so I went on the appointed evening to the Lester Pearson Building for the event. I was greeted by Mr. Jamieson and some of his officials and mingled with some of the other guests. I was informed that it was possible that the prime minister, Mr. Trudeau, might attend and some extra time would be allowed before dinner actually began to accommodate a possible late arrival. I was enjoying myself in conversation with people about national and international matters, and the time slipped by quickly. While in the midst of one of these conversations, the prime minister arrived without my notice and suddenly inserted himself in the semicircle of guests of which I was a part.

Seeming to want to capture attention and looking surprised at my attendance, he exclaimed, "Oh, Mr. Peckford, you are here, what a surprise! I was thinking the other day that I should visit Newfoundland soon. Would I need a passport?"

This sudden verbal thrust caught me off guard momentarily. There was a silence in the group (since it was clear to all that this wasn't just some humorous verbal action) and a sudden unease permeated the group.

"Well, Mr. Prime Minister," I said, recuperating, "you know, now that you have informed me of your intentions, I will later this evening contact our immigration people and inform them of your intentions. I am sure that a speedy approval process will ensure that your visit will be a smooth one."

Abruptly as he had entered the group, the prime minister took a speedy exit to another part of the room.

Most are familiar with the more public encounter at the nationally televised First Ministers Conference on the Constitution when the prime minister tried to associate me with the Quebec Separatists movement as a result of my support for a general social policy/ measure that the Quebec government had introduced. This was the unseemly aspect of the man. So quick to try to make an association of his adversary on erroneous information. Effective repartee is more elevated than this! Of course, the press and some apologists lapped up this supposed brilliant wit!

The prime minister later pursued this in his book *Memoirs* in which he says on page 248: "I recall Premier Brian Peckford saying that his view of Canada was closer to Lévesque's than it was to Trudeau's."

And later on page 325 he says: "I suggested out of a sense of irony—lost, I think, on the Newfoundland Premier—that Brian Peckford should read out the terms of the agreement because he was the one who had said he was closest to Lévesque's view of Canada."

Of course, he forgot to mention that the reason for him asking me to read the terms was the fact that he was aware that I had a proposal to present that was endorsed by most of the provinces, who had also supported my presenting it to the conference, and which later formed the basis for the agreement which he, himself, later acknowledged to the press.

Blinded by anyone suggesting that they agreed with parts of someone else's vision of Canada, especially views of his arch-enemy (it was Quebec's insistence like Alberta and Saskatchewan's insistence on the importance of the division of powers versus Trudeau's unilateralism that I was supporting, as well as a non-constitutional Quebec program), one can almost understand why he would continue to remember that part of my comments and why they were what stayed in his mind later when he was writing. He could not be wrong.

Allan Gotlieb, who worked for Trudeau in Washington as our ambassador, says this about Trudeau in his book *The Washington Diaries* on page 13: ". . . he holds to all his opinions with absolute conviction. He can never be wrong, so he defends them all to the considerable limit of his intellectual powers."

Gordon Robertson, a colleague of Trudeau's in his early years in Ottawa, later a clerk of the Cabinet in Trudeau's time, says tellingly in his book *Memories of a Very Civil Servant* on page 378: "Trudeau was philosophically and temperamentally less suited than Pearson, or King, or St. Laurent to the Federal system of Government with its constant need for agreement and compromise." Later, Robertson muses: "It is amazing really that a man of rigidity could carry on as PM of a country built on flexibility and compromise."

Perhaps the most galling of all the few encounters I had with the man concerned the fishery. Like economics, this was an area with which the prime minister had little understanding. I had been trying for years to sit down with the man and have a one-on-one talk about the Atlantic ground fishery: how the Europeans were over-fishing and that the toothless North Atlantic Fishery Organization (NAFO) was doing a disservice to fishery science and how the federal government was not doing its part to defend this fishery. I was convinced that if I had an hour or so I could show him through maps and facts how reasonable our position really was.

Finally a meeting was arranged. There were four people in attendance: the prime minister and his adviser, Michael Kirby, later to be appointed to the Senate, and myself and my adviser, Cyril Abery, now deceased, my deputy minister of Intergovernmental Affairs. Unfortunately, the meeting came on the heels of one of the prime minister's international trips. After the pleasantries were over, I was eager to provide an overview of the North Atlantic ground fishery and the present crucial issues. The prime minister was really not with us that day. He proceeded to describe his recent tour and seemed eager to talk of his meetings with the presidents of France and Germany. He seemed pleased at having walked with the high priests of Europe. Obviously, I was unimpressed as I could see the precious minutes roll by, subtracting from the allotted sixty minutes that were available and still no fishery issues bring discussed. So, characteristically and not without some risk, I interrupted the prime minister and told him that while I appreciated the importance of his trip and its many interesting dimensions, I was really eager to discuss the purpose of the meeting, the fishery. With his reluctant co-operation I proceeded to explain the complexities of the North Atlantic ground fishery in less than thirty minutes. Mr. Kirby was trying to be helpful and understanding of my dilemma and interjected profitably on a number of occasions to elucidate a particular point that I had made. But with such a time frame and the obvious disinterest of the prime minister, little was accomplished. I uttered a few inoffensive platitudes to the press afterwards and that was that.

It is sad that a prime minister who had the support of so many Newfoundlanders was so disengaged in the province's most important industry of the time. It is ironic that in his early years he could talk so eloquently of foreign domination and forgot it now on the Atlantic fishery. In a speech to l'Institut Canadien des Affaires Publiques in the early 1950s, he said, "The meaning to these figures is obvious: in key sectors of the Canadian economy, non-residents are in a position to take decisions quite foreign to the welfare of Canadians."

The disinterest of the prime minister and the federal government to take meaningful action during these years led over time, with other factors, to the almost complete shutdown of the province's ground fishery, putting tens of thousands out of work and causing the federal government to spend hundreds of millions on financial support to families and retraining and dislocating whole communities.

RENÉ LÉVESQUE

Lévesque was a different quintal of fish. Although hopelessly misguided on the Constitutional issue as it related to Quebec's place in the federal family, he was an engaging individual, worldly wise, amusing, and possessed of a lively mind. He bridged the world of ideas and the practical political waters with ease. It was this singular characteristic that kept Trudeau uneasy in his presence. I remember a number of dinners of first ministers where Trudeau and Lévesque would spar, a sort of ping-pong dialogue. The striking thing I remember is how upset Trudeau would become with Lévesque as a result of some very pertinent point Lévesque had just made that Trudeau found difficult to handle, all the while Lévesque seemed very much at ease, with that impish grin in full view.

I had an interesting encounter with Lévesque at one of the Eastern Premiers New England Governors' conferences. This was in Vermont. Of course, Quebec and Newfoundland were in that on again–off again mode of tackling the Churchill Falls issues: Quebec eager to become involved with Newfoundland in the Lower Churchill project and Newfoundland insisting that changes to the Upper Churchill contract must precede, or be a part of, any new arrangement with Quebec regarding Churchill River developments. We had both been involved before so we were not new to the issues, and we both got along personally notwithstanding our views on the nature of Canada and our past differences on the Churchill issue. Unlike many politicians, Lévesque could agree to disagree and you could still have a relationship.

Almost inevitably at these gatherings, the Churchill Falls issue arose, especially with the press, which needed fodder for their papers unlikely to be found from the mundane subjects of such meetings and to justify their presence. This being a much smaller stage where interaction with the press was closer and contact with the first ministers was easier than at the larger gatherings, this subject was a natural target for them.

Both Lévesque and I were eager to see if we could break the impasse and so we agreed to stay over an extra day after the formal part of the conference was completed. Lévesque invited me to spend an afternoon with him and his female partner aboard a yacht on Lake Champlain, which was adjacent to where the conference was being held. He thought that a pleasant casual afternoon away from the confines of a room would be more conducive to our talks.

And so I joined Lévesque for the afternoon, meandering around the lake under the watchful eye of two security boats. Lévesque liked to swim. No sooner were we out in the middle of the lake when he donned his bathing suit, insisted I do the same, and before I knew it, we were both overboard in the cool waters of Lake Champlain. A succession of on the boat-in the water episodes ensued, and then a relaxing time musing, interspersed with some fine scotch. It was then that we got to the subject of Churchill Falls and we both expressed the view that there must be some way to solve this disagreement between the provinces and move ahead. We undertook to revisit our files when we returned home and try to creatively find ways to a solution. Several weeks later I wrote Lévesque, and although some talks occurred, little had really changed. Like the Constitution, Lévesque (although musing about flexibility) seemed incapable of seeing it through. One could argue that the ideologues of Morin and Parizeau blocked any Constitutional flexibility, and a similar hard-line bent at Hydro Quebec prevented anything on that front from being realized. A more sinister view is that the crafty Lévesque was just trying to see if he could lure me into another negotiating exercise in the hopes of wearing me down and, with a few concessions on the margins, get substantially the deal he wanted.

One other incident I remember involved the eight provinces (the Gang of Eight) during the tumultuous Constitutional struggles of the early eighties. We were meeting at a hotel in Montreal and of course we were deeply engaged in debating various elements of Constitutional change and what our common position would be. Premier Lougheed and Premier Lévesque became involved in a heated exchange over some specific issue; Lougheed, in responding to a particular point Lévesque had made, used language that upset Lévesque. He became very agitated, as did Lougheed, and the incident almost came to blows but was quickly diffused by a number of us and civility was restored. It was the only time I saw either of them really lose their cool.

BRIAN MULRONEY

Mr. Mulroney became president of the Iron Ore Company of Canada in 1977 when I was minister of Mines and Energy. One of the company's main assets was the large iron ore mine and pellet plant in Labrador City, Labrador. It was inevitable, then, that we would have involvement one with the other.

It should be noted that I had recently supported his rival, Joe Clark, for the leadership of the federal Progressive Conservative Party, which Mr. Clark won. However, this seemed to be firmly behind him in his relationship with me as minister; at no time could I detect, either directly or indirectly, any action that would have led me to believe that my opposition to his leadership bid in any way impaired our dealings. In this regard, he was one of the very few I had met who could act so magnanimously in such circumstances.

My first contact was when Mr. Mulroney, as president of IOC, requested a meeting to review the status of the company's operation in the province. He wanted to brief Cabinet, the premier, and the minister on present operations and future plans. I arranged for this presentation and we were all very impressed by his performance; his grasp of the issues and understanding of the operation was exceptional, especially since we were all well aware that he was not a geologist and had little mining or mine processing experience.

Not long after this initial contact, labour issues at Labrador City reached a critical stage. Mr. Mulroney decided to become personally involved and I accompanied him to Labrador City for meetings with the management and a hostile union leadership. He was successful in lessening the tensions in meeting with the union leadership, highlighting the financial position of the company and showing that he was not playing games with the union but that the facts demanded some responsibility on all sides for a peaceful solution. This was achieved as a result of this intervention and impressively showcased an able negotiator and leader.

It was in these visits to Labrador City that I first became aware of Mr. Mulroney's fondness for alcohol, having on one occasion literally put him to bed one evening. He was up at the crack of dawn the next morning, alert and ready for the business of the day. What was most amazing for those of us who were aware of this problem was how scrupulously disciplined he became later as prime minister in completely conquering this.

We were both big sports fans and had occasion to attend hockey and American football games together on my visits to IOC headquarters in Montreal and to Cleveland, Ohio, where some of the ownership group of the company were headquartered. It was during such visits that I met Mila Mulroney, truly a lady of commitment and class.

It wasn't long before the leadership of the federal Progressive Conservative Party was once again a hot topic, given the problems of the short-lived Clark government. Once again, I would not be a supporter of Mr. Mulroney as he again sought the leadership. Under ordinary circumstances I would have supported this second effort, but Newfoundlander John Crosbie was also running and of course my allegiance was first and foremost to one of our own. However, I was a vocal and ardent supporter of him and his government in two elections.

But we did have one significant disagreement and this one was over the fishery. The federal bureaucracy and most of the federal ministers in both Liberal and Progressive Conservative governments were entrenched—as they are to this day—in the mistaken notion that some better sharing of fishery powers between the federal and provincial governments would somehow be injurious to the stability of the country. Mr. Mulroney was unable to change.

Two large national issues, to which he directed his attention, displayed his prowess and skill. On the constitutional front, Mr. Mulroney was masterful, open, and genuinely attempted to bring the country together. Tragically, this was sabotaged by a jealous and vindictive Pierre Elliott Trudeau and others of his ilk, manufacturing false fears on a weary population. The Meech Lake Accord, history has proven, would have been a reasonable accommodation.

On the economic front, Mr. Mulroney's free-trade initiative, which led to the Canada/U.S. Free Trade Agreement was truly a remarkable achievement. In this his government had frequent and extensive consultation with all the provinces and industry and is one of the most important bilateral arrangements of the century. Mountains of empirical evidence have accumulated demonstrating the significant positive effect that it has had on both countries. The false nationals of the day (the Liberal opportunists who promised to tear up the agreement when elected) and the New Democratic Party have all been silenced by the results. People forget that Mr. Mulroney was loudly and falsely attacked as a traitor to his country because of his passionate advocacy of this milestone.

But for me, Mr. Mulroney will go down in history as Newfoundland's best friend. He understood the place. Bill Marshall says it was Mulroney's understanding of the Churchill Falls issue that made him support the offshore:

> I believe that his knowledge of that plight cemented his resolve to see that we were treated fairly in the offshore settlement. Certainly, he took a marked personal interest in the matter and his resolve to see an agreement that was fair to Newfoundland and Labrador without compromising legitimate national interests was evident at each meeting.

Without Brian Mulroney there would be no Atlantic Accord, and without the Accord Newfoundland and Labrador would not be a "have" province today. And this book would have been much different.

Sadly, if a poll was taken today asking who had the greatest positive impact upon Newfoundland and Labrador's fortunes, the majority would likely say Mr. Trudeau.

Perhaps this book will help to change that view.

THE ATLANTIC ACCORD
MEMORANDUM OF AGREEMENT BETWEEN THE GOVERNMENT OF CANADA AND THE GOVERNMENT OF NEWFOUNDLAND AND LABRADOR ON OFFSHORE OIL AND GAS RESOURCE MANAGEMENT AND REVENUE SHARING

THE ATLANTIC ACCORD

1. The Government of Canada and the Government of Newfoundland and Labrador have reached an Accord on joint management of the offshore oil and gas resources off Newfoundland and Labrador and the sharing of revenues from the exploitation of these resources. The Accord will be implemented, to the extent possible, through mutual and parallel legislation to be introduced by both governments into the Parliament of Canada and the Legislature of Newfoundland and Labrador.

PURPOSES OF THE ACCORD

2. The purposes of this Accord are:

    (a) to provide for the development of oil and gas resources offshore Newfoundland for the benefit of Canada as a whole and Newfoundland and Labrador in particular;

    (b) to protect, preserve, and advance the attainment of national self-sufficiency and security of supply;

    (c) to recognize the right of Newfoundland and Labrador to be the principal beneficiary of the oil and gas resources off its shores, consistent with the requirement for a strong and united Canada;

    (d) to recognize the equality of both governments in the management of the resource, and ensure that the pace and manner of development optimize the social and economic benefits to Canada as a whole and to Newfoundland and Labrador in particular;

    (e) to provide that the Government of Newfoundland and Labrador can establish and collect resource revenues as if these resources were on land, within the province;

(f) to provide for a stable and fair offshore management regime for industry;

(g) to provide for a stable and permanent arrangement for the management of the offshore adjacent to Newfoundland by enacting the relevant provisions of this Accord in legislation of the Parliament of Canada and the Legislature of Newfoundland and Labrador and by providing that the Accord may only be amended by the mutual consent of both governments; and

(h) to promote within the system of joint management, insofar as is appropriate, consistency with the management regimes established for other offshore areas in Canada.

JOINT MANAGEMENT

3. The two parties agree to establish the Canada-Newfoundland Offshore Petroleum Board, hereinafter called "the Board", to administer the relevant provisions of the Canada-Newfoundland Atlantic Accord Implementation Act as enacted by the Parliament of Canada and the Legislature of Newfoundland and Labrador, and other relevant legislation.

4. The Board shall consist of seven members: three of whom shall be appointed by the Government of Canada and three of whom shall be appointed by the Government of Newfoundland and Labrador. The Chairman shall be jointly appointed by both governments. Members of the Board shall not be public servants of Canada or Newfoundland and shall be subject to conflict of interest guidelines.

5. In the event that after three months of consultation, the two governments fail to agree on the Chairman, the Chairman shall be chosen by a panel consisting of one nominee from each government who shall agree on a third person to chair the panel. In the event that the nominees fail to agree on the Chairman of the panel, the Chairman shall be selected by the Chief Justice of Newfoundland. The decision of the panel shall be binding on both governments.

6. The first members of the Board shall be appointed by each government for staggered terms of four, five and six years respectively in order that only two members retire in any one year. The Chairman shall be appointed for

a term of seven years. Subsequently, members and the Chairman shall be appointed for terms of six years. On completion of a term, members and the Chairman may be reappointed for further terms. They shall hold office during good behaviour. Each government may appoint one alternate member to serve as a member in the absence of one of the members nominated by that government.

7. The quorum of the Board shall be four of the members.

8. The offices of the Board and its staff shall be located in Newfoundland.

9. The Board may from time to time establish or change its rules and procedures including provisions for reasonable notice of meetings.

10. The Board may review and make recommendations to the two governments with respect to proposed amendments to the legislation implementing the Accord and the regulations made thereunder.

11. The Board shall keep the Government of Canada and the Government of Newfoundland and Labrador informed of its decisions in a timely manner.

12. Both governments agree that the Board should make its decisions on the basis of consensus. Members of the Board are not to act as nominees of the government which appointed them. In the absence of consensus, decisions will be made by the Board on majority vote.

13. The Board shall provide both governments with full and complete access to all information held by the Board. In addition, the Board shall require applicants, permittees, and licencees to concurrently file copies of all material filed with the Board with both Governments.

14. The Board shall report promptly and concurrently to the designated department or Agency of both governments any significant event or information received by the Board.

15. The Board shall meet at least once monthly and at any other time at the call of the Chairman, or at the call of any two members. The Board shall also meet when requested by either one or both of the two governments, to review any matter referred to it by a government.

SOME DAY THE SUN WILL SHINE

16. The Board shall select and appoint a Chief Executive Office through an open competitive process. Alternatively, the two governments may appoint the Chairman of the Board as Chief Executive Officer. The appointment of a separate Chief Executive Officer is subject to the approval of both governments. Failing agreement, the arbitration process set out for the appointment of the Chairman shall apply for the selection of a Chief Executive Officer. The Chief Executive Officer shall be fully accountable to the Board.

17. The Board shall, upon the recommendation of the Chief Executive Officer, appoint sufficient staff to fully carry out its functions under the Accord legislation. The staff shall be selected on the basis of merit, generally following a public competition and shall be employees of the Board. When requested by the Board, both governments will take action to facilitate mobility between employment in the federal and provincial public services and employment in the Board, including secondments and portable pensions.

18. The Chief Executive Officer shall prepare a budget for the Board on an annual basis. Following approval of the budget by the Board, it shall be submitted to both governments for their consideration and approval. The budget shall be sufficient to permit the Board to carry out its duties under the legislation implementing the Accord. Each government shall pay one-half of the approved annual cost of Board operations.

19. The Board shall establish, maintain and operate a facility in Newfoundland for the storage and curatorship of all geophysical records and geological and hydrocarbon samples relating to the offshore area.

20. The Board shall prepare an annual report and submit it to both governments by the end of the first quarter of the following calendar year. The report, which shall contain an audited financial statement and a description of the Board's activities during the previous year, shall be tabled in the House of Commons and the House of Assembly by the Minister of Energy, Mines and Resources and the designated Newfoundland Minister respectively. Provision will also be made in the legislation implementing the Accord for the Government of Canada and the Government of Newfoundland and Labrador to have access to the books and accounts of the Board for the purposes of an audit.

333

DECISIONS IN RELATION TO OFFSHORE MANAGEMENT

21. For the purposes of defining the role of the Board and Ministers, decisions on offshore resources shall be divided as follows:

    (a) decisions, made by Parliament, the Government of Canada, or Federal Ministers (clause 22);

    (b) decisions made by the Newfoundland Legislature, the Newfoundland Government or Provincial Minister (clause 23);

    (c) decisions made by the Board subject to no ministerial review or directives (clause 24); and

    (d) decisions made by the Board subject to the approval of the appropriate Minister (Fundamental Decisions, clause 25), or subject to directions from the Ministers of both governments (clause 33a).

22. Decisions made by Parliament, the Government of Canada or Federal Ministers alone comprise:

    (a) decisions related to Canadianization policy (e.g., discretionary Canadian Ownership requirements);

    (b) decisions made under legislation of general application not specifically related to oil and gas exploration and production (e.g., Fisheries Act, Canada Shipping Act, Immigration Act); and

    (c) decisions related to the application of federal taxes.

23. Decisions made by the Newfoundland Legislature, the Newfoundland Government, or Provincial Ministers alone comprise:

    (a) the royalty regime and other provincial-type revenues (see clause 37);

    (b) decisions related to provincial laws of general application having effect in the offshore pursuant to clause 61.

24. The Board shall make all other decisions relating to the regulation and management of petroleum-related activities in the offshore area. Except for fundamental decisions, as set out in clause 25, all decisions of the Board shall be final. Without limiting the generality of the above, such final decisions shall include:

(a) The Declaration of Discoveries:
- declaration of significant discoveries and commercial discoveries

(b) Production Licence
- granting and renewal of a production licence
- exclusion of lands from a production licence

(c) Compliance Functions:
- prosecution, notices, and orders regarding offenses

(d) The Administration of Regulations Respecting "Good Oilfield Practice":
- orders relating to waste
- entry into pooling and unitization agreements
- administration of technical regulations related to safety, environmental protection, resource conservation, and other matters during the exploration, development and production phases
- production installation, facility and operations approvals, certification of fitness
- oil and gas committee appellate functions

(e) The Exercise of Emergency Powers (which may be vested in the Chief Executive Officer) Respecting Safety, Spills and Conservation:
- orders to prevent waste (excluding waste from flaring of gas or unsound recovery methods)
- taking action or directing action to repair, remedy or mitigate the impacts of an oil spill
- orders, evidence of financial responsibility, inquiries.

25. Where a fundamental decision is made by the Board, notice of that decision will be transmitted to both governments before the decision becomes final. Both governments will then consider the decision and advise the Board whether its decision may stand and be put into effect or whether either one or both of the governments disagree with the decision. Fundamental decisions primarily affecting pace and mode of exploration and pace of production are:

(a) Rights Issuance, comprising

i) the calling for proposals relating to the granting of an interest in lands and the selection of the proponent to whom an interest is to be granted;

ii) the direct issuance of an interest in lands;

iii) the determination of the terms and conditions to be contained in an Exploration Agreement;

iv) the variation of the terms and conditions contained in an Exploration Agreement; and

v) the continuation of any provisional lease or the variation in the conditions now applying in such lease.

(b) Extraordinary Powers, comprising the issuance of orders:

i) directing an interest holder to drill a well;

ii) requiring the commencement, continuation, increase or suspension of production;

iii) cancelling the rights of an interest holder; and,

iv) requiring an interest holder to introduce specific measures to prevent waste.

Fundamental decisions primarily affecting the mode of development are:

(c) Approval of the development plan with respect to:

i) the choice of production system,

ii) the planned level of recovery of the resource in place,

iii) the pace and timing of the implementation of the project, and

iv) any fundamental revision to any of the foregoing.

26. It is the objective of this Accord that consensus be sought and reached between the two governments with respect to fundamental decisions as defined in clause 25. Where agreement cannot be reached between governments on a fundamental decision within thirty days following receipt of the Board's decision, the following shall apply:

(a) in the national interest, and subject to clause 26(b), the Federal Minister will be responsible for approving a fundamental decision taken by the Board until a period when national self-sufficiency and security of supply are reached, or, having been reached, are lost. Once Canada reaches a period in which self-sufficiency and security of supply are reached, the Provincial Minister will have the power to approve a fundamental decision taken by the Board, subject to the normal exercise of the Government of Canada's authority over exports. The determination of whether self-sufficiency and security of supply, as defined in clause 28, have been reached will be made in the manner set out in clause 27; and

(b) the Provincial Minister will be responsible for approving fundamental decisions taken by the Board primarily affecting the mode of development as defined in clause 25(c), subject to the Federal Minister's right to override the Provincial Minister's approval or veto if it unreasonably delays the attainment of self-sufficiency and security of supply.

27. In the absence of agreement, the determination of whether self-sufficiency and security of supply as defined in clause 28 have been attained, and whether a decision by the Provincial Minister has caused an unreasonable delay in the attainment of self-sufficiency and security of supply, will be made by a three person arbitration panel as provided for under clause 5 of this Accord. Both governments agree to accept the decision of the arbitration panel as final and binding for the purposes of this Accord.

28. National self-sufficiency is achieved in any calendar year when the volume of suitable crude oil and equivalent substances available from domestic Canadian hydrocarbon productive capacity is adequate to supply the feedstock requirements of Canadian refineries necessary to satisfy the refined product requirements of Canada. Suitable crude oil and equivalent substances are those which are appropriate for processing in Canadian refineries and which are potentially deliverable to Canadian refineries.

Security of supply is realized when the achievement of self-sufficiency as defined above is anticipated in each of the next ensuing five calendar years, giving full consideration to anticipated additions to productive capacity, and anticipated adjustments to refining capacity.

In determining the above requirements, the volumes of crude oils having the quality characteristics required for the production of speciality refined products and which are not available from Canadian sources shall be excluded.

29. To minimize the regulatory uncertainty faced by industry associated with potential shifts in the role of Federal and Provincial Ministers, the determination of self-sufficiency and security of supply will be fixed for periods of five years. Each determination shall be conclusive and binding on the parties. For the first 5-year period, which commences on the proclamation of legislation implementing this Accord, both governments agree that the requirement of selfsufficiency and security of supply has not been met.

30. In the event of a sudden domestic or import supply shortfall, the Board will undertake to increase production, if requested by the federal government, consistent with good oil field practice. In addition, should Canada's obligations under the International Energy Agency (IEA) oil-sharing agreement be triggered, the Federal Minister would, during the period these obligations continue, be able to direct the Board to take such measures as are necessary to comply with Canada's obligations under the IEA and as are fair and equitable in relation to other hydrocarbon producing regions of Canada.

31. The contribution of petroleum resources from the offshore area to the achievement of selfsufficiency and security of supply shall be equitable in relation to the other hydrocarbon producing regions of Canada.

SUSPENSIVE VETOES

32. Where a government exercises its authority under this Accord with respect to a fundamental decision, the other government may delay the execution of that decision for a period of three months in order to give further opportunity to reach consensus.

MINISTERIAL DIRECTIVES

33. (a) In the public interest, Ministers may jointly direct the Board in writing concerning:

   i) fundamental decisions (described in clause 25);

   ii) the public review process (clause 34);

   iii) Canada and Newfoundland benefits; and

   iv) studies and the provision of policy advice.

The Board shall carry such directives into effect.

(b) During the first month of each calendar year the Board shall provide to both Ministers a plan outlining the Board's intentions regarding the areas to be made available for exploration and development during that calendar year. If, upon review, it is felt that the proposed plan does not provide for an adequate level of effort towards the achievement of self-sufficiency and security of supply, the appropriate Minister as determined under Clause 26(a) may reject the plan and inform the Board of the reasons for so doing and the Board shall bring forward an alternate plan consistent with these views.

PUBLIC REVIEW

34. In relation to any prospective development, the Board shall conduct a public review. If the Board decides that it is in the public interest, It may waive the holding of a public review, subject to clause 33(a). If a public review is conducted, the Board may:

(a) establish terms of reference and a timetable that will permit a comprehensive review of the project, including aspects falling within the retained jurisdiction of the Federal and Provincial Governments;

(b) name a commissioner or panel, and may request both governments to confer upon the commissioner or panel powers of inquiry under the Public Enquiries Act of Newfoundland and Labrador or the Inquiries Act of Canada;

(c) name to a panel members proposed by the Federal and Provincial Governments, in recognition of their jurisdiction;

(d) require a project proponent to submit a preliminary development plan, and as needed an environmental impact statement and a socio-economic impact statement, including a preliminary benefits plan; and

(e) cause the commissioner or panel to hold public hearings in appropriate locations in the province and report to the Board and the relevant Ministers.

Not more than 270 days shall elapse between the receipt of the plan by the Board and its decision with respect to the plan.

PRICING

35. The Government of Newfoundland and Labrador will be a full participant in negotiations and consultations with the Government of Canada from time to time in the same manner as the governments of other producing provinces for the establishment of the price of oil and natural gas in the offshore area.

REVENUE SHARING

36. The principles of revenue sharing between Canada and Newfoundland with respect to revenues from petroleum-related activities in the offshore area shall be the same as those which exist between the Government of Canada and other hydrocarbon producing provinces with respect to revenues from petroleum-related activities on land. The federal legislation implementing the Accord, therefore, will permit the Government of Newfoundland and Labrador to establish and collect resource revenues and provincial taxes of general application as if these petroleum-related activities were on land within the province, through incorporation by reference of Newfoundland laws (as amended from time to time), or through other appropriate legislative mechanisms.

37. On the basis of the foregoing, Newfoundland shall receive the proceeds of the following revenues from petroleum related activity in the offshore area:

    (a) royalties;

    (b) a corporate income tax which is the same as the generally prevailing provincial corporate
income tax in the province;

    (c) a sales tax that is the same as the generally prevailing provincial sales tax in the province;

    (d) any bonus payments;

    (e) rentals and licence fees; and

    (f) other forms of resource revenue and provincial taxes of general application, consistent with the spirit of this Accord, as may be established from time to time.

38. The Board shall collect royalties, bonus payments, rentals and licence fees. These revenues and other offshore revenues referred to in clause 37 shall be remitted to the Government of Newfoundland and Labrador.

EQUALIZATION OFFSET PAYMENTS

39. The two governments recognize that there should not be a dollar for dollar loss of equalization payments as a result of offshore revenues flowing to the Province. To achieve this, the Government of Canada shall establish equalization offset payments. These payments shall commence on April 1 of the first fiscal year following the attainment of cumulative production of fifteen million barrels of offshore production of oil or the energy equivalent production of natural gas and shall be in two parts.

    Offset payments (Part I) will be made equivalent to the loss in fiscal equalization payments resulting from any future changes to the floor provisions of the Federal-Provincial Fiscal Arrangements and Federal Post-Secondary Education and Health Contributions Act, 1977, as amended 1982, with respect to the phaseout of equalization entitlements, if the changes are detrimental to Newfoundland. These Part I offset payments will apply for a period of twelve years from commencement of production.

    In addition, the Government of Canada will make offset payments (Part II) equivalent to 90 percent of any decrease in the fiscal equalization payment to Newfoundland in respect of a fiscal year in comparison with the payment for the immediately preceding fiscal year, as calculated under the prevailing Federal-Provincial Fiscal Arrangements and Federal Post-Secondary Education and Health Contributions Act, 1977, as amended from time to time and, taking into account for both years, the offset component entitlement under Part I.

    Beginning in the fifth fiscal year of offshore production, this offset rate shall be reduced by ten percentage points and by ten percentage points in each subsequent year.

CROWN SHARE

40. The costs and benefits of any Crown share in the offshore area which may be retained by the Government of Canada will be established by the Canada-Newfoundland Atlantic Accord Implementation Act. The costs and benefits thereof will be shared equitably by both governments.

CROWN CORPORATIONS

41. Crown corporations and agencies involved in oil and gas resource activities in the offshore area shall be subject to all taxes, royalties and levies.

DEVELOPMENT FUND

42. The Government of Canada and the Government of Newfoundland and Labrador hereby establish an Offshore Development Fund. The purposes of this Fund are to defray the social and economic infrastructure costs related to the development of oil and gas in the offshore area in the period before production begins, and to ensure that the provincial economy is well positioned to reap the economic benefits of offshore development. This Fund shall be in addition to the funding provided by the Government of Canada for regional development and other similar initiatives in Newfoundland.

    The Fund will consist of a $300 million grant, cost shared 75 per cent federal and 25 per cent provincial. Contributions to the Fund will be made over a five year period commencing April 1, 1985 on a schedule to be agreed by Ministers on the basis of project requirements.

43. A Development Fund Committee comprised of two representatives from each of the Federal and Provincial Governments shall be established to monitor and review the implementation of this Fund.

44. Both Ministers may propose projects, normally falling within provincial jurisdiction, for funding. Expenditures will be made by mutual consent.

OIL POLLUTION AND FISHERIES COMPENSATION REGIME

45. The legislation implementing the Accord will establish an oil pollution compensation regime with respect to absolute liability for oil spill damages and debris, requiring appropriate financial security. Together with the relevant provisions of the Canada Shipping Act that establish the Maritimes Pollution Claims Fund, or its successors, and any industry-sponsored programs for non-attributable damages, this shall be accepted as the basis of an oil spill damage compensation regime that recognizes the various causes and sources of pollution damage.

46. This regime shall include provisions to compensate fishermen with respect to absolute liability for attributable oil spill and debris-related damages. The Board shall also promote and monitor industry-sponsored fishermen's compensation policies for damages of a non-attributable nature.

47. A committee consisting of representatives from the Government of Canada,

the Government of Newfoundland and Labrador, the petroleum industry, and the fishery industry will review and monitor these provisions.

MANAGEMENT OFFICES

48. The Board shall seek to ensure that all companies which operate in the offshore area establish offices in the province with appropriate levels of decision-making. In this spirit, the Government of Canada shall ensure, where possible, that Petro-Canada maintains an office in the province with responsibility for its operations in the offshore area.

49. The Government of Canada shall establish in the province, where possible, regional offices with appropriate levels of decision-making for all departments directly involved in activities relating to the offshore area.

ECONOMIC GROWTH AND DEVELOPMENT

50. It is the objective of both governments to ensure that the offshore area is managed in a manner which will promote economic growth and development in order to optimize benefits accruing to Newfoundland in particular and to Canada as a whole.

51. The legislation implementing the Accord shall provide that before the start of any work program for exploration or field development, a plan must be submitted satisfactory to the Board for the employment of Canadians and, in particular, members of the provincial labour force and for providing manufacturers, consultants, contractors and service companies in Newfoundland and other parts of Canada with a full and fair opportunity to participate in the supply of goods and services used in that work or activity.

In its review of Canada and Newfoundland benefits plans, the Board shall seek to ensure that first consideration is given to services provided from within Newfoundland, and to goods manufactured in Newfoundland, where such goods and services are competitive in terms of fair market price, quality, and delivery.

The Board shall also require that any such plans include particular provisions, consistent with the Canadian Charter of Rights and Freedoms, to ensure that individuals resident in Newfoundland are given first consideration for training and employment opportunities in the work program for which the plan was submitted.

52. Plans submitted to the Board, for the use of goods and services and for employment, including plans for any specified purchases, shall be reviewed by the Board in consultation with both governments which shall advise the Board on the extent to which they provide for full, fair and competitive access. Both governments will attempt to provide a common view to the Board, but where this is not possible, the decision on employment and procurement plans approval shall rest with the Board. The Board shall have the authority to approve such plans subject to the power of joint ministerial direction set out in clause 33.

53. The appropriate Federal and Provincial Ministers shall conclude a Memorandum of Understanding regarding the coordination of industrial and employment benefits by the Board and with respect to the industrial and employment benefits review and evaluation procedures to be followed by both governments and the Board.

REGIONAL SECURITY OF SUPPLY

54. Hydrocarbons produced from the offshore area will be made available to Newfoundland and Labrador on commercial terms to meet both total end use consumption and the feedstock requirements of industrial facilities in place on the day that legislation implementing this Accord is proclaimed. Similarly, feedstock availability shall be ensured, on commercial terms, for new industrial facilities in Newfoundland and Labrador, provided such feedstock is excess to feedstock required to meet the demand of presently existing industrial capacity in eastern Canada.

RESEARCH AND DEVELOPMENT AND EDUCATION AND TRAINING

55. Benefits plans submitted pursuant to clause 51 shall provide for expenditures to be made on research and development, and education and training, to be conducted within the province. Expenditures made by companies active in the offshore pursuant to this requirement shall be approved by the Board.

ENVIRONMENTAL STUDIES REVOLVING FUND

56. The Environmental Studies Revolving Fund (ESRF) will continue to be considered a national program with a central administration. One Newfoundland member of the Board will be appointed to the ESRF Advisory Board. In addition, the ESRF annual budget will be reviewed by the Board,

and the application of related levies in the Newfoundland offshore shall be subject to Board approval.

LEGISLATION

57. Each government shall, within one year of the signing of this Accord, introduce the legislation necessary to implement the Accord and support it as a government measure.

58. The legislation implementing the Accord shall replace and supersede the federal Canada Oil and Gas Act and the Oil and Gas Production and Conservation Act and the provincial Petroleum and Natural Gas Act as it applies in the offshore area. All other federal and provincial legislation which is presently applicable to the management of the oil and gas resources in the offshore area will continue to apply.

59. Notwithstanding clause 58, to the extent that the provisions of the Canada Oil and Gas Act and the Oil and Gas Production and Conservation Act and Regulations are consistent with this Accord, they will be retained in the legislation and regulations implementing the Accord.

60. Except by mutual consent, neither government will introduce amendments to the legislation or regulations implementing the Accord.

61. The Government of Canada will introduce in Parliament legislation to extend federal laws to apply to activities in the offshore, and apply appropriate provincial laws, including social legislation such as occupational health and safety legislation and other legislation designed to protect workers.

62. Federal courts shall be invested with jurisdiction in the offshore area in respect of any matter to the same extent as if the matter had arisen within their ordinary jurisdiction. Provincial courts shall be invested with jurisdiction in the offshore region in respect of any matter arising under the laws made applicable by Parliament to the offshore region to the same extent as if the matter had arisen within their ordinary territorial jurisdiction. For the purpose of this paragraph, the offshore region shall be deemed to be within the territorial limits of the judicial centre of St. John's as defined in the District Court Act, 1977.

COORDINATION

63. The Board shall conclude Memoranda of Understanding with the government departments and agencies having continuing responsibilities in the offshore area for environmental and safety regulation and for emergency measures with a view to ensuring effective coordination and minimum duplication.

CONSTITUTIONAL ENTRENCHMENT

64. The Government of Canada agrees that should the Government of Newfoundland and Labrador achieve the requisite support among the other provinces for the constitutional entrenchment of the Accord that it would introduce a mutually agreeable resolution into Parliament.

TRANSITIONAL

65. Pending the enactment of legislation implementing the Accord, the Government of Canada and the Government of Newfoundland and Labrador agree to take all possible steps to set up the Board and administer existing legislation within the spirit of this Accord.

66. Subject to clause 36, interests created before the proclamation of the legislation implementing the Accord shall continue and shall be administered by the Board in accordance with the legislation.

OTHER MINERALS

67. In the event that exploration, production and development of minerals other than petroleum in the offshore area become feasible in the future, the two governments agree to enter into discussions regarding their exploration, development and production.

AREA COVERED BY ACCORD

68. The area covered by this Accord is that area below the low water mark lying off the coast of Newfoundland and Labrador out to the outer edge of the continental margin, coming within Canada's jurisdiction being north and east and south of the appropriate lines of demarcation between Newfoundland, the adjacent provinces, and the Northwest Territories.

Dated at St. John's this 11th day of February, 1985

(signature)

Brian Mulroney
Prime Minister of Canada

(signature)

A. Brian Peckford
Premier of Newfoundland and
Labrador and Minister for
Intergovernmental Affairs

(signature)

Pat Carney
Minister of Energy, Mines
and Resources

(signature)

William W. Marshall
President of the Executive
Council and Minister Responsible
for Energy

(signature)

John C. Crosbie
Minister of Justice
and Attorney General
of Canada

BIBLIOGRAPHY

Alexander, David. *The Decay of Trade: An Economic History of the Newfoundland Saltfish Trade, 1935–1965.* St. John's: ISER Books, 1977.

Andrieux, J.P. *Newfoundland's Cod War: Canada or France?* St. John's: OTC Press, 1987.

Bannister, Jerry. "Making History: Cultural Memory in Twentieth-Century Newfoundland." *Newfoundland and Labrador Studies* 18, no. 2 (2002): 175–94.

Bavington, Dean. *Managed Annihilation: An Unnatural History of the Newfoundland Cod Collapse.* Vancouver: UBC Press, 2010.

Browne, William J. *Eighty-Four Years a Newfoundlander: Memoirs of William J. Browne, Vol. 1, 1897–1949.* St. John's: Dicks & Company, 1981.

Crosbie, John C. *No Holds Barred: My Life in Politics.* Toronto: McClelland & Stewart, 1997.

Cuff, Harry, and Leslie Harris, eds. *Where Once We Stood: The Newfoundland Quarterly 100th Anniversary Anthology.* St. John's: Harry Cuff Publications, 2001.

Cuff, Robert H. ed. *A Coaker Anthology*. St. John's: Creative Publishers, 1986.

Cuff, Robert H., and Melvin Baker, eds. *Dictionary of Newfoundland and Labrador Biography*. St. John's: Harry Cuff Publications, 1990.

Dawson, Robert MacGregor. *The Government of Canada*. 3rd ed. Toronto: University of Toronto Press, 1948.

Fitzgerald, John Edward, ed. *Newfoundland at the Crossroads: Documents on Confederation with Canada*. St. John's: Terra Nova Publishing, 2002.

Gilmore, Bill. "The Acquisition of Dominion Statehood Reconsidered." *Virginia Journal of International Law* 22 (1982): 481–517.

———. "Aspects of United Kingdom Treaty Practice with Respect to Newfoundland." *Canadian Yearbook of International Law* 24 (1986): 213–46.

———. "Hot Pursuit and Constructive Presence in Canadian Law Enforcement." *Marine Policy* 12 (1988): 105–11.

———. "Law, Constitutional Convention and the Union of Newfoundland and Canada." *Offshore Investment* 18 (1989): 111–26.
———. "Legal and Institutional Aspects of the Organisation of Eastern Caribbean Studies." *Review of International Studies* 11 (1985): 311–28.
———. "Newfoundland and the League of Nations." *Canadian Yearbook of International Law* 18 (1980): 201–17.

———. "Newfoundland and the Paris Peace Conference." *British Journal of Canadian Studies* 1:282–301.

————. "The Newfoundland Continental Shelf Dispute in the Supreme Court of Canada." *Marine Policy* 8 (1984): 323–29.

————. "Newfoundland Offshore Mineral Rights." *Marine Policy* 7 (1983): 175–96.

————. "Problems in Paradise: Public Corruption and Constitutional Change in the Turks and Caicos Islands." *Public Law* (1988): 32–43.

————. "Requiem for Associated Statehood?" *Review of International Studies* 8 (1982): 9–25.

————. "The Search for Constitutional Change in the US Virgin Islands." *Social and Economic Studies* 33 (1984): 143–61.

Gotlieb, Allan. *The Washington Diaries, 1981–1989.* Toronto: McClelland & Stewart, 2006.

Graham, Ron. *The Last Act: Pierre Trudeau, the Gang of Eight and the Fight for Canada.* Toronto: Penguin Group (Canada), 2011.

Gunn, Gertrude. *The Political History of Newfoundland, 1832–1864.* Toronto: University of Toronto Press, 1966.

Gwyn, Richard. *Smallwood: The Unlikely Revolutionary.* Toronto: McClelland & Stewart, 1968.

Harrington, Michael. *Prime Ministers of Newfoundland.* St. John's: Harry Cuff Publications, 1991.

Harris, L. *Independent Review of the State of the Northern Cod Stock.* Report prepared for the Department of Fisheries and Oceans, Ottawa, 1990.

Hatton, Joseph, and Rev. M. Harvey. *Newfoundland: Its History, Its Present Condition, and Its Prospects in the Future*. Boston: Doyle & Whittle, 1883.

Henke, Janice Scott. *Seal Wars! An American Viewpoint*. St. John's: Breakwater Books, 1985.

Hillier, James, and Peter Neary, eds. *Newfoundland in the Nineteenth and Twentieth Centuries: Essays in Interpretations*. Toronto: University of Toronto Press, 1980.

Hogg, Peter W. *Constitutional Law of Canada*. Toronto: Carswell, 1977.

Horwood, Harold. *Joey: The Life and Political Times of Joey Smallwood*. Toronto: Stoddart, 1989.

House, J. D. *The Challenge of Oil: Newfoundland's Quest for Controlled Development*. St. John's: ISER Books, 1985.

Innis, Harold A. *The Cod Fisheries: The History of an International Economy*. Toronto: University of Toronto Press, 1954.

Kurlansky, Mark. *Cod: A Biography of the Fish that Changed the World*. Toronto: Penguin Books, 1997.

Laird, M. *Bibliography of the Natural History of Newfoundland and Labrador*. Toronto: Academic Press, 1980.

Leeson, Howard. *The Patriation Minutes*. Edmonton: Centre for Constitutional Studies, University of Alberta, 2011.

Lougheed, Peter. *Constitutional Patriation: The Lougheed-Lévesque Correspondence*. With an introduction by J. Peter Meekison. Kingston: Institute of Intergovernmental Relations, Queen's University, 1999.

MacKay, R.A., ed. *Newfoundland Economic, Diplomatic, and Strategic Studies*. Toronto: Oxford University Press, 1946.

Martin, C. *No Fish and Our Lives: Some Survival Notes for Newfoundland*. St. John's: Creative Publishers, 1992.

McLintock. A.H. *The Establishment of Constitutional Government in Newfoundland, 1783–1832: A Study of Retarded Colonisation*. London: Longmans, Green, 1941.

Neary, Peter. *Newfoundland in the North Atlantic World, 1929–1949*. Montreal and Kingston: McGill-Queen's University Press, 1988.

————, ed. *The Political Economy of Newfoundland, 1929–1972*. Vancouver: Copp Clarke Publishing, 1973.

Neary, Peter, and Patrick O'Flaherty. *Part of the Main: An Illustrated History of Newfoundland and Labrador*. St. John's: Breakwater Books, 1983.

Noel, S.J.R. *Politics in Newfoundland*. Toronto: University of Toronto Press, 1971.

O'Flaherty, Patrick. *Lost Country: The Rise and Fall of Newfoundland, 1843–1933*. St. John's: Long Beach Press, 2005.

————. *Old Newfoundland: A History to 1843*. St. John's: Long Beach Press, 1999.

Peckford, A. Brian. *The Past in the Present: A Personal Perspective on Newfoundland's Future*. St. John's: Harry Cuff Publications, 1983.

Pottle, Herbert. *Newfoundland, Dawn without Light: Politics, Power & People in the Smallwood Era*. St. John's: Breakwater Books, 1979.

Prowse, D.W.A. *History of Newfoundland: From the English, Colonial and Foreign Records.* London: Macmillan, 1895.

Reeves, John. *History of the Government of the Island of Newfoundland.* London, 1793. Reprinted New York: Johnson Reprint Corporation, 1967.

Robertson, Gordon. *Memories of a Very Civil Servant: Mackenzie King to Pierre Trudeau.* Toronto: University of Toronto Press, 2000.

Rose, George A. *Cod: An Ecological History of the North Atlantic Fisheries.* St. John's: Breakwater Books, 2007.

Ross, W. Gillies. *Arctic Whalers, Icy Seas: Narratives of the Davis Strait Whale Fishery.* Toronto: Irwin Publishing, 1985.

Rowe, Frederick W. *A History of Newfoundland and Labrador.* Toronto: McGraw-Hill Ryerson, 1980.

Ryan, Shannon. *Fish Out of Water: The Newfoundland Saltfish, 1814–1914.* Newfoundland History Series 2. St. John's: Breakwater Books, 1986.

Scammell, A.R. *Collected Works of A.R. Scammell.* St. John's: Harry Cuff Publications, 1990.

Sheppard, Robert, and Michael Valpy. *The National Deal: The Fight for a Canadian Constitution.* Toronto: Fleet Books, 1982.

Sinclair, Peter R. ed. *A Question of Survival: The Fisheries and Newfoundland Society.* St. John's: ISER Books, 1988.

Smith, Philip. *Brinco: The Story of Churchill Falls.* Toronto: McClelland & Stewart, 1975.

Tait, R.H. *Newfoundland: A Summary of the History and Development of Britain's Oldest Colony from 1497 to 1939*. Harrington, NJ: Harrington Press, 1939.

Trudeau, Pierre. *Against the Current: Selected Writings, 1939–1996*. Edited by Gerard Pelletier. Toronto: McClelland & Stewart, 1996.

———. *Memoirs*. Toronto: McClelland & Stewart, 1993.

Vardy, David, and Eric Dunn. *New Arrangements for Fisheries Management in Newfoundland and Labrador*. Report prepared for the Royal Commission on Renewing and Strengthening Our Place in Canada, St. John's, 2003.

Walsh, Bren. *More Than a Poor Majority: The Story of Newfoundland's Confederation with Canada*. St. John's: Breakwater Books, 1985.

Warner, William W. *Distant Water: The Fate of the North Atlantic Fisherman*. Boston: Little, Brown, 1983.

Wood, David G. *The Lougheed Legacy*. Toronto: Key Porter Books, 1985.

Zulaika, Joseba. *Terranova: The Ethos and Luck of Deep-Sea Fishermen*. St. John's: ISER Books, 1981.

INDEX

BRIAN PECKFORD WAS BORN in Whitbourne, Newfoundland, on August 27, 1942, and grew up in Whitbourne, Marystown, and Lewisporte. Peckford is a former premier of the province of Newfoundland and Labrador and holds a Bachelor of Education degree, having also completed postgraduate work in English Literature, Education, Psychology, and French Literature. Prior to entering politics, he was a high school teacher in rural Newfoundland.

He was first elected to the House of Assembly in 1972 at the age of twenty-nine. He was appointed parliamentary assistant to the premier, Honourable Frank Moores, in 1973. The following year he was appointed minister of Municipal Affairs and Housing and in 1976 held the portfolios of minister of: Mines and Energy; and Rural and Northern Development. At the age of thirty-six, he was elected leader of the provincial Progressive Conservative Party and premier of the province, becoming the youngest first minister in over 100 years.

It was Peckford's administration that fought for and achieved a new, groundbreaking arrangement with the federal government called the Atlantic Accord, which has become the template for all exploration and development of offshore oil and gas resources in Canada. It is under this arrangement that the oil fields of Hibernia, Terra Nova, and White Rose have been developed and are producing today. It is as a result of the revenues from these developments that the province of Newfoundland and Labrador has achieved "have" status, the first time since becoming a part of Canada in 1949. Peckford retired from public life in 1989 and established his own consulting business serving government and business clients in North America and Europe.

In 1982, Peckford received the Vanier Award as an outstanding young Canadian. That same year he was sworn to the Privy Council of Canada by her majesty the Queen, and he published a book in 1983 entitled *The Past in the Present* expressing his views on Newfoundland and Labrador's economic history and prospects. In 1986, he received an honorary Doctor of Laws degree from Memorial University and served on the board of the Canadian Broadcasting Corporation and as chair of its Human Resources Committee from 1993 to 1998. He was appointed, in 1998, as a one-person inquiry by the Government of British Columbia to investigate the state of Fraser River salmon stocks and management issues related to the fishery. Two reports were issued in ninety days, on budget. In 2001, he received an Outstanding Contribution Award from the Newfoundland Ocean Industries Association for his work on offshore oil and gas issues. In 2007, he was appointed Chancellor of Sprott Shaw Degree College.

In 2008, Mr. Peckford was chair of a federal government–appointed expert panel to review federal chronic disease policy, especially diabetes, and to present a report to the federal Health minister. The report was completed on time and on budget. Peckford is currently a director of Strongbow Exploration Inc., a public junior mining company with exploration interests in British Columbia, North West Territories, Nunavut, and the United States. He and his wife, Carol, reside in Qualicum Beach on Vancouver Island.

Although Peckford is well-known for his persistent efforts to improve the financial and economic condition of his native province, there are other firsts for which he and his administrations are responsible, including the first aquaculture legislation, first Department of Environment, first pay equity policy, first Arts Council, first Status of Women Council, first community college system, and the first and only Fine Arts degree program and building at the Grenfell Campus of Memorial University in Corner Brook.

Brian Peckford can be reached via email at brianpeckford@gmail.com.